Italian verb handbook

Carole Shepherd

Berlitz Publishing Company, Inc.
Princeton Mexico City Dublin Eschborn Singapore

Italian Verb Handbook

Published by Berlitz Publishing Company, Inc.
400 Alexander Park, Princeton, NJ 08540 USA
9-13 Grosvenor St., London W1X 9FB UK

Reprinted August 1998
Printed in Canada
ISBN 2-8315-6394-1

The Author:

Carole Shepherd is an experienced teacher, author and language consultant.

The Series Editor:

Christopher Wightwick was formerly principal inspector of Modern Languages for England and UK representative on the Council of Europe Modern Languages Project.

CONTENTS

How to Use This Handbook

This Handbook aims to provide a full description of the Italian verb system for all learners and users of the Italian language. It provides the following information:

• a chapter explaining the verb system in Italian;

• the conjugation of one hundred six verbs, grouped to show the common patterns underlying the system;

• a subject index to The Verb System in Italian;

• a verb index, containing over twenty-two hundred verbs with their English meanings and references to the pattern(s) they follow.

An important feature of the book is that examples, showing many of the verbs in use, are given throughout The Verb System in Italian and the Model Verbs.

THE VERB SYSTEM IN ITALIAN

Use the Contents and Subject Index to find your way around this section, which describes the functions and forms of verbs in general. It provides information on the use of tenses, word order, the way verbs govern other parts of speech, and the way verbs are formed. It also describes methods of avoiding the passive, and it explains features such as the reflexive forms, the subjunctive, and the auxiliary verbs. It explains the main features of predictability and irregularity, and it illustrates key irregular verbs.

MODEL VERBS

Use the Verb Index to find your way around this section, which gives the full conjugation of two key model verbs — i.e., of **lodare,** in both its active and passive voice; and of **entrare**, in its active voice. This section provides models for for all three groups of regular verbs plus the full range of spelling-change verbs, followed by all useful irregular verbs. This makes a total of one hundred six model verbs.

The conjugation of each verb is given in all usable tenses. Tenses that have any irregularity are given in full, with the irregularity in bold type. For tenses that are predictable, particularly compound tenses, only the first person singular form is given, as this is sufficient to enable you to predict the other forms within those tenses. Therefore, if a tense is not given in full, you can assume that it is regular.

For simple tenses, just look at the two model verbs (**lodare** and **entrare**) or at the appropriate verb of the five regular verbs (**parlare, vendere, dormire, finire,** and **lavarsi**) to figure out the endings needed. For compound tenses, check the Verb System in Italian to decide which tense of which auxiliary verb is necessary, then look up the appropriate auxiliary verb (**avere** or **essere**) in the Model Verbs.

Where appropriate, the model verb pages also contain the following:

• A list of other verbs that follow the same pattern. If possible, all such verbs are given. If, however, they are too numerous to list, a selection of the most useful ones is given. There are, of course, verbs that stand alone, having no others following their model.

• Notes indicating the main features of this pattern and any variations or additional features affecting any of the verbs that basically follow that model.

• Short dialogues, narratives, or sentences that illustrate some of the different tenses and usages of these verbs.

For further information on how the verb system works, refer to The Verb System in Italian.

THE SUBJECT INDEX

The Subject Index gives section references for all the main grammatical terms used in The Verb System in Italian.

VERB INDEX

For each of the twenty-two hundred or so verbs listed, the Verb Index gives information on whether it is transitive (*tr*), intransitive (*intr*), or reflexive (*refl*), together with its English meaning. It also lists common secondary meanings and the main idiomatic expressions based on common verbs. Finally, each entry is referred to the model verb whose pattern it follows:

acquistare (*tr*) acquire, get 3

There are verbs that have more than one predictable or unpredictable variation from the norm. Such verbs have two numbers after them, and both model verb pages should be consulted in these cases.

assorbire (*tr*) absorb, soak up 5, 6

HOW TO FIND THE INFORMATION YOU WANT

If you want to check on the form, meaning, or use of a verb, look it up in the Verb Index. This shows:

• which verbs are model verbs (indicated by **[M]**);

vendere (*tr*) sell, retail 4 **[M]**

• which verbs take **essere** (indicated by *)

***andare** (*intr*) go, ride (in car) 21 **[M]**

• which verbs take **avere** when transitive and **essere** when intransitive (indicated by a †)

†salire (*intr/tr*) go up, climb, mount, come in (of tide) 77 **[M]**

• any preposition normally accompanying the verb;

***abituarsi a** (*intr/refl*) become accustomed to, get used to 7

• whether the verb is transitive (*tr*), intransitive (*intr*), or reflexive (*refl*);

camminare (*intr*) step, tread, walk 3

• the main English meaning of the verb, along with any important idiomatic uses;

colpire (*tr*) impress, knock against, shock, smack, strike, hit 6

colpire a morte (*tr*) shoot dead 6

• a number indicating the model verb, which gives the congugation of the verb, points out its irregularities, and lists verbs that follow a similar pattern.

chiudere (*tr*) close, shut, zip up 30 **[M]**

If you want further information on the form or use of the verb, turn to the verb reference given.

Note: *The rules regarding the use of accents in Italian require that there should be an acute accent on closed vowels and a grave accent on open vowels [*➤ Berlitz *Italian Grammar Handbook 2a]. However, modern usage tends to prefer the grave accent, particularly on* ***à, ò, ù*** *and* ***ì****, and this usage is employed throughout the Handbook.*

A

THE VERB SYSTEM IN ITALIAN

1 What Verbs Do

1a *Full Verbs*

The great majority of verbs tell us about the action, state of mind, or changing situation of the subject of the sentence. We call these verbs *full* verbs.

***Abito* in Italia.**	*I live* in Italy.
***Abbiamo* un appartamento.**	*We have* an apartment.

1b *Auxiliary Verbs*

A much smaller group of verbs is used to add something to the sense of the full verb—for example, to make a compound tense or to add a comment on an action. These are called *auxiliary* (helping) verbs.

***Sto* studiando l'italiano.**	I am studying Italian.
***Ho* comprato una macchina.**	I (have) bought a car.
***Sono* andato in città.**	I went into town.

1c *Dual-Purpose Verbs*

Most auxiliary verbs can be used either with their full meanings or as auxiliaries. For example, the verb **stare**—used mostly to express the position or the state or condition of something or somebody—is also used as an auxiliary verb to form the present progressive tense, which describes an action actually in progress.

***Sta* in casa.**	She is in the house.
***Sta* preparando da mangiare.**	She is preparing something to eat.

 What Verbs Govern

A sentence can contain many items of information other than what is given by the subject and the main verb. Some of these items depend directly on the main verb and cannot be removed without leaving the sentence incomplete. These are said to be governed by the verb.

2a *Intransitive Verbs*

Some verbs do not normally govern an object [▶ 2c], though the sentence may, of course, contain expressions that add to the meaning. These verbs are called *intransitive* verbs and are usually marked in the verb lists and dictionaries as (intr) or (i).

Torno subito.	I'll come back right away.

'I'll come back' makes sense in itself. The 'right away' gives us some extra information.

2b *Verbs Linking Equals: The Complement*

A small number of verbs act as a link between the subject and another word or phrase, which is called the complement of the verb. Usually, the complement is a noun or a phrase referring to the same person or thing as the subject.

Mio padre *è* dottore.	My father *is* a doctor.

2c *Transitive Verbs*

Many verbs take a *direct object.* These verbs are *transitive.* They are usually marked in dictionaries and verb lists as (tr). A direct object answers the question *what?* or *whom?* Intransitive verbs cannot have a direct object.

Giorgio ha comprato *un cane.*	Giorgio bought *a dog.*

Here the dog is what Giorgio bought, so it is the direct object of 'bought.'

2d *Verbs That Can Be Both Transitive and Intransitive*

Many verbs can be both transitive and intransitive in Italian. They may be listed as (intr/tr) in verb lists.

Maria parla troppo.	Maria talks too much.
Giovanni parla inglese.	Giovanni speaks English.

2e *Verbs with Two Objects: Direct and Indirect*

Some transitive verbs describe the transfer of the direct object to another person (or possibly thing). This person is then the *indirect object* of the verb. With some verbs the idea can be extended to include people indirectly affected by the action of the verb. The indirect object answers the question *to whom?* or *for whom?* However, in English the 'to' or the 'for' is not always stated.

Sandro ha comprato dei fiori per la mamma.	Sandro bought some flowers for his mother.
Le ha comprato dei fiori.	He bought her some flowers.
Ha dato i fiori alla mamma.	He gave the flowers to his mother.
Le ha dato i fiori.	He gave her the flowers.

Here the flowers are the direct object and the mother/her—the recipient—is the indirect object.

2f *Reflexive Verbs*

(i) Some verbs express an action that is turned back on the subject; in other words, the object is the same person or the same thing as the subject. These are called *reflexive* verbs [➤10]. In English, these verbs may use one of the '-self' pronouns.

Mi diverto sempre in Italia.	I always enjoy myself in Italy.
Ci siamo divertiti molto.	We enjoyed ourselves a lot.

(ii) Sometimes people are doing the action not to themselves but to each other, in which case the subject is usually plural. As a result, it is only possible to use one of the plural forms of the verb—that is, the **noi, voi,** or **loro** form.

Si sono incontrati ieri.	They met (each other) yesterday.
Ci telefoniamo spesso.	We often phone each other.

(iii) In many cases the Italian reference to '-self' or 'each other' is not expressed in English.

Mi sveglio alle sette.	I wake up at seven.
Mi alzo subito.	I get up immediately.
Mi lavo nel bagno.	I get washed in the bathroom.

(iv) With some verbs the reflexive idea has largely disappeared in English, but the reflexive grammatical form in Italian still applies.

Me ne sono accorta che l'uomo mi guardava.	I noticed that the man was looking at me.
Non si rende conto che sono straniera.	He does not realize that I am a foreigner.

(v) Normally reflexive verbs do not have another direct object; but if they do, the past participle agrees with that object rather than the reflexive pronoun, which then becomes an indirect object.

Mi sono tagliato il dito.	I cut my finger.
Mi sono rotta la gamba.	I have broken my leg.
Mi sono lavate le mani.	I washed my hands.

However, usage varies; and you may find that Italians make a past participle agree with the subject even when there is a direct object.

Alberto s'è tolto la camicia.	Alberto took off his shirt.

In these examples, the English uses a possessive adjective whereas Italian uses a reflexive pronoun.

(vi) Reflexive verbs are often used where a passive would be used in English.

Qui si vendono mele.	Apples are sold here.
Qui si parla inglese.	English is spoken here.

2g Verbs Governing Verbs

(i) Verbs followed by an infinitive

This is quite a common structure in Italian, which has many expressions based on a *modal* auxiliary verb [➤3].

***Vorrei* partire alle otto.**	*I'd like* to leave at eight.
***Devo* essere in città alle nove.**	*I must* be in town at nine.
***Sai* nuotare?**	*Do you know how to* swim?
***Possiamo* andare in piscina insieme.**	*We can* go to the swimming pool together.

(ii) Verbs followed by a preposition and an infinitive

Italian also has a number of these structures, which are very similar to *(i)*, but with a preposition between the auxiliary verb and the main verb. The Verb Index lists which verbs take which prepositions.

Andiamo *a* mangiare adesso!	Let's go to eat now!
Cerca *di* venire stasera.	Try to come tonight.
Ho dimenticato *di* comprare il giornale.	I forgot to buy the newspaper.
Sono usciti *senza* salutarmi.	They went out without saying good-bye to me.

(iii) Use of the gerund

As in English, Italian has a way of describing an action in progress. In English the verb 'to be' and the present participle of the verb are used, while in Italian the verb **stare** and the gerund can be used.

***Sto studiando* l'italiano.**	*I am studying* Italian.
***Stavo leggendo* quando è arrivato Luigi.**	*I was reading* when Luigi arrived.

2h Position of Verbs in the Sentence

(i) *Subject pronouns*

Generally speaking, the position of verbs in an Italian sentence is similar to that in English. However, one important difference is that Italian verbs are usually found without a subject pronoun. This is because each verb ending is clear and distinct, not just in the written but also in the spoken form. However, the pronouns are used when necessary for emphasis, contrast, or clarity.

***Io* vado in città, ma *tu* devi rimanere qui.**	*I* am going into town, but *you* must stay here.
—Chi ha rotto il bicchiere?	—Who broke the glass?
—L'ha rotto *lui,* mamma.	—*He* broke it, mom / mum.

In the last example the pronoun comes after the verb for greater emphasis on the person who broke the glass.

(ii) *Questions*

Questions in English are usually formed by inverting the verb and the subject or by using the verb 'to do.' Such inversion is not so common in Italian, since the subject pronoun is rarely used except for emphasis, contrast, or clarity. Instead, questions often look exactly the same as statements but are indicated by voice intonation—the voice is raised at the end of the question. In a written form, the question is made visible, as in English, by the question mark.

Tuo padre ha una macchina nuova.	Your father has a new car.
Tuo padre ha una macchina nuova?	Does your father have a new car?
Hai visto Carlo ieri.	You saw Carlo yesterday.
Hai visto Carlo ieri?	Did you see Carlo yesterday?

(iii) *Negative expressions*

Negative expressions are straightforward in Italian. The English word 'not' is translated by the Italian **non,** which is placed immediately before the verb and any dependent object pronouns.

— *Non* vado al cinema stasera.	— I'm *not* going to the movies / cinema this evening.
— Perchè *non* ci accompagni?	— Why do*n't* you come with us?
— *Non* mi sento bene.	— I do*n't* feel well.
***Non* lo so.**	I do*n't* know.

Non can be combined with other negative expressions (**mai, nessuno, niente,** etc.) usually placed after the main verb.

***Non* vedo *nessuno* fuori.**	I don't see anyone outside.
***Non* è *niente,* non ti preoccupare.**	It's nothing, don't worry.
***Non* ho *mai* visto quel film.**	I have never seen that film.

Note: **Nessuno** can begin a sentence, in which case there is no need for the **non.** This does not affect the position of the verb in the sentence.

***Nessuno* vuole venire.**	Nobody wants to come.

3 Attitudes to Action: Modal Verbs

3a The Function of Modal Verbs

Modal verbs, as mentioned in 2g(i), modify full verbs to express additional points of view such as possibility, desire, and obligation. They create moods for the verbs that follow. They are used in the appropriate persons and tenses followed by the infinitives of the full verbs.

3b Modal Verbs and Their Meanings

These are the main modal auxiliary verbs used in Italian:

(i) *potere 'can,' 'be able to'*

Non *posso* venire domani.	*I can*'t come tomorrow.

(ii) *volere 'want to,' 'wish,' 'like'*

Non *voleva* andarci.	He *did*n't *want to* go there.

(iii) *dovere 'have to,' 'must,' 'be obliged to,' 'ought to,' 'should'*

***Dovete* ascoltare il professore.**	*You should* listen to the teacher.

(iv) *sapere 'know how to,' 'be able to'*

—*Sai* suonare il flauto?	—*Do you know how to* play the flute?
—No, ma *so* giocare a tennis!	—No, but *I know how to* play tennis!

Note: Object pronouns may precede the modal verb or be attached to the end of the infinitive.

***Te lo* posso dire adesso.**	I can tell *(it to) you* now.
Posso dir*telo* adesso.	I can tell *(it to) you* now.

4 Verb Forms Not Related to Time

Verbs are very important words, in that a single verb form will usually give three pieces of information: *what* is happening, *when* it is happening, and *who* is doing it. However, there are some verb forms that do not specify time or person.

4a The Infinitive

The part of the verb that you will find in a verb list or dictionary, and also in the Verb Index of this book, is the *infinitive.* In English this is the word preceded by 'to,' for example, 'to love.' In Italian the infinitive form of all regular verbs ends in one of the following: **-are, -ere, -ire** (for example, **amare, vendere, capire, dormire**).

4b The Participles and the Gerund

(i) The present participle

The present participle in Italian has lost its verbal force and in most cases is used as an adjective or a noun. It is usually formed by adding **-ante** or **-ente** to the stem of the infinitive.

il capitolo *seguente*	the *following* chapter
gli *amanti*	the *lovers*

(ii) The present gerund

The present gerund is often used to describe an action in progress. Its most common use is with the auxiliary verb **stare** to form the present, imperfect, and sometimes future progressive tenses. However, it can be used by itself, provided that its subject and that of the verb in the sentence are the same. The gerund is formed by adding **-ando** or **-endo** to the stem of the infinitive, is invariable, and *never* takes a preposition before it. Care must be taken that the action being referred to actually take place at the same time as that of the main verb — i.e., present, past, or future.

***Sto finendo* l'esercizio.**	*I am finishing* the exercise.
Il bambino *sta dormendo* nella culla.	The baby *is sleeping* in the cradle.
Cosa *stavate facendo?*	What *were you doing?*
Cammino lungo la strada *parlando* con Anna.	I walk along the road *while speaking* to Anna.
Papà ci rispose *sorridendo.*	Father answered us *smiling.*

Note the difference between the following:

Studio l'italiano a scuola.	I study Italian at school.
Sto studiando l'italiano adesso.	I am studying Italian now (i.e., at this precise moment).

(iii) *The past participle*

This form is used to describe an action that is finished. In Italian it ends in **-ato** (**-are** verbs), **-uto** (**-ere** verbs), or **-ito** (**-ire** verbs). It is mainly used with the verb **avere** or the verb **essere** to form the perfect tense and other compound tenses; but it is also used in other ways, including as an adjective and to form the passive. When used with **avere** in compound tenses, it does not agree with the subject, but can agree with a preceding direct object and *must* agree with a preceding direct object *pronoun.*

When used with **essere** it almost always agrees with the subject [but for reflexive usage ➤2f(v)].

***Ho comprato* una casa nuova.**	*I have bought* a new house.
***Fu costruita* da Salvatore.**	*It was built* by Salvatore.
L'*ho invitata* a pranzo.	*I invited* her to dinner (*if in Italy*) / lunch (*if in USA*).
La mia amica *è partita* alle nove.	My friend *left* at nine.
***Ho lasciato* la porta aperta.**	*I left* the door open.

In the examples given above, the past participle is used as part of the compound tense of the active transitive / intransitive verb of the sentence in all but the second example, where it is used as part of a passive construction. In the final example the second past participle is used as an adjective. When used in a passive construction or as an adjective or with the verb **essere,** the past participle follows the same rules of agreement as an adjective.

4c *The Verb* Piacere

piacere 'like,' 'be pleasing to,' 'please'

The construction of **piacere** is different from that of most other verbs, and it works the other way around than that of its English equivalents 'like' and 'please.' The subject of the verb in Italian becomes the direct object of the verb in English, and the subject of the verb in English becomes the indirect object of the verb in Italian.

Mi *piace* studiare	I *like* studying (i.e., '*Studying pleases / is pleasing* to me').
Mi *piacciono* i film di Fellini.	I *like* Fellini's movies (i.e., 'Fellini's movies *please / are pleasing* to me').

If the indirect object of the verb is a noun, it is usually preceded by the preposition **a.**

***A mio padre* piace molto leggere il giornale.**	*My father* likes to read the newspaper a lot. (i.e., 'Reading the newspaper pleases *my father* a lot / is very pleasing to *my father*).

An indirect object pronoun may be accompanied by **a** + a disjunctive pronoun for emphasis.

***A me* non *mi* piacciono le banane.**	*I* don't like bananas (i.e., Bananas don't please / are not pleasing *to me*).

5 The Use of Tenses

5a What Are Tenses?

Tenses are grammatical structures that record when an event happened. Both the number of tenses and the names given to them vary from language to language. Many tenses are formed from the stem of the infinitive—this is the part that remains when the **-are, -ere,** or **-ire** ending has been removed (for example, the stem of **parlare** is **parl-**). We may speak of simple and compound tenses.

(i) *Simple tenses*

These are formed by adding specific endings to the stem of the verb, which may also change.

(ii) *Compound tenses*

These are formed with the help of the auxiliary verbs **avere, essere,** and **stare** plus a participle or a gerund.

Thus a simple tense is a one-word form, while a compound tense is a form of two or more words.

5b Auxiliary Verbs

(i) *The progressive tenses*

The progressive tenses are used to describe actions that are in progress at the time being referred to—present, past (imperfect), or sometimes future. In English they are easily identifiable, since they are formed by the appropriate form of the verb 'to be' followed by the main verb in the '-ing' form. Italian uses a similar structure with the verb **stare** in the appropriate tense followed by the gerund of the main verb. The two main tenses of **stare** used in Italian are the present and the imperfect. However, you should note that Italian uses these forms less frequently than English does, and only when the action is in progress at the time being described.

Quando è arrivato, *stavo leggendo* un libro.	When he arrived, *I was reading* a book.

Andare is sometimes used to form the progressive tenses when a cumulative progression is indicated.

Gianna *andava parlando* di questo progetto per ore e ore.	Gianna *went on talking* about this project for hours and hours.

(ii) The compound past tenses

In Italian these tenses are formed with the appropriate forms of the verb **avere** or **essere** and the past participle.

***Ho visto* Gianluca ieri.**	*I saw* Gianluca yesterday.
***Aveva incontrato* Sara.**	*He had met* Sara.
***Sono andata* in città.**	*I went* into town.
***Era partito* presto.**	*He had left* early.

(iii) The past gerund

The past gerund is formed by combining the present gerund of **avere** or **essere** with the past participle of the verb. It is used to translate the perfect participle in English (i.e., having bought, having understood, and so forth).

***Avendo comprato* il giornale, tornai a casa.**	*Having bought* the newspaper, I returned home.
***Essendo partite* le mie amiche, andai a dormire.**	My friends *having left,* I went to sleep.

Note: As in the second example, the past gerund often has a subject of its own, unlike the present gerund used in the present progressive tense.

6 Statements of Probable Fact: The Indicative

Verb forms and tenses that make a positive statement are said to be in the *indicative.* [Contrast this with the subjunctive ➤ 8.]

In all verbs there are some tenses whose stems and endings can be predicted if you know one of the other parts of the verb. Parts that cannot be predicted in this way have to be learned. It is helpful to know how to obtain the stem, to which the endings for each tense are added, and any spelling adjustments that may need to be made. The following sections tell you how to form each tense, explaining how to get the stem and giving you the endings; and they list the main uses for each one.

6a The Present Tenses

(i) The present indicative

The present indicative of regular verbs is formed as follows:

FIRST CONJUGATION	SECOND CONJUGATION	THIRD CONJUGATION	
amare 'love'	***vendere*** 'sell'	***dormire*** 'sleep'	***finire*** 'finish'
am**o**	vend**o**	dorm**o**	fin**isco**
am**i**	vend**i**	dorm**i**	fin**isci**
am**a**	vend**e**	dorm**e**	fin**isce**
am**iamo**	vend**iamo**	dorm**iamo**	fin**iamo**
am**ate**	vend**ete**	dorm**ite**	fin**ite**
am**ano**	vend**ono**	dorm**ono**	fin**iscono**

Note that the following groups of verbs undergo spelling changes or other modifications, mainly for pronunciation purposes:

• Verbs ending in **-are** whose stems end in **-c** or **-g** insert an **h** before an **i** or an **e.**

pagare pago, **paghi, paghiamo,** pagate, pagano
cercare cerco, **cerchi,** cerca, **cerchiamo,** cercate, cercano

• Verbs ending in **-iare** have only one **i** in the **tu** form if the **i** of the stem is not stressed.

studiare	**studi**	(The stress falls on the first syllable.)

• Verbs ending in **-iare** retain the **i** if the stem is stressed.

sciare	**scii**	(The stress is on the first **i.**)

• Verbs ending in **-durre** are not irregular once the first person singular is known, as this is based on a **-ducere** ending.

produrre	**produco,** etc.
ridurre	**riduco,** etc.
tradurre	**traduco,** etc.

• Verbs **bere, dire,** and **fare** are formed from the obsolete **-ere** infinitives **bevere, dicere,** and **facere;** and if classified as second conjugation verbs, they are regular in some parts of the present tense.

bere (bevere)	bevo, bevi, beve, beviamo, bevete, bevono
dire (dicere)	dico, dici, dice, diciamo, **dite,** dicono
fare (facere)	**faccio, fai, fa, facciamo, fate, fanno**

• Some verbs add another vowel (turning into a diphthong) in the first, second, and third person singular and third person plural.

morire	**muoio, muori, muore,** moriamo, morite, **muoiono**
sedere	**siedo, siedi, siede,** sediamo, sedete, **siedono**

For irregular verbs, see Model Verbs.

The present tense in Italian can be used to convey the following ideas:

• What the situation is now.

Studio l'italiano a una scuola serale.	I study Italian at a night school.

• What happens sometimes or usually.

Ogni giorno esco alle sette.	I go out every day at seven.

• What is going to happen soon.

Quest'estate vado in Italia.	This summer I am going to Italy.

• What has been happening up to now and may be continuing to happen.

Abito a Firenze da due anni.	I have been living in Florence for two years.
Aspettiamo da una mezz'ora.	We have been waiting for half an hour.

(ii) The present progressive

This is formed by using the present tense of **stare** plus the gerund [▶ 5b(i)].

studiare → studiando **prendere → prendendo** **finire → finendo**

There are three irregular gerunds formed from obsolete forms of the **-ere** infinitive.

VERB	OBSOLETE INFINITIVE	GERUND
dire	**(dicere)**	**dicendo**
fare	**(facere)**	**facendo**
bere	**(bevere)**	**bevendo**

Sto bevendo **un bicchiere di vino.**	*I am drinking* a glass of wine.
Sto leggendo **il giornale.**	*I am reading* the newspaper.

6b The Past Tenses

(i) The imperfect indicative

The imperfect tense of all verbs is formed by taking off the **-re** ending of the infinitive and adding the following endings:

-vo, -vi, -va, -vamo, -vate, -vano

comprare 'buy'	***vendere*** 'sell'	***dormire*** 'sleep'
compra**vo**	vende**vo**	dormi**vo**
compra**vi**	vende**vi**	dormi**vi**
compra**va**	vende**va**	dormi**va**
compra**vamo**	vende**vamo**	dormi**vamo**
compra**vate**	vende**vate**	dormi**vate**
compra**vano**	vende**vano**	dormi**vano**

The following irregular imperfect tenses are formed from obsolete forms of the infinitive:

Verb	*Obsolete Infinitive*	*Imperfect*
dire	**(dicere)**	**dicevo,** etc.
fare	**(facere)**	**facevo,** etc.
bere	**(bevere)**	**bevevo,** etc.

Verbs ending in **-durre:**

produrre	**producevo,** etc.
tradurre	**traducevo,** etc.

Verbs ending in **-arre:**

attrarre	**attraevo,** etc.
distrarre	**distraevo,** etc.

The verb **essere** is the only verb to have a completely irregular form.

essere **ero, eri, era, eravamo, eravate, erano**

The imperfect tense is used for:

- repeated or habitual actions in the past.
- descriptions of things or of people in the past.
- ongoing actions in the past, often as a setting to other actions.

Ogni anno *andava* in Francia.	*He used to go* to France every year.
***Era* una ragazza molto povera.**	*She was* a very poor girl.
***Parlava* con Antonio quando sono entrata.**	*He was speaking* to Antonio when I came in.

(ii) The imperfect progressive tense

This is formed by using the appropriate form of the imperfect tense of **stare** followed by the gerund [for usage ➤ 5b(i)]:

***Stavo scrivendo* quando ha telefonato Leonardo.**	*I was writing* when Leonardo called / telephoned.

(iii) The past definite

The past definite of regular verbs is formed by adding the following endings to the stem of the infinitive.

-are	**-ai, -asti, -ò, -ammo, -aste, -arono**
-ere	**-ei (-etti), -esti, -é (-ette), -emmo, -este, -erono (-ettero)**
-ire	**-ii, -isti, -í, -immo, -iste, -irono**

trovare 'find'	***vendere*** 'sell'	***capire*** 'understand'
trov**ai**	vend**ei** / vend**etti**	cap**ii**
trov**asti**	vend**esti**	cap**isti**
trov**ò**	vend**é** / vend**ette**	cap**í**
trov**ammo**	vend**emmo**	cap**immo**
trov**aste**	vend**este**	cap**iste**
trov**arono**	vend**erono** / vend**ettero**	cap**irono**

Note: There is stress on the ending of the third person plural.

For irregular verbs ➤ Model Verbs 17–106. Although there are a considerable number of verbs that are irregular in the past definite, many of these are irregular only in the first and third person singular and third person plural, as in the following example:

chiedere — **chiesi,** chiedesti, **chiese,** chiedemmo, chiedeste, **chiesero**

Note the irregular past definite of **avere** and **essere.**

avere	***essere***
ebbi	**fui**
avesti	**fosti**
ebbe	**fu**
avemmo	**fummo**
aveste	**foste**
ebbero	**furono**

The past definite is used to describe completed actions in the past, which have no further correlation to the present. It is mainly used in literary and formal writing, though in some parts of Italy it is an alternative to the perfect tense.

Tornando a casa, *incontrai* Carlo.	While I was returning home, *I met* Carlo.
***Comprai* una macchina due mesi fa.**	*I bought* a car two months ago.

Note: The verb **nascere** needs special attention: **è nato** is used for someone still living; **era nato** is used for someone who has recently died; **nacque** is used for someone long dead.

La bambina *è nata* stamattina.	The baby girl *was born* this morning.
Il morto *era nato* novantadue anni fa.	The dead man *was born* ninety-two years ago.
Dante Alighieri *nacque* secoli fa.	Dante Alighieri *was born* centuries ago.

(iv) *Other past tenses*

The remainder of the past tenses in Italian are compound tenses. They are formed using the appropriate tense of the auxiliary verb **avere** or **essere** and the past participle of the verb [▶ 5b(ii)].

(v) *The present perfect tense*

The present perfect tense is formed in Italian by using the present tense of **avere** or **essere** and the past participle of the verb. To form the past participle of regular verbs, remove the infinitive ending and add the appropriate ending.

-are	**-ato**
-ere	**-uto**
-ire	**-ito**

comprare	***vendere***	***finire***
ho comprato	**ho venduto**	**ho finito**
hai comprato	**hai venduto**	**hai finito**
ha comprato	**ha venduto**	**ha finito**
abbiamo comprato	**abbiamo venduto**	**abbiamo finito**
avete comprato	**avete venduto**	**avete finito**
hanno comprato	**hanno venduto**	**hanno finito**

andare	***venire***	***lavarsi***
sono andato / a	**sono venuto / a**	**mi sono lavato / a**
sei andato / a	**sei venuto / a**	**ti sei lavato / a**
è andato / a	**è venuto / a**	**si è lavato / a**
siamo andati / e	**siamo venuti / e**	**ci siamo lavati / e**
siete andati / e	**siete venuti / e**	**vi siete lavati / e**
sono andati / e	**sono venuti / e**	**si sono lavati / e**

Note: Most intransitive verbs, most impersonal verbs, and all reflexive verbs take **essere** in the present perfect tense. In the Verb Index these are marked *.

Some of the most common verbs taking **essere** are as follows:

andare (andato)	go	**restare (restato)**	stay
arrivare (arrivato)	arrive	**rimanere (rimasto)**	remain
cadere (caduto)	fall	**riuscire (riuscito)**	succeed
†correre (corso)	run	**salire (salito)**	go up
essere (stato)	be	**scendere (sceso)**	go down
morire (morto)	die	**scoppiare (scoppiato)**	burst
nascere (nato)	be born	**sembrare (sembrato)**	seem
parere (parso)	appear	**tornare (tornato)**	return
partire (partito)	leave	**uscire (uscito)**	go out
piacere (piaciuto)	please	**venire (venuto)**	come

Note: **†Correre** can take **avere** when used with a direct object.

Giovanni ha corso un grave rischio quel giorno.	Giovanni ran a great risk that day.

All verbs marked † in the Verb Index take **essere** when used intransitively and **avere** when used transitively.

Many past participles are irregular and will need to be learned.

The perfect tense is used to describe:

- a single completed action in the past.

Ho letto il suo libro.	I read his book.

- an action taking place in the past but continuing up to the present.

Fino adesso Anna ha scritto tre libri.	Up to now Anna has written three books.

- an action that has recently taken place.

Oggi Antonio è venuto a trovarmi.	Antonio came to see me today.
Stamattina sono andata al mercato.	I went to the market this morning.
Abbiamo finito i compiti!	We have finished the homework!
Maria ha scritto due lettere stasera.	Maria has written two letters this evening.

(vi) *The pluperfect tense*

The pluperfect tense is formed with the imperfect tense of **avere** or **essere** and the past participle of the verb.

comprare	***vendere***	***finire***
avevo comprato	**avevo venduto**	**avevo finito**
avevi comprato	**avevi venduto**	**avevi finito**
aveva comprato	**aveva venduto**	**aveva finito**
avevamo comprato	**avevamo venduto**	**avevamo finito**
avevate comprato	**avevate venduto**	**avevate finito**
avevano comprato	**avevano venduto**	**avevano finito**

andare	***venire***	***lavarsi***
ero andato / a	**ero venuto / a**	**mi ero lavato / a**
eri andato / a	**eri venuto / a**	**ti eri lavato / a**
era andato / a	**era venuto / a**	**si era lavato / a**
eravamo andati / e	**eravamo venuti / e**	**ci eravamo lavati / e**
eravate andati / e	**eravate venuti / e**	**vi eravate lavati / e**
erano andati / e	**erano venuti / e**	**si erano lavati / e**

The pluperfect tense is used to take a step back in time in the past. It corresponds to the English 'had.'

Antonio aveva scritto due righe.	Antonio had written a note ('two lines').
Avevo mangiato bene.	I had eaten well.
Ero arrivato tardi.	I had arrived late.

(vii) *The past anterior*

The past anterior has the same meaning as the pluperfect tense. It, too, corresponds to the English 'had' and is formed with the past definite tense of **avere** or **essere** and the past participle of the verb.

comprare	***vendere***	***finire***
ebbi comprato	**ebbi venduto**	**ebbi finito**
avesti comprato	**avesti venduto**	**avesti finito**
ebbe comprato	**ebbe venduto**	**ebbe finito**
avemmo comprato	**avemmo venduto**	**avemmo finito**
aveste comprato	**aveste venduto**	**aveste finito**
ebbero comprato	**ebbero venduto**	**ebbero finito**

andare	*venire*	*lavarsi*
fui andato / a	**fui venuto / a**	**mi fui lavato / a**
fosti andato / a	**fosti venuto / a**	**ti fosti lavato / a**
fu andato / a	**fu venuto / a**	**si fu lavato / a**
fummo andati / e	**fummo venuti / e**	**ci fummo lavati / e**
foste andati / e	**foste venuti / e**	**vi foste lavati / e**
furono andati / e	**furono venuti / e**	**si furono lavati / e**

The past anterior is rarely used in speech.

It can only be used in subordinate clauses introduced by a conjunction of time when the verb of the main clause is in the past definite.

Quando ebbi finito, me ne andai.	When I finished, I left.
Non appena fu arrivato, squillò il telefono.	As soon as he arrived, the phone rang.

6c *The Future Tenses*

(i) *The simple future*

The present tense in Italian can be used to denote the future.

Dove vai in vacanza?	Where are you going on vacation / holiday?
Vado in Italia quest'estate.	I am going to Italy this summer.
A che ora arriva Paolo?	What time is Paolo arriving?
Arriva alle otto.	He is arriving at eight.

(ii) *The future*

The future tense in Italian is formed by adding these modified forms of the present tense of **avere** to the infinitive of the verb minus the final **-e.**

-ò, -ai, -à, -emo, -ete, -anno

Note: **-are** verbs change their stems from **-ar** to **-er** in the future.

comprare	***vendere***	***finire***
comprer**ò**	vender**ò**	finir**ò**
comprer**ai**	vender**ai**	finir**ai**
comprer**à**	vender**à**	finir**à**
comprer**emo**	vender**emo**	finir**emo**
comprer**ete**	vender**ete**	finir**ete**
comprer**anno**	vender**anno**	finir**anno**

The verbs **avere** and **essere** have irregular future stems.

avr-	**avrò**	**sar-**	**sarò**

The following verbs have contracted stems (i.e., they lose the characteristic vowel of the infinitive ending).

andare	**andrò**	**potere**	**potrò**
cadere	**cadrò**	**sapere**	**saprò**
dovere	**dovrò**	**vedere**	**vedrò**
morire	**morrò**	**vivere**	**vivrò**

Some verbs and their compounds undergo a slight modification to their spelling so that the stem doubles the **-r.**

bere	**berrò**	**valere**	**varrò**
parere	**parrò**	**venire**	**verrò**
rimanere	**rimarrò**	**volere**	**vorrò**
tenere	**terrò**		

A few verbs retain the vowel of the infinitive ending.

dare	**darò**	**stare**	**starò**
fare	**farò**		

Verbs ending in **-ciare** and **-giare** drop the **i** before the **-er** of the future tense.

cominciare	**comincerò**	**mangiare**	**mangerò**

Verbs ending in **-care** or **-gare** add an **h** after the **c** or the **g** throughout the future tense to retain the hard sound.

cercare	**cercherò**	**pagare**	**pagherò**

The future tense is used to refer to what is going to happen.

Andrò a Roma l'anno prossimo.	I shall go to Rome next year.

It is used in dependent clauses that start with **se** or a conjunction of time if the main verb is in the future.

Se lo vedrò, glielo spiegherò.	If I see him, I shall explain it to him.
Quando arriverà, gliene parlerò.	When he arrives, I shall speak to him about it.

It can also denote probability.

Sarà un coltello?	Is it (perhaps) a knife?
Saranno i miei genitori alla porta.	It must be my parents at the door.

(iii) The future perfect

The future perfect tense is used to take a step forward from a time in the past. It expresses the idea of 'will have,' or it indicates probability. It is formed with the future tense of **avere** or **essere** and the past participle of the verb.

comprare	***vendere***	***finire***
avrò comprato	avrò venduto	avrò finito
avrai comprato	avrai venduto	avrai finito
avrà comprato	avrà venduto	avrà finito
avremo comprato	avremo venduto	avremo finito
avrete comprato	avrete venduto	avrete finito
avranno comprato	avranno venduto	avranno finito

andare	***venire***	***lavarsi***
sarò andato / a	sarò venuto / a	mi sarò lavato / a
sarai andato / a	sarai venuto / a	ti sarai lavato / a
sarà andato / a	sarà venuto / a	si sarà lavato / a
saremo andati / e	saremo venuti / e	ci saremo lavati / e
sarete andati / e	sarete venuti / e	vi sarete lavati / e
saranno andati / e	saranno venuti / e	si saranno lavati / e

Quando avrò finito i compiti, guarderò la televisione.	When I have finished the homework, I shall watch television.
Saranno andati al bar.	They will / must have gone to the bar.
Avrà perso la borsa.	She must have lost her bag.

6d The Conditional

(i) The present conditional

The present tense of the conditional mood is formed by adding the following endings to the future stem:
-ei, -esti, -ebbe, -emmo, -este, -ebbero.

comprare	*vendere*	*finire*
comprer**ei**	vender**ei**	finir**ei**
comprer**esti**	vender**esti**	finir**esti**
comprer**ebbe**	vender**ebbe**	finir**ebbe**
comprer**emmo**	vender**emmo**	finir**emmo**
comprer**este**	vender**este**	finir**este**
comprer**ebbero**	vender**ebbero**	finir**ebbero**

Note: The irregular future stems in 6c also apply to the conditional.

The conditional is used to express an English conditional form.

***Dovrei* andare a scuola.**	*I should* go to school.
***Vorrei* comprare dei fiori.**	*I would like* to buy some flowers.

It is also used to express a wish more politely.

***Potrei* avere un po' di zucchero?**	*Could I* have some sugar?
Mi *accompagneresti* domani?	*Will you come with* me tomorrow?

The verb **gradire** 'like to,' 'appreciate,' can also be used in the conditional to stress politeness.

***Gradirei* una risposta alla mia lettera.**	*I would like* a reply to my letter.
***Gradiremmo* sapere i prezzi da Voi praticati.**	*We would like* to know your prices.

(ii) The conditional perfect

The perfect tense of the conditional mood is used to convey the idea of 'would have' or that the statement reported is hearsay. It is formed with the present conditional of **avere** or **essere** and the past participle of the verb.

comprare	*vendere*	*finire*
avrei comprato	avrei venduto	avrei finito
avresti comprato	avresti venduto	avresti finito
avrebbe comprato	avrebbe venduto	avrebbe finito
avremmo comprato	avremmo venduto	avremmo finito
avreste comprato	avreste venduto	avreste finito
avrebbero comprato	avrebbero venduto	avrebbero finito

andare	***venire***	***lavarsi***
sarei andato / a	sarei venuto / a	mi sarei lavato / a
saresti andato / a	saresti venuto / a	ti saresti lavato / a
sarebbe andato / a	sarebbe venuto / a	si sarebbe lavato / a
saremmo andati / e	saremmo venuti / e	ci saremmo lavati / e
sareste andati / e	sareste venuti / e	vi sareste lavati / e
sarebbero andati / e	sarebbero venuti / e	si sarebbero lavati / e

Note: According to the sequence of tenses in Italian, when the main verb is in the past tense, any subordinate conditional clause must also be in the past.

Avrei voluto imparare il giapponese.	I would have liked to learn Japanese.
Lasciò detto che sarebbe tornato alle otto.	He left word to say that he would be returning at eight.
A quanto dicono i giornali, la disoccupazione sarebbe cresciuta durante gli ultimi dieci anni.	From what the newspapers say, unemployment has increased during the last ten years.

7 Requests and Commands: The Imperative

7a *The Informal Imperative:* Tu, Noi, Voi

Apart from the **tu** form of **-are** verbs, the imperative of regular verbs is the same as the present indicative.

tu *form*	***noi*** *form*	***voi*** *form*
parla	**parliamo**	**parlate**
vendi	**vendiamo**	**vendete**
dormi	**dormiamo**	**dormite**
finisci	**finiamo**	**finite**

A few verbs are irregular in the **tu** and, occasionally, the **voi** forms.

andare	**va**	andate
avere	**abbi**	**abbiate**
dare	**dà**	date
dire	**di'**	dite
essere	**sii**	**siate**
fare	**fa**	fate
sapere	**sappi**	**sappiate**
stare	**sta**	state

Pronouns are attached to the end of the informal imperative.

Parla alla mamma!	Speak to mom / mum!
Andiamo in Italia!	Let's go to Italy!
Trovate quei libri!	Find those books!
Fammi un piacere!	Do me a favor / favour!
Digli che venga a casa mia.	Tell him to come to my house.

7b *Informal Negative Imperative*

The informal negative **tu** form of the imperative is formed by adding **non** before the infinitive. Pronouns are attached to the end of the infinitive, which then drops the **-e.**

The informal negative **noi** or **voi** form is formed by placing **non** before the corresponding informal imperative form.

Non vendere quella gonna!	Don't sell that skirt!
Non parlargli!	Don't speak to him!
Non andarci!	Don't go there!
Non facciamo i compiti!	Let's not do our homework!
Non finite l'articolo!	Don't finish the article!

7c *Polite Imperative:* Lei, Loro

All formal imperatives are formed using the **Lei** or **Loro** form of the present subjunctive. Any irregularity in the present subjunctive will, of course, occur in these imperatives [➤8] as well.

Note: • The formal form **Loro** is now often replaced by the less formal **voi** form, which avoids the use of the subjunctive.

• With the exception of **loro** 'to them,' pronouns come before the imperative form of the verb.

Mi passi il sale, per favore.	(Would you) pass me the salt, please.
Gli dia quella penna per favore.	(Would you) give him that pen, please.
Mi mostri il libro che ha comprato.	(Would you) show me the book you have bought.
Finiscano adesso.	Finish now.

Areas of Uncertainty: The Subjunctive

8a The Present Subjunctive

(i) The present subjunctive of regular verbs is formed by adding the following endings to the stem of the infinitive.

-are	**-i, -i, -i, -iamo, -iate, -ino**
-ere	**-a, -a, -a, -iamo, -iate, -ano**
-ire	**-a, -a, -a, -iamo, -iate, -ano** (verbs like **dormire**)
-ire	**-isca, -isca, -isca, -iamo, -iate, -iscano** (verbs like **finire**)

parlare	*vendere*	*dormire*	*finire*
parl**i**	vend**a**	dorm**a**	fin**isca**
parl**i**	vend**a**	dorm**a**	fin**isca**
parl**i**	vend**a**	dorm**a**	fin**isca**
parl**iamo**	vend**iamo**	dorm**iamo**	fin**iamo**
parl**iate**	vend**iate**	dorm**iate**	fin**iate**
parl**ino**	vend**ano**	dorm**ano**	fin**iscano**

(ii) The present subjunctive of most irregular verbs is formed from the first person singular of the irregular present indicative.

andare	vada, vada, vada, andiamo, andiate, vadano
bere	beva, beva, beva, beviamo, beviate, bevano
dire	dica, dica, dica, diciamo, diciate, dicano
dovere	deva / debba, deva / debba, deva / debba, dobbiamo, dobbiate, devono / debbano
fare	faccia, faccia, faccia, facciamo, facciate, facciano
morire	muoia, muoia, muoia, moriamo, moriate, muoiano
parere	paia, paia, paia, paiamo, paiate, paiano
potere	possa, possa, possa, possiamo, possiate, possano
rimanere	rimanga, rimanga, rimanga, rimaniamo, rimaniate, rimangano
scegliere	scelga, scelga, scelga, scegliamo, scegliate, scelgano
tenere	tenga, tenga, tenga, teniamo, teniate, tengano
tradurre	traduca, traduca, traduca, traduciamo, traduciate, traducano
uscire	esca, esca, esca, usciamo, usciate, escano
venire	venga, venga, venga, veniamo, veniate, vengano
volere	voglia, voglia, voglia, vogliamo, vogliate, vogliano

However, the present subjunctive of some other irregular verbs is formed from the **noi** form of the present indicative.

avere	abbia, abbia, abbia, abbiamo, abbiate, abbiano
dare	dia, dia, dia, diamo, diate, diano
essere	sia, sia, sia, siamo, siate, siano
sapere	sappia, sappia, sappia, sappiamo, sappiate, sappiano
stare	stia, stia, stia, stiamo, stiate, stiano

8b The Imperfect Subjunctive

The imperfect subjunctive of regular verbs is formed by adding the following endings to the stem of the infinitive.

-are	**-assi, -assi, -asse, -assimo, -aste, -assero**
-ere	**-essi, -essi, -esse, -essimo, -este, -essero**
-ire	**-issi, -issi, -isse, -issimo, -iste, -issero**

comprare	***vendere***	***finire***
compr**assi**	vend**essi**	fin**issi**
compr**assi**	vend**essi**	fin**issi**
compr**asse**	vend**esse**	fin**isse**
compr**assimo**	vend**essimo**	fin**issimo**
compr**aste**	vend**este**	fin**iste**
compr**assero**	vend**essero**	fin**issero**

The following verbs are irregular.

dare	**dessi,** etc.	**stare**	**stessi,** etc.
essere	**fossi,** etc.		

All verbs with contracted infinitives revert to their obsolete forms in the imperfect subjunctive.

bere	**bevessi,** etc.	**fare**	**facessi,** etc.
dire	**dicessi,** etc.		

Note also verbs in **-durre** and **-arre.**

produrre	**producessi,** etc.	**trarre**	**traessi,** etc.

8c Compound Subjunctive Tenses

The compound subjunctive tenses are formed by using the appropriate subjunctive tense of the auxiliary verb **avere** or **essere,** followed by the past participle of the main verb.

(i) *The perfect subjunctive*

This is formed by using the present subjunctive of **avere** or **essere** with the past participle of the verb.

parlare	**abbia parlato,** etc.	**capire**	**abbia capito,** etc.
accorgersi	**mi sia accorto,** etc.		

(ii) *The pluperfect subjunctive*

The pluperfect subjunctive is formed by using the imperfect subjunctive of **avere** or **essere** with the past participle of the verb.

parlare	**avessi parlato,** etc.
capire	**avessi capito,** etc.
accorgersi	**mi fossi accorto,** etc.

8d *Use of the Subjunctive*

The subjunctive is used:

- as a polite imperative [➤ 7c].

Mi dia un piatto per favore.	(Would you) give me a plate, please.
Venga pure!	Please do come!

- in many subordinate clauses introduced by **che.**

(i) *to express commands, following the verbs:*

dire	tell
ordinare	order
proibire	forbid, prohibit

Ha ordinato che io venga con te.	He has ordered that I come with you.
Digli che ci accompagni al teatro.	Tell him to accompany us to the theater.
Proibisco che tu esca stasera.	I forbid you to go out tonight.

(ii) *to express preference, desire to, or insistence, following the verbs:*

aspettare	await	**attendere**	await
aspettarsi	expect	**augurarsi**	wish, hope

desiderare	wish, want	**piacere**	like
impedire	prevent	**preferire**	prefer
insistere	insist	**sperare**	hope
lasciare	let	**suggerire**	suggest
permettere	permit, allow	**volere**	want, wish, like

Ha voluto che si parlasse inglese qui.	He wanted English to be spoken here.
Preferisce che tu rimanga in Italia.	He prefers that you stay in Italy.
Non permetto che tu esca stasera!	I won't allow you to go out tonight!
Impedì che visitassero la nonna.	He prevented them from visiting grandmother.

(iii) to express opinion, doubt, ignorance, or denial, following the verbs:

credere	believe	**(non) dire**	(not) say
dubitare	doubt	**negare**	deny
pensare	think	**(non) sapere**	(not) know
ritenere	consider, think		

Penso che Domenico abbia ragione.	I think Domenico is right.
Dubito che Gianni venga stasera.	I doubt that Gianni is coming this evening.
Non dico che Antonia abbia ragione.	I am not saying that Antonia is right.
Non so se abbia molto denaro.	I don't know if he has much money.
Nego che Gianni abbia rotto quella finestra.	I deny that Gianni broke that window.
Non dico che non sia vero.	I am not saying it isn't true.

Note: However, if there is no doubt at all, the indicative may be used with verbs expressing positive opinion.

Credo che Luigi potrà aiutarci.	I believe/am sure that Luigi will be able to help us.

(iv) *to express emotions, following the verbs:*

avere paura	be afraid	**essere sconvolto**	be upset
dispiacere	be sorry, regret	**essere sorpreso**	be surprised
essere arrabbiato	be angry	**essere spiacente**	be sorry
essere contento	be happy, pleased	**essere triste**	be sad
essere deluso	be disappointed	**meravigliarsi**	be amazed
essere felice	be happy, pleased	**rincrescere**	regret
essere infelice	be unhappy, displeased	**stupirsi**	be surprised
essere scontento	be unhappy, displeased	**temere**	fear

Mi dispiace che Giovanni non ci accompagni.	I am sorry that Giovanni is not coming with us.
Sono contenta che tu sia venuta ad incontrarmi.	I am pleased that you have come to meet me.
Mi meraviglio che tu sia riuscito ad aprirla.	I am amazed that you managed to open it.

If the subject is the same in both halves of the sentence, an infinitive construction is preferred.

Sono contenta di incontrarti.	I am pleased to meet you.

- after many impersonal verbs followed by **che.**

accade	it happens	**è peggio**	it is worse
basta	it is enough	**è possibile**	it is possible
bisogna	it is necessary	**è preferibile**	it is preferable
capita	it happens	**è probabile**	it is probable
conviene	it is better / advisable	**è strano**	it is strange
è bene	it is a good thing	**è un peccato**	it is a pity
è difficile	it is difficult	**è utile**	it is useful
è facile	it is easy	**importa**	it matters / is important
è impossibile	it is impossible		
è improbabile	it is unlikely	**occorre**	it is necessary
è inutile	it is useless / pointless	**pare**	it seems / appears
è male	it is a bad thing	**può darsi**	it may be
è meglio	it is better	**sembra**	it seems
è naturale	it is natural	**succede**	it happens
è necessario	it is necessary	**vale la pena**	it is worth it

Note that the verbs are given here in the present tense, but they may well be found in other tenses.

Pare che abbia ragione.	It appears that he/she is right (that you are right).
Bisogna che vadano subito a vedere Giuliana.	They must go to see Giuliana immediately.
È meglio che esca adesso.	It's better that he/she go out (that you go out) now.
È un peccato che tu non sia qui.	It's a pity that you not be here.
Sembrava che avesse già visto quel film.	It seemed that he/she had already seen that film (that you had already seen that film).
Non è possibile che Simone sia uscito a quest'ora.	It is not possible that Simone has gone out at this time.

Note that many of these impersonal expressions may be followed by the infinitive in Italian, as in English.

È meglio uscire adesso.	It is better to go out now.

- after certain conjunctions.

a condizione che	on condition that	**perché**	so that, in order that
a meno che (non)	unless	**prima che**	before
a patto che	on condition that	**purché**	provided that, on condition that
affinché	so that	**qualora**	in case, if
benché	although, even though, even if	**quand'anche**	even if
caso mai	should, in the event that	**salvo che (non)**	unless, provided that
come se	as if	**se, quando qualora**	if
finché non	until	**sebbene**	although, even though, even if
in maniera che	so that	**senza che**	without
in/di modo che	so that	**seppure**	even though, even if
malgrado che	in spite of the fact that	**supponendo che**	supposing that
nel caso che	in case		
nonostante che	in spite of the fact that		
per paura che (non)	for fear that		

Telefonagli prima che esca.	Call him before he goes out.
Benché piova, voglio partire.	Although it is raining, I want to leave.
Caso mai faccia brutto tempo domani, possiamo andare al cinema.	Should the weather be bad tomorrow, we can go to the movies/cinema.
Gli ho dato i soldi perché andasse al cinema.	I gave him some money so that he could go to the movies/cinema.

Note: • **Perché** takes the indicative when it means 'because.' **In modo che** and **in maniera che** also take the indicative when they mean 'with the result that' (i.e., when the action has clearly happened).

• **Se** often takes the indicative in the present and future tenses, and when it means 'whether;' but it can *never* be followed by a conditional. When the main verb is in the present or perfect conditional, the verb of the **se** conditional clause must be in the imperfect or the pluperfect subjunctive, according to the sense.

Oggi la scuola è chiusa perché è festa nazionale.	Today school is closed because it's a national holiday.
Se mi avesse parlato, avrei detto di sì.	If he had spoken to me, I would have said yes.
Se andasse a trovare la nonna, sarei molto contenta.	I she were to go and see her grandmother, I would be very pleased.

• in indirect statements expressing doubt and in some indirect questions, although it is not always obligatory.

Si dice che il professore sia un uomo alto e bello.	They say that the teacher is a tall, handsome man.
Mi hanno chiesto come fossi venuto in Italia.	They asked me how I had come to Italy.
Il capitano domandò dove andassero i ragazzi.	The captain asked where the boys were going.
Mi domando perché Anna abbia parlato così.	I wonder why Anna spoke like that.
Chi ha chiesto se Antonella potesse venire alla festa?	Who asked whether Antonella could come to the party?

• after indefinite pronouns and adjectives.

chiunque	whoever	**qualunque**	whichever
comunque	however, no matter how	**qualunque cosa**	whatever
dovunque	wherever	**qualsiasi cosa**	whatever

Chiunque venga con me, deve essere disposto a guidare.	Whoever comes with me must be willing to drive.
Qualunque decisione prenda, fammela sapere domani.	Whichever decision you make, let me know tomorrow.
Qualunque cosa lo faccia, trovo sempre difficoltà.	Whatever I do, I always find difficulties.

• after a negative, a comparative, or a superlative in the previous clause.

Non c'è nessuno qui che sappia parlare tedesco.	There is no one here who knows how to speak German.
Questa donna è più intelligente che non sembri.	This woman is more intelligent than she appears.
Giovanni è l'uomo più pigro che io abbia mai conosciuto.	Giovanni is the laziest man I have ever known.
Anna è l'unica persona che sia in grado di scrivere una tale lettera.	Anna is the only person capable of writing such a letter.

Note that, in the second example, the word **non** must be inserted before the verb. Note also that the words **primo, ultimo, unico,** and **solo** are treated as superlatives for this purpose.

• in certain exclamations.

Fossi pazzo!	If I were crazy!
Volesse il cielo!	God willing! ('Would to heaven!')
Fosse possibile!	If only it were possible!

8e *The Sequence of Tenses with the Subjunctive*

The most usual combinations of tenses are as follows:

(i) *Main clause in the present, future, or present perfect indicative —*

subordinate clause in the present or perfect subjunctive.

Spero che tu abbia ragione.	I hope you are right.
Mi ha chiesto come abbiano viaggiato.	He asked me how they had traveled.

(ii) *Main clause in the imperfect, present perfect, past definite, pluperfect indicative; in the present conditional, conditional perfect —*

subordinate clause in the imperfect or pluperfect subjunctive.

Pensavano che arrivasse alle otto.	They thought he was arriving at eight.
Bisognerebbe che lo studente cambiasse corso.	It would be necessary for the student to change course.
Impedì che venissero domani.	He stopped them from coming tomorrow.
Sperava che fossero partiti l'altro ieri.	He hoped that they had left the day before yesterday.

[For a more detailed explanation ➤Berlitz *Italian Grammar Handbook.*]

9 Things Done to You: The Passive

9a The True Passive

The passive is formed when the object of the sentence becomes the subject.

L'uomo ha costruito la casa.	The man built the house.
La casa è stata costruita dall' uomo.	The house was built by the man.

The object of the first sentence 'the house' has become the subject of the second.

(i) The passive with **essere**

In Italian the passive is usually formed by using an appropriate tense of the verb **essere** and the past participle of the verb. Here are the first person singular forms of the verb **lodare** 'praise' in the passive [➤ **lodare 1** for full passive forms].

PRESENT INDICATIVE
sono lodato/a

IMPERFECT
ero lodato/a

PAST DEFINITE
fui lodato/a

FUTURE
sarò lodato/a

PRESENT CONDITIONAL
sarei lodato/a

PRESENT SUBJUNCTIVE
sia lodato/a

IMPERFECT SUBJUNCTIVE
fossi lodato/a

PRESENT PERFECT
sono stato/a lodato/a

PLUPERFECT
ero stato/a lodato/a

PAST ANTERIOR
fui stato/a lodato/a

FUTURE PERFECT
sarò stato/a lodato/a

CONDITIONAL PERFECT
sarei stato/a lodato/a

PERFECT SUBJUNCTIVE
sia stato/a lodato/a

PLUPERFECT SUBJUNCTIVE
fossi stato/a lodato/a

Note: The past participle always agrees in number and gender with the subject of the sentence, as in the following examples:

Il pranzo è servito.	Dinner / lunch is (being) served.
La cena è servita.	Supper is (being) served.
La finestra fu rotta ieri.	The window was broken yesterday.
I ladri sono stati visti in città.	The thieves have been seen in town.

(ii) The use of ***venire***

With verbs of action **venire** very often replaces **essere** as an auxiliary verb.

La porta era chiusa.	The door was closed. (*state*)
La porta venne chiusa.	The door was (had just been) closed. (*action*)

Venire can act as an auxiliary verb in place of **essere** only in simple tenses, not compound ones.

Io vengo lodato / io sono lodato.	I am praised.
But	
Sono stato lodato.	I have been praised.

Note: Since **sono stato lodato** is a compound tense, **venire** cannot be used.

(iii) The use of ***andare***

With verbs of losing, wasting, destroying, **andare** can be used to form the passive.

Una buona parola non va mai sprecata.	A good word is never wasted.
Andarono perduti dei documenti importantissimi.	Important documents were lost / went missing.

However, **andare** is more often used to indicate obligation.

Quella sedia va messa nell'angolo.	That chair should be put in the corner.
Costruirò la scuola come va costruita.	I shall build the school as it should be built.

9b Alternatives to the Passive

There are several ways of avoiding the passive.

- By using a reflexive verb.

Come si scrive il tuo nome?	How do you write your name?

- By using the indefinite pronoun **si.**

Si dice che sia fuggito.	It is said (They say) that he has fled.

- By using the third person plural form of the verb.

Dicono che la bottega sia aperta oggi.	They say that the shop is open today.

10 Reflexive Verbs

In section 2f you have encountered a general explanation of reflexive verbs. Many verbs can be used both reflexively and as ordinary transitive verbs.

10a *Reflexive Pronouns*

The full set of reflexive pronouns can be seen in the present tense of this reflexive verb.

lavarsi	'to wash oneself'/'get washed'
mi lavo	I wash myself
ti lavi	you wash yourself (*informal*)
si lava	he / she washes her- / himself you wash yourself (*formal*)
ci laviamo	we wash ourselves
vi lavate	you wash yourselves
si lavano	they wash themselves

Note: The pronouns can be contracted to **m', t', s',** in front of a vowel, although this is not obligatory.

10b *Position of Reflexive Pronouns*

Reflexive pronouns obey the same rules as other pronouns:

• they come *before* the verb in all tenses of the indicative and subjunctive.

• they come after the verb with the infinitive; and with the **tu, noi,** and **voi** forms of the imperative.

Mi alzo alle sette ogni mattina.	I get up at seven every morning.
Bisogna alzarsi quando entra il maestro.	You need (It is necessary) to stand up when the teacher comes in.
Siediti qui accanto a me!	Sit down here next to me!
Sedetevi, ragazzi!	Sit down, boys!

10c *Reflexive Verbs and* Ne

Some verbs are not only reflexive, but they also take **ne** — for example:

andarsene 'to go away' / 'leave'

me	**ne**	**vado**
te	**ne**	**vai**
se	**ne**	**va**
ce	**ne**	**andiamo**
ve	**ne**	**andate**
se	**ne**	**vanno**

Note how the **-i** of the reflexive pronoun becomes an **-e** when followed by **ne.**

Verbs with **ne** are very often used colloquially.

scapparsene	slip away	**starsene seduto / a**	sit

Sono stanca, me ne vado adesso!	I am tired, I am going now!
Se ne sta seduta senza aiutare la mamma!	She just sits there without helping mom/mum!

10d Other Uses of the Reflexive

(i) The reflexive is often used in Italian when a possessive adjective would be used in English.

Si lavano le mani.	They wash their hands.
Vi asciugate i capelli.	You dry your hair.

(ii) Plural reflexive verbs can be used to describe actions done to 'each other.'

Si amano tanto.	They love each other so much.
Si scrivono ogni giorno.	They write to each other every day.

(iii) A number of idiomatic phrases are formed with the reflexive verb and the feminine pronoun **la:**

Quel professore se la prende con tutti.	That teacher argues with everyone.
Ce la godiamo sempre qui alla spiaggia.	We always enjoy (it) here at the beach.

 Types of Verb in Italian

11a *Predictability*

Within each tense in Italian there are six different forms of the verb, each one corresponding to a particular person, as follows:

first person singular	**io**	I
second person singular	**tu**	you (*informal singular*)
third person singular	**lui**	he
	lei	she
	Lei	you (*formal singular*)
first person plural	**noi**	we
second person plural	**voi**	you (*informal/formal plural*)
third person plural	**loro**	they
	Loro	you (*formal plural*)

Note: 'He,' 'she,' and 'you' (*formal singular*) share the same verb form. **Loro** is rarely found nowadays and is frequently replaced by **voi.**

11b *Regular Verbs*

Regular verbs are those verbs for which you can predict any part of any tense from the spelling of the infinitive. Infinitives in Italian end in **-are, -ere,** and **-ire.** Verbs in which some parts cannot be predicted in this way are said to be *irregular.* Many common **-ere** verbs are irregular in Italian, but often only in their past participle and definite past forms. Some verbs also have an irregular, shortened future stem and an irregular present subjunctive/formal imperative form.

11c *Spelling-Change Verbs*

Some verbs make spelling changes in certain tenses.

(i) Verbs ending in **-care** and **-gare** insert an **h** after the **c** and the **g** when these letters are followed by **e** or **i.**

dimenticare	**dimentichi, dimentichiamo, dimenticherò,** etc.
pregare	**preghi, preghiamo, pregherò,** etc.

(ii) Verbs ending in **-ciare** and **-giare** drop the **i** before another **i** or an **e.**

lasciare	**lasci, lascerò,** etc.
mangiare	**mangi, mangerò,** etc.
viaggiare	**viaggi, viaggerò,** etc.

(iii) Other verbs in **-iare** that have an unstressed **i** in the first person singular drop the **i** before another **i.**

fischiare	**fischi, fischiamo,** etc.
studiare	**studi, studiamo,** etc.
imbrogliare	**imbrogli, imbrogliamo,** etc.

(iv) Verbs in **-iare** that have an unstressed **i** in the first person singular keep the **i** before another **i** when it is stressed.

rinviare	**rinvii,** but **rinviamo,** etc.
sciare	**scii,** but **sciamo,** etc.

(v) Verbs ending in **-scere** insert an **i** before the **u** of the past participle only.

conoscere	**conosciuto,** but **conoscono,** etc.
mescere	**mesciuto,** but **mescono,** etc.
pascere	**pasciuto,** but **pascono,** etc.

(vi) Some verbs change their stem vowels in certain persons of the present tense, in order to facilitate pronunciation.

sedersi	**mi siedo, ti siedi, si siede,** ci sediamo, vi sedete, **si siedono**
muoversi	mi muovo, ti muovi, si muove, **ci moviamo, vi movete,** si muovono

11d Compound Verbs

Prefixes can be added to any verb as long as it makes sense.

(i) The following are the most common prefixes:

• **ri-** can be used to indicate repetition, like 're-' in English.

cominciare	begin	**ricominciare**	begin again
fare	do	**rifare**	redo
leggere	read	**rileggere**	reread

• **s-** can sometimes be added to create the opposite meaning.

chiudere	close	**schiudere**	open
coprire	cover	**scoprire**	uncover, discover
gelare	freeze	**sgelare**	thaw

• **mal-** gives the meaning of 'bad,' 'badly,' or 'evil'.

trattare	treat	**maltrattare**	mistreat
intendere	understand	**malintendere**	misunderstand

(ii) Some common base verbs have a variety of prefixes, which often correspond to similar prefixes in English.

• The verb **porre** 'place,' 'put,' has many compounds.

comporre	compose	**posporre**	postpone
decomporre	decompose	**presupporre**	presuppose
disporre	dispose	**proporre**	propose
imporre	impose	**supporre**	suppose
opporre	oppose		

• The verb **tenere** 'hold' has many compounds that correspond to the English ending '-tain.'

contenere	contain	**ritenere**	retain
detenere	detain	**sostenere**	sustain
mantenere	maintain	**trattenere**	detain

• Similarly, the verb **venire** 'come' has a number of compounds.

avvenire	happen	**provenire**	come from, originate from
convenire	agree, suit	**sopravvenire**	arrive, happen
divenire	become	**svenire**	faint
intervenire	intervene		

(iii) Finally, there are a number of verbs ending in **-durre.**

condurre	lead, drive	**ridurre**	reduce
dedurre	deduce	**riprodurre**	reproduce
indurre	induce	**sedurre**	seduce
introdurre	introduce	**tradurre**	translate
produrre	produce		

B

MODEL VERBS

Index of Model Verbs

An * before a verb indicates that this verb takes **essere.**

A † before a verb indicates that this verb takes **essere** when intransitive, but **avere** when transitive.

If the verb is usually used impersonally, this is indicated by (*Imp.*)

THE COMPLETE SYSTEM OF TENSES IN ITALIAN

Model Regular Verbs		*Number*
lodare	praise	1
***entrare**	enter, come in; get in	2
Regular Verbs		
parlare	speak	3
vendere	sell	4
dormire	sleep	5
finire	finish	6
***lavarsi**	wash oneself	7
Verbs with Obsolete Infinitives		
bere	drink	8
dire	say	9
fare	do	10
Spelling-Change Verbs		
dimenticare	forget	11
mangiare	eat	12
fischiare	whistle	13
***sedersi**	sit down	14
muovere	move	15
nuocere	be bad for, harm	16
Irregular Verbs		
accendere	turn on, light	17
affiggere	post / put (up), attach; fix	18
affliggere	suffer from, afflict	19
alludere	allude	20
***andare**	go	21
annettere	attach, add, annex	22

ACTIVE VOICE

Example of a verb using **avere** in the compound tenses

PRESENT GERUND	***PAST PARTICIPLE***
lodando	lodato

PRESENT INDICATIVE
lodo
lodi
loda
lodiamo
lodate
lodano

PRESENT PERFECT
ho lodato
hai lodato
ha lodato
abbiamo lodato
avete lodato
hanno lodato

PRESENT PROGRESSIVE
sto lodando
stai lodando
sta lodando
stiamo lodando
state lodando
stanno lodando

IMPERFECT PROGRESSIVE
stavo lodando
stavi lodando
stava lodando
stavamo lodando
stavate lodando
stavano lodando

IMPERFECT
lodavo
lodavi
lodava
lodavamo
lodavate
lodavano

PAST DEFINITE
lodai
lodasti
lodò
lodammo
lodaste
lodarono

PLUPERFECT
avevo lodato
avevi lodato
aveva lodato
avevamo lodato
avevate lodato
avevano lodato

PAST ANTERIOR
ebbi lodato
avesti lodato
ebbe lodato
avemmo lodato
aveste lodato
ebbero lodato

IMPERATIVE
loda (tu) lodi (Lei) lodiamo (noi) lodate (voi) lodino (Loro)

FUTURE
loderò
loderai
loderà
loderemo
loderete
loderanno

FUTURE PERFECT
avrò lodato
avrai lodato
avrà lodato
avremo lodato
avrete lodato
avranno lodato

PRESENT CONDITIONAL
loderei
loderesti
loderebbe
loderemmo
lodereste
loderebbero

CONDITIONAL PERFECT
avrei lodato
avresti lodato
avrebbe lodato
avremmo lodato
avreste lodato
avrebbero lodato

PRESENT SUBJUNCTIVE
lodi
lodi
lodi
lodiamo
lodiate
lodino

PERFECT SUBJUNCTIVE
abbia lodato
abbia lodato
abbia lodato
abbiamo lodato
abbiate lodato
abbiano lodato

IMPERFECT SUBJUNCTIVE
lodassi
lodassi
lodasse
lodassimo
lodaste
lodassero

PLUPERFECT SUBJUNCTIVE
avessi lodato
avessi lodato
avesse lodato
avessimo lodato
aveste lodato
avessero lodato

PASSIVE VOICE

For notes on other ways of expressing the passive ➤ 9b The Verb System in Italian.

PRESENT INDICATIVE
sono lodato / a
sei lodato / a
è lodato / a
siamo lodati / e
siete lodati / e
sono lodati / e

IMPERFECT
ero lodato / a
eri lodato / a
era lodato / a
eravamo lodati / e
eravate lodati / e
erano lodati / e

PLUPERFECT
ero stato / a lodato / a
eri stato / a lodato / a
era stato / a lodato / a
eravamo stati / e lodati / e
eravate stati / e lodati / e
erano stati / e lodati / e

PRESENT PERFECT
sono stato / a lodato / a
sei stato / a lodato / a
è stato / a lodato / a
siamo stati / e lodati / e
siete stati / e lodati / e
sono stati / e lodati / e

PAST DEFINITE
fui lodato / a
fosti lodato / a
fu lodato / a
fummo lodati / e
foste lodati / e
furono lodati / e

PAST ANTERIOR
fui stato / a lodato / a
fosti stato / a lodato / a
fu stato / a lodato / a
fummo stati / e lodati / e
foste stati / e lodati / e
furono stati / e lodati / e

Note: ➤ The Verb System in Italian for explanations of the tenses. It is important to remember that all forms have the basic part or stem **lod-**, which contains the meaning of the verb. Many tenses are simple tenses, in which endings are added to this stem to form one word; other tenses are compound tenses, in which an auxiliary verb is used in the appropriate tense and form in front of the appropriate gerund or past participle of the verb.

FUTURE
sarò lodato / a
sarai lodato / a
sarà lodato / a
saremo lodati / e
sarete lodati / e
saranno lodati / e

PRESENT CONDITIONAL
sarei lodato / a
saresti lodato / a
sarebbe lodato / a
saremmo lodati / e
sareste lodati / e
sarebbero lodati / e

PRESENT SUBJUNCTIVE
sia lodato / a
sia lodato / a
sia lodato / a
siamo lodati / e
siate lodati / e
siano lodati / e

IMPERFECT SUBJUNCTIVE
fossi lodato / a
fossi lodato / a
fosse lodato / a
fossimo lodati / e
foste lodati / e
fossero lodati / e

FUTURE PERFECT
sarò stato / a lodato / a
sarai stato / a lodato / a
sarà stato / a lodato / a
saremo stati / e lodati / e
sarete stati / e lodati / e
saranno stati / e lodati / e

CONDITIONAL PERFECT
sarei stato / a lodato / a
saresti stato / a lodato / a
sarebbe stato / a lodato / a
saremmo stati / e lodati / e
sareste stati / e lodati / e
sarebbero stati / e lodati / e

PERFECT SUBJUNCTIVE
sia stato / a lodato / a
sia stato / a lodato / a
sia stato / a lodato / a
siamo stati / e lodati / e
siate stati / e lodati / e
siano stati / e lodati / e

PLUPERFECT SUBJUNCTIVE
fossi stato / a lodato / a
fossi stato / a lodato / a
fosse stato / a lodato / a
fossimo stati / e lodati / e
foste stati / e lodati / e
fossero stati / e lodati / e

Remember that in Italian, the subject pronouns (**io, tu,** etc.) are not normally needed because the verb endings which are very clear in both spoken and written forms, tell you who the subject of the verb is. Pronouns are only used for emphasis, contrast, or clarity.

For notes on other ways of expressing the passive ➤ 9b The Verb System in Italian.

Example of a verb using **essere** in the compound tenses

PRESENT GERUND	*PAST PARTICIPLE*
entrando	entrato

PRESENT INDICATIVE	*PRESENT PERFECT*
entro	sono entrato / a
entri	sei entrato / a
entra	è entrato / a
entriamo	siamo entrati / e
entrate	siete entrati / e
entrano	sono entrati / e
PRESENT PROGRESSIVE	***IMPERFECT PROGRESSIVE***
sto entrando	stavo entrando
stai entrando	stavi entrando
sta entrando	stava entrando
stiamo entrando	stavamo entrando
state entrando	stavate entrando
stanno entrando	stavano entrando
IMPERFECT	***PAST DEFINITE***
entravo	entrai
entravi	entrasti
entrava	entrò
entravamo	entrammo
entravate	entraste
entravano	entrarono
PLUPERFECT	***PAST ANTERIOR***
ero entrato / a	fui entrato / a
eri entrato / a	fosti entrato / a
era entrato / a	fu entrato / a
eravamo entrati / e	fummo entrati / e
eravate entrati / e	foste entrati / e
erano entrati / e	furono entrati / e

Note: 1) Verbs taking **essere** are marked with an * in all the notes to the model verb pages and in the Verb Index.
2) All compound tenses using **essere** require gender agreements of the past participle—this may be masculine singular (**-o**), feminine singular (**-a**), feminine plural (**-e**), or masculine plural (**-i**).

IMPERATIVE
entra (tu) entri (Lei) entriamo (noi) entrate (voi) entrino (Loro)

FUTURE	***FUTURE PERFECT***
entrerò	sarò entrato / a
entrerai	sarai entrato / a
entrerà	sarà entrato / a
entreremo	saremo entrati / e
entrerete	sarete entrati / e
entreranno	saranno entrati / e

PRESENT CONDITIONAL	***CONDITIONAL PERFECT***
entrerei	sarei entrato / a
entreresti	saresti entrato / a
entrerebbe	sarebbe entrato / a
entreremmo	saremmo entrati / e
entrereste	sareste entrati / e
entrerebbero	sarebbero entrati / e

PRESENT SUBJUNCTIVE	***PERFECT SUBJUNCTIVE***
entri	sia entrato / a
entri	sia entrato / a
entri	sia entrato / a
entriamo	siamo entrati / e
entriate	siate entrati / e
entrino	siano entrati / e

IMPERFECT SUBJUNCTIVE	***PLUPERFECT SUBJUNCTIVE***
entrassi	fossi entrato / a
entrassi	fossi entrato / a
entrasse	fosse entrato / a
entrassimo	fossimo entrati / e
entraste	foste entrati / e
entrassero	fossero entrati / e

Dubito che Gianna *sia* ancora *entrata.*	I doubt that Gianna *has come in* yet.
Le ragazze *sono entrate* in macchina.	The girls *got into* the car.

First conjugation, regular -**are** verb

PRESENT GERUND	***PAST PARTICIPLE***
parlando	parlato

PRESENT INDICATIVE	***PRESENT PERFECT***
parlo	ho parlato
parli	hai parlato
parla	ha parlato
parliamo	abbiamo parlato
parlate	avete parlato
parlano	hanno parlato

PRESENT PROGRESSIVE	***IMPERFECT PROGRESSIVE***
sto parlando	stavo parlando

IMPERFECT	***PAST DEFINITE***
parlavo	parlai
parlavi	parlasti
parlava	parlò
parlavamo	parlammo
parlavate	parlaste
parlavano	parlarono

Similar verbs

accompagnare	accompany	**guardare**	look, watch
aiutare	help	**lavare**	wash
***arrivare**	arrive	**lavorare**	work
chiamare	call	**portare**	carry; wear
***entrare**	enter	**trovare**	find

Note: The regular **-are** verb conjugation is very large. As most regular verbs belong to this conjugation, only a small selection of the most useful verbs of the group are given above. In the Verb Index the main meanings of each verb are given. Several can also be found in the reflexive form, e.g., **lavare** 'to wash,' **lavarsi** 'to get washed.'

The only **-are** verbs that are irregular are **andare, dare, fare, stare.** These are dealt with in the Irregular Verbs section.

IMPERATIVE
parla (tu) parli (Lei) parliamo (noi) parlate (voi) parlino (Loro)

PLUPERFECT
avevo parlato

PAST ANTERIOR
ebbi parlato

FUTURE
parlerò

FUTURE PERFECT
avrò parlato

PRESENT CONDITIONAL
parlerei

CONDITIONAL PERFECT
avrei parlato

PRESENT SUBJUNCTIVE
parli

PERFECT SUBJUNCTIVE
abbia parlato

IMPERFECT SUBJUNCTIVE
parlassi

PLUPERFECT SUBJUNCTIVE
avessi parlato

—Con chi *stai parlando?*	—Whom *are you speaking* with?
—*Stavo parlando* con Gianni. Adesso *sto parlando* con Antonia.	—*I was speaking* with Gianni. Now *I am speaking* with Antonia.
—*Hai parlato* con Giuseppe?	—*Have you spoken* with Giuseppe?
—No, ma gli *parlerò* domani.	—No, but *I'll speak* with him tomorrow.
—Dubito che Giuseppe *abbia parlato* con tuo fratello.	—I doubt that Giuseppe *has spoken* with your brother.
—Guarda, *porta* una valigia molto pesante.	—Look, *he is carrying* a very heavy suitcase.
—Lo *chiamerò* ... Ti possiamo *aiutare?*	—*I'll call* him. . . . Can we *help* you?
—Sì, grazie, mi *accompagnerete* a casa?	—Yes, please, *will you accompany* me home?

Second conjugation, regular **-ere** verb

PRESENT GERUND	***PAST PARTICIPLE***
vendendo	venduto

PRESENT INDICATIVE	***PRESENT PERFECT***
vendo	ho venduto
vendi	hai venduto
vende	ha venduto
vendiamo	abbiamo venduto
vendete	avete venduto
vendono	hanno venduto

PRESENT PROGRESSIVE	***IMPERFECT PROGRESSIVE***
sto vendendo	stavo vendendo

IMPERFECT	***PAST DEFINITE***
vendevo	vendei / vendetti
vendevi	vendesti
vendeva	vendé / vendette
vendevamo	vendemmo
vendevate	vendeste
vendevano	venderono / vendettero

Similar verbs

The following **-ere** verbs are regular and follow the pattern of **vendere**.

battere	beat	**ripetere**	repeat
credere	believe	**temere**	fear
ricevere	receive		

Note: Many verbs of the **-ere** conjugation are either irregular, often in the past participle and past definite forms, or subject to spelling variations. The three verbs **bere, dire, fare,** which are given in full later [➤8, 9, 10], also belong to this conjugation.

IMPERATIVE
vendi (tu) venda (Lei) vendiamo (noi) vendete (voi) vendano (Loro)

PLUPERFECT
avevo venduto

PAST ANTERIOR
ebbi venduto

FUTURE
venderò

FUTURE PERFECT
avrò venduto

PRESENT CONDITIONAL
venderei

CONDITIONAL PERFECT
avrei venduto

PRESENT SUBJUNCTIVE
venda
venda
venda
vendiamo
vendiate
vendano

PERFECT SUBJUNCTIVE
abbia venduto

IMPERFECT SUBJUNCTIVE
vendessi
vendessi
vendesse
vendessimo
vendeste
vendessero

PLUPERFECT SUBJUNCTIVE
avessi venduto

In addition, many **-ere** verbs can have both a reflexive and a nonreflexive form.

Note that the following present tense endings are the same as those of the **-are** verbs:

- the first person singular and plural
- the second person singular

Third conjugation, regular **-ire** verb

PRESENT GERUND	***PAST PARTICIPLE***
dormendo	dormito

PRESENT INDICATIVE
dormo
dormi
dorme
dormiamo
dormite
dormono

PRESENT PERFECT
ho dormito
hai dormito
ha dormito
abbiamo dormito
avete dormito
hanno dormito

PRESENT PROGRESSIVE
sto dormendo

IMPERFECT PROGRESSIVE
stavo dormendo

IMPERFECT
dormivo
dormivi
dormiva
dormivamo
dormivate
dormivano

PAST DEFINITE
dormii
dormisti
dormí
dormimmo
dormiste
dormirono

PLUPERFECT
avevo dormito

PAST ANTERIOR
ebbi dormito

Similar verbs

Some **-ire** verbs conjugate like **dormire,** others like **finire** [> 6]. A few are irregular, and you will find these in the Verb Index.

The most commonly used verbs like **dormire** are:

bollire	boil	***pentirsi**	repent
consentire	consent	**seguire**	follow
***divertirsi**	amuse oneself	**sentire**	feel, hear
†fuggire	flee	**servire**	serve
***partire**	leave	**soffrire**	suffer

Note: 1) The gerund and the following present tense endings are the same as those of the **-ere** verbs:

IMPERATIVE
dormi (tu) dorma (Lei) dormiamo (noi) dormite (voi) dormano (Loro)

FUTURE
dormirò

FUTURE PERFECT
avrò dormito

PRESENT CONDITIONAL
dormirei

CONDITIONAL PERFECT
avrei dormito

PRESENT SUBJUNCTIVE
dorma
dorma
dorma
dormiamo
dormiate
dormano

PERFECT SUBJUNCTIVE
abbia dormito

IMPERFECT SUBJUNCTIVE
dormissi
dormissi
dormisse
dormissimo
dormiste
dormissero

PLUPERFECT SUBJUNCTIVE
avessi dormito

- the first person singular and plural
- the second person singular
- the third person singular and plural

2) The verb **riempire,** 'fill,' follows the **dormire** pattern, with the exception of the gerund **riempiendo** and the present tense, where it adds an **i** before the endings of the first and third person singular and the third person plural: riemp**i**o, riempi, riemp**i**e, riempiamo, riempite, riemp**i**ono.

—Ti *senti* meglio oggi?	—*Do you feel* better today?
—Sì, *ho dormito* molto bene stanotte.	—Yes, *I slept* very well last night.
***Riempie* le tasche di caramelle.**	*He is filling* his pockets with candies.

Third conjugation, regular **-ire** verb adding **-isc-**

PRESENT GERUND	***PAST PARTICIPLE***
finendo	finito

PRESENT INDICATIVE

fin**isc**o
fin**isc**i
fin**isc**e
finiamo
finite
fin**isc**ono

PRESENT PERFECT

ho finito
hai finito
ha finito
abbiamo finito
avete finito
hanno finito

PRESENT PROGRESSIVE

sto finendo

IMPERFECT PROGRESSIVE

stavo finendo

IMPERFECT

finivo
finivi
finiva
finivamo
finivate
finivano

PAST DEFINITE

finii
finisti
finí
finimmo
finisti
finirono

Similar verbs

Some **-ire** verbs insert **-isc-** between the stem and the ending in the singular and in the third person plural of the present indicative and of the present subjunctive. These are indicated in the Verb Index by 6.

Some **-ire** verbs can follow the pattern of either **dormire** or **finire.** The most common are:

applaudire	applaud	**preferire**	prefer
assorbire	absorb	**smentire**	deny
capire	understand; realize	**spedire**	send, dispatch
inghiottire	swallow	**suggerire**	suggest
mentire	lie	**tossire**	cough
nutrire	nourish		

IMPERATIVE
finisci (tu) finisca (Lei) finiamo (noi) finite (voi) finiscano (Loro)

PLUPERFECT
avevo finito

PAST ANTERIOR
ebbi finito

FUTURE
finirò

FUTURE PERFECT
avrò finito

PRESENT CONDITIONAL
finirei

CONDITIONAL PERFECT
avrei finito

PRESENT SUBJUNCTIVE
fin**isc**a
fin**isc**a
fin**isc**a
finiamo
finiate
fin**isc**ano

PERFECT SUBJUNCTIVE
abbia finito

IMPERFECT SUBJUNCTIVE
finissi
finissi
finisse
finissimo
finiste
finissero

PLUPERFECT SUBJUNCTIVE
avessi finito

***Finisco* i compiti e usciamo.**	*I finish* my homework, and we go out.
— *Capisci* quando parla il tuo corrispondente?	— *Do you understand* your pen pal when he speaks?
— Sì, ma *preferisco* quando mi *spedisce* una lettera!	— Yes, but *I prefer* it when *he sends* me a letter!
— Il mio corrispondente *ha suggerito* un buon dizionario.	— My pen pal *has suggested* a good dictionary.
— *Preferirei* un buon traduttore. Sarebbe meno lavoro per me!	— *I would prefer* a good translator. It would be less work for me.

Reflexive, regular **-are** verb

PRESENT GERUND	***PAST PARTICIPLE***
lavandosi	lavato

PRESENT INDICATIVE
mi lavo
ti lavi
si lava
ci laviamo
vi lavate
si lavano

PRESENT PERFECT
mi sono lavato / a
ti sei lavato / a
si è lavato / a
ci siamo lavati / e
vi siete lavati / e
si sono lavati / e

PRESENT PROGRESSIVE
mi sto lavando

IMPERFECT PROGRESSIVE
mi stavo lavando

IMPERFECT
mi lavavo

PAST DEFINITE
mi lavai

Note: Reflexive verbs can be either **-arsi, -ersi,** or **-irsi** verbs. As such, they follow the conjugation of the corresponding nonreflexive verbs—i.e., **-are, -ere,** or **-ire** verbs—whether regular or irregular.

In all cases the pronouns **mi, ti, si, ci, vi, si,** will be used. In front of a vowel these can be contracted to **m', t', s', c', v', s'.** Before another pronoun they change to: **me, te, se, ce, ve, se.**

These pronouns normally precede the verb. However, they follow the verb in the following cases:

- in the **tu, noi,** and **voi** imperative forms
- with the past participle
- with the infinitive
- with the gerund

N.B. All reflexive verbs use **essere** in their compound tenses.

IMPERATIVE
lavati (tu) si lavi (Lei) laviamoci (noi) lavatevi (voi) si lavino (Loro)

PLUPERFECT
mi ero lavato / a

PAST ANTERIOR
mi fui lavato / a

FUTURE
mi laverò

FUTURE PERFECT
mi sarò lavato / a

PRESENT CONDITIONAL
mi laverei

CONDITIONAL PERFECT
mi sarei lavato / a

PRESENT SUBJUNCTIVE
mi lavi

PERFECT SUBJUNCTIVE
mi sia lavato / a

IMPERFECT SUBJUNCTIVE
mi lavassi

PLUPERFECT SUBJUNCTIVE
mi fossi lavato / a

Similar verbs

There are many reflexive verbs. Only some of the most common are listed here:

***abbronzarsi**	tan	***interessarsi a / di**	take an interest in
***abituarsi**	get used to	***perdersi**	get lost
***accomodarsi**	come in; sit down	***pettinarsi**	comb one's hair
***alzarsi**	get up, stand up	***preoccuparsi**	worry
***arrabbiarsi**	get angry	***sbrigarsi**	hurry up
***avvicinarsi a**	approach	***scusarsi**	apologize
***chiamarsi**	be called	***sentirsi**	feel
***divertirsi**	enjoy oneself	***svegliarsi**	wake up
***fermarsi**	stop	***vergognarsi**	be ashamed
***incontrarsi**	meet	***vestirsi**	get dressed

— *Svegliati,* Paolo, sono già le sette!
— Ma, mamma, non voglio *alzarmi!*
— *Vergognati, lavati* e *vestiti* subito!
— *Mi alzerò* alle sette e mezzo.

— *Wake up,* Paolo, it's seven o'clock already.
— But mom / mum, I don't want *to get up.*
— *You should be ashamed — wash up* and *get dressed* immediately!
— *I'll get up* at seven-thirty.

Obsolete infinitive **bevere**

PRESENT GERUND	*PAST PARTICIPLE*
bevendo	bevuto

IMPERATIVE
bevi (tu) beva (Lei) beviamo (noi) bevete (voi) bevano (Loro)

PRESENT INDICATIVE bevo	*PRESENT PERFECT* ho bevuto
PRESENT PROGRESSIVE sto bevendo	*IMPERFECT PROGRESSIVE* stavo bevendo
IMPERFECT bevevo	*PAST DEFINITE* **bevvi** / bevetti / bevei bevesti **bevve** bevemmo beveste **bevvero**
PLUPERFECT avevo bevuto	*PAST ANTERIOR* ebbi bevuto
FUTURE **berrò**	*FUTURE PERFECT* avrò bevuto
PRESENT CONDITIONAL **berrei**	*CONDITIONAL PERFECT* avrei bevuto
PRESENT SUBJUNCTIVE beva	*PERFECT SUBJUNCTIVE* abbia bevuto
IMPERFECT SUBJUNCTIVE bevessi	*PLUPERFECT SUBJUNCTIVE* avessi bevuto

Note: ➤10 **fare** for notes on verbs with obsolete infinitives.

Obsolete infinitive **dicere**

PRESENT GERUND	***PAST PARTICIPLE***
dicendo	**detto**

IMPERATIVE
di' (tu) dica (Lei) diciamo (noi) **dite** (voi) dicano (Loro)

PRESENT INDICATIVE
dico
dici
dice
diciamo
dite
dicono

PRESENT PERFECT
ho detto

PRESENT PROGRESSIVE
sto dicendo

IMPERFECT PROGRESSIVE
stavo dicendo

IMPERFECT
dicevo

PAST DEFINITE
dissi
dicesti
disse
dicemmo
diceste
dissero

PLUPERFECT
avevo detto

PAST ANTERIOR
ebbi detto

FUTURE
dirò

FUTURE PERFECT
avrò detto

PRESENT CONDITIONAL
direi

CONDITIONAL PERFECT
avrei detto

PRESENT SUBJUNCTIVE
dica

PERFECT SUBJUNCTIVE
abbia detto

IMPERFECT SUBJUNCTIVE
dicessi

PLUPERFECT SUBJUNCTIVE
avessi detto

Obsolete infinitive **facere**

PRESENT GERUND	*PAST PARTICIPLE*
facendo	**fatto**

PRESENT INDICATIVE
faccio
fai
fa
facciamo
fate
fanno

PRESENT PERFECT
ho fatto

PRESENT PROGRESSIVE
sto facendo

IMPERFECT PROGRESSIVE
stavo facendo

IMPERFECT
facevo

PAST DEFINITE
feci
facesti
fece
facemmo
faceste
fecero

Similar verbs

contraffare	counterfeit
disfare	undo; unpack
soddisfare	satisfy

Note: The three verbs with obsolete infinitives (**bere** 8, **dire** 9, and **fare** 10) are exceptions. As can be seen above, sometimes the stem returns to the obsolete infinitive; other times it doesn't, thus being shorter.

—Dimmi, cosa *hai fatto* ieri sera?	—Tell me, what *did you do* last night?
—*Ho detto* a Stefano di venire a trovarmi.	—*I told* Stefano to come and see me.
—E cosa *avete fatto?*	—And what *did you do?*
—*Abbiamo bevuto* una birra e abbiamo mangiato una pizza.	—*We drank* a beer and ate a pizza.

IMPERATIVE
fa (tu) faccia (Lei) facciamo (noi) **fate** (voi) facciano (Loro)

PLUPERFECT
avevo fatto

PAST ANTERIOR
ebbi fatto

FUTURE
farò

FUTURE PERFECT
avrò fatto

PRESENT CONDITIONAL
farei

CONDITIONAL PERFECT
avrei fatto

PRESENT SUBJUNCTIVE
faccia
faccia
faccia
facciamo
facciate
facciano

PERFECT SUBJUNCTIVE
abbia fatto

IMPERFECT SUBJUNCTIVE
facessi

PLUPERFECT SUBJUNCTIVE
avessi fatto

To say you are having or getting something done, you use **fare** immediately followed by the infinitive. Note the use of **fare** in the following examples:

***Ho fatto* riparare la macchina.**	*I have had* the car repaired.
***Hai fatto* tradurre quella lettera?**	*Have you had* that letter translated?
Gianni mi *ha fatto* aspettare un'ora!	Gianni *made* me wait one hour.
***Fammi* vedere!**	*Let me* see!
Le *faccio* entrare?	*Shall I let* them in?

Verbs ending in **-care / -gare**

PRESENT GERUND	***PAST PARTICIPLE***
dimenticando	dimenticato

PRESENT INDICATIVE
dimentico
dimentic**hi**
dimentica
dimentic**hiamo**
dimenticate
dimenticano

PRESENT PERFECT
ho dimenticato

PRESENT PROGRESSIVE
sto dimenticando

IMPERFECT PROGRESSIVE
stavo dimenticando

IMPERFECT
dimenticavo

PAST DEFINITE
dimenticai

Similar verbs

cercare	search, look for	**pagare**	pay
leccare	lick	**pregare**	pray

Note: Verbs ending in **-care** or **-gare** insert an **h** after the **c** and the **g** when these letters are followed by **e** or **i.** In all other respects these verbs are regular.

IMPERATIVE

dimentica (tu)	dimentic**hi** (Lei)	dimentic**hiamo** (noi)
dimenticate (voi)	dimentic**hino** (Loro)	

PLUPERFECT
avevo dimenticato

PAST ANTERIOR
ebbi dimenticato

FUTURE
dimentic**herò**

FUTURE PERFECT
avrò dimenticato

PRESENT CONDITIONAL
dimentic**herei**

CONDITIONAL PERFECT
avrei dimenticato

PRESENT SUBJUNCTIVE
dimentic**hi**

PERFECT SUBJUNCTIVE
abbia dimenticato

IMPERFECT SUBJUNCTIVE
dimenticassi

PLUPERFECT SUBJUNCTIVE
avessi dimenticato

***Ho dimenticato* dove ho messo la penna.**	*I have forgotten* where I put my pen.
***Ho cercato* dappertutto.**	*I have searched* everywhere.
Chi mi *pagherà* una nuova se l'ho persa?	Who *will pay* for a new one for me if I lost it?
Adesso *pregherò*.	Now *I shall pray.*

12 mangiare — eat

Verbs ending in **-ciare / -giare**

PRESENT GERUND	***PAST PARTICIPLE***
mangiando	mangiato

PRESENT INDICATIVE
mangio
mang**i**
mangia
mang**iamo**
mangiate
mangiano

PRESENT PERFECT
ho mangiato

PRESENT PROGRESSIVE
sto mangiando

IMPERFECT PROGRESSIVE
stavo mangiando

IMPERFECT
mangiavo

PAST DEFINITE
mangiai

Similar verbs

cominciare	begin	**pronunciare**	pronounce
lasciare	leave; allow	**viaggiare**	travel

Note: Verbs ending in **-ciare** or **-giare** drop the **i** before another **i** or before an **e.**

IMPERATIVE
mangia (tu) mang**i** (Lei) mang**iamo** (noi) mangiate (voi) mang**ino** (Loro)

PLUPERFECT
avevo mangiato

PAST ANTERIOR
ebbi mangiato

FUTURE
mang**erò**

FUTURE PERFECT
avrò mangiato

PRESENT CONDITIONAL
mang**erei**

CONDITIONAL PERFECT
avrei mangiato

PRESENT SUBJUNCTIVE
mang**i**

PERFECT SUBJUNCTIVE
abbia mangiato

IMPERFECT SUBJUNCTIVE
mangiassi

PLUPERFECT SUBJUNCTIVE
avessi mangiato

— *Viaggi* spesso in Italia?	— *Do you travel* to Italy often?
— Sì, so che ci *mangerò* molto bene.	— Yes, I know that *I will eat* very well there.
— *Lasci* i figli a casa?	— *Do you leave* your children at home?
— No, *viaggiamo* tutti insieme.	— No, *we* all *travel* together.

Verbs ending in **-iare**

PRESENT GERUND	***PAST PARTICIPLE***
fischiando	fischiato

PRESENT INDICATIVE
fischio
fisch**i**
fischia
fisch**iamo**
fischiate
fischiano

PRESENT PERFECT
ho fischiato

PRESENT PROGRESSIVE
sto fischiando

IMPERFECT PROGRESSIVE
stavo fischiando

IMPERFECT
fischiavo

PAST DEFINITE
fischiai

Similar verb

pigliare take, catch

Note: Verbs in **-iare** drop the **i** before another **i.**

IMPERATIVE
fischia (tu) fischi (Lei) fischiamo (noi) fischiate (voi) fischino (Loro)

PLUPERFECT
avevo fischiato

PAST ANTERIOR
ebbi fischiato

FUTURE
fischierò

FUTURE PERFECT
avrò fischiato

PRESENT CONDITIONAL
fischierei

CONDITIONAL PERFECT
avrei fischiato

PRESENT SUBJUNCTIVE
fischi

PERFECT SUBJUNCTIVE
abbia fischiato

IMPERFECT SUBJUNCTIVE
fischiassi

PLUPERFECT SUBJUNCTIVE
avessi fischiato

Perché *fischi?*	Why *are you whistling?*
Chi dorme non *piglia* pesci. (*Proverbio*)	The early bird *catches* the worm. (*Lit.* He who sleeps *catches* no fish.) (*Proverb*)

Verb ending in **-ersi** with a change of vowel in the present indicative and present subjunctive

PRESENT GERUND
sedendosi

PAST PARTICIPLE
seduto

PRESENT INDICATIVE
mi siedo / seggo
ti siedi
si siede
ci sediamo
vi sedete
si siedono / seggono

PRESENT PERFECT
mi sono seduto / a

PRESENT PROGRESSIVE
mi sto sedendo

IMPERFECT PROGRESSIVE
mi stavo sedendo

IMPERFECT
mi sedevo

PAST DEFINITE
mi sedei / sedetti

Similar verbs

possedere possess, have
sedere be seated, sit

Note: The main irregular features of the verb are

- the present indicative and the present subjunctive tenses

IMPERATIVE
siediti (tu) **si sieda** (Lei) sediamoci (noi) sedetevi (voi) **si siedano** (Loro)

PLUPERFECT
mi ero seduto / a

PAST ANTERIOR
mi fui seduto / a

FUTURE
mi sederò

FUTURE PERFECT
mi sarò seduto / a

PRESENT CONDITIONAL
mi sederei

CONDITIONAL PERFECT
mi sarei seduto / a

PRESENT SUBJUNCTIVE
mi sieda / segga
ti sieda / segga
si sieda / segga
ci sediamo
vi sediate
si siedano / seggano

PERFECT SUBJUNCTIVE
mi sia seduto / a

IMPERFECT SUBJUNCTIVE
mi sedessi

PLUPERFECT SUBJUNCTIVE
mi fossi seduto / a

— *Siediti* qui accanto a me!	— *Sit* here next to me!
— No, grazie, non *mi siedo,* ho fretta.	— No thank you, *I'll* not *sit down,* I'm in a hurry.
— Mi dispiace che non *ti sieda,* ho tanto da dirti.	— I am sorry that *you won't sit down*, I have a lot to tell you.
***Possiede* una memoria prodigiosa.**	*He has* an exceptional memory.
Giovanni *sedeva* in una poltrona vicino alla finestra.	Giovanni *was sitting* in an armchair near the window.

Verb ending in **-ere** with a change of vowel in the present indicative, past definite, present subjunctive, and past participle

PRESENT GERUND	***PAST PARTICIPLE***
muovendo	**mosso**

PRESENT INDICATIVE

muovo
muovi
muove
moviamo
movete
muovono

PRESENT PERFECT

ho mosso

PRESENT PROGRESSIVE

sto muovendo

IMPERFECT PROGRESSIVE

stavo muovendo

IMPERFECT

muovevo

PAST DEFINITE

mossi
movesti
mosse
movemmo
moveste
mossero

Similar verbs

commuovere	move, affect
promuovere	promote, pass (*exams*)
smuovere	shift; dissuade

Note: A few verbs change their vowels like **muovere.** These are indicated in the Verb Index by 15.

IMPERATIVE
muovi (tu) muova (Lei) **moviamo** (noi) **movete** (voi) muovano (Loro)

PLUPERFECT
avevo mosso

PAST ANTERIOR
ebbi mosso

FUTURE
muoverò

FUTURE PERFECT
avrò mosso

PRESENT CONDITIONAL
muoverei

CONDITIONAL PERFECT
avrei mosso

PRESENT SUBJUNCTIVE
muova
muova
muova
moviamo
moviate
muovano

PERFECT SUBJUNCTIVE
abbia mosso

IMPERFECT SUBJUNCTIVE
muovessi

PLUPERFECT SUBJUNCTIVE
avessi mosso

Ci *moviamo?*	*Shall we move?*
Nessuno *si è mosso.*	No one *moved.*
***Mosse* la sedia.**	*He moved* the chair.
Era* veramente *commossa.	*She was* really *moved.*
Non *fu promosso* quest'anno.	*He did* not *pass* this year.
***Promosse* il nuovo progetto.**	*He promoted* the new project.
Se Stefano ha deciso è difficile *smuoverlo.*	If Stefano has decided, it is difficult to *dissuade him.*

Verb ending in **-ere** with a change of vowel in the present indicative, past definite, and present subjunctive

PRESENT GERUND
nocendo / nuocendo

PAST PARTICIPLE
nociuto / nuociuto

PRESENT INDICATIVE
noccio / nuoccio
nuoci
nuoce
nociamo / nuociamo
nocete / nuocete
nocciono / nuocciono

PRESENT PERFECT
ho nociuto / nuociuto

PRESENT PROGRESSIVE
sto nuocendo

IMPERFECT PROGRESSIVE
stavo nuocendo

IMPERFECT
nocevo / nuocevo

PAST DEFINITE
nocqui
nocesti / nuocesti
nocque
nocemmo
noceste
nocquero

IMPERATIVE
nuoci (tu) **noccia** (Lei) **nociamo** (noi) **nocete** (voi) **nocciano** (Loro)

PLUPERFECT
avevo nociuto / nuociuto

PAST ANTERIOR
ebbi nociuto / nuociuto

FUTURE
nocerò / nuocerò

FUTURE PERFECT
avrò nociuto / nuociuto

PRESENT CONDITIONAL
nocerei / nuocerei

CONDITIONAL PERFECT
avrei nociuto / nuociuto

PRESENT SUBJUNCTIVE
noccia / nuoccia
noccia
noccia
nociamo
nociate
nocciano

PERFECT SUBJUNCTIVE
abbia nociuto / nuociuto

IMPERFECT SUBJUNCTIVE
nocessi / nuocessi

PLUPERFECT SUBJUNCTIVE
avessi nociuto / nuociuto

Dubito che il gelato *noccia* al bambino. — I doubt that the ice cream *will be bad for* the child.

Non *nuoce* a nessuno. — *He harms* no one.

Non gli *nocerei*. — *I would* not *harm* him.

Non *nuocerà* ripeterglielo. — *It won't hurt* to tell him again.

Verbs ending in **-endere**

PRESENT GERUND	*PAST PARTICIPLE*
accendendo	**acceso**

PRESENT INDICATIVE
accendo

PRESENT PERFECT
ho acceso

PRESENT PROGRESSIVE
sto accendendo

IMPERFECT PROGRESSIVE
stavo accendendo

IMPERFECT
accendevo

PAST DEFINITE
accesi
accendesti
accese
accendemmo
accendeste
accesero

Similar verbs

appendere	hang	**offendere**	offend
difendere	defend	**sospendere**	suspend
dipendere	depend on	**spendere**	spend
intendere	intend		

For **prendere, rendere, scendere,** and their compounds ➤ Model Verbs 66, 71, and 79.

Note: The main irregular features of the verb are

- the past definite tense
- the past participle

IMPERATIVE

accendi (tu)	accenda (Lei)	accendiamo (noi)
accendete (voi)	accendano (Loro)	

PLUPERFECT
avevo acceso

PAST ANTERIOR
ebbi acceso

FUTURE
accenderò

FUTURE PERFECT
avrò acceso

PRESENT CONDITIONAL
accenderei

CONDITIONAL PERFECT
avrei acceso

PRESENT SUBJUNCTIVE
accenda

PERFECT SUBJUNCTIVE
abbia acceso

IMPERFECT SUBJUNCTIVE
accendessi

PLUPERFECT SUBJUNCTIVE
avessi acceso

Accese **la luce.**	*He turned on* the light.
Hai acceso **il gas?**	*Have you turned on* the gas?
Difesero **la patria dal nemico.**	*They defended* their country from the enemy.
Sa ***difendere*** **la sua opinione.**	He knows how to *hold his own.*
Ho difeso **la causa del ragazzo ferito.**	*I pleaded* the case for the injured boy.
Non credo che ***abbiano difeso*** **la città.**	I don't think that *they defended* the city.
Ho speso **50.000 lire oggi.**	*I spent* 50,000 lire today.
Spese **80.000 lire per quella collana.**	*He spent* 80,000 lire on that necklace.
Sospesi **la lampada al soffitto.**	*I hung* the lamp from the ceiling.
L'affare ***fu sospeso*** **a causa della sua partenza.**	The business *was adjourned* because of his departure.

PRESENT GERUND	***PAST PARTICIPLE***
affiggendo	**affisso**

PRESENT INDICATIVE
affiggo

PRESENT PERFECT
ho affisso

PRESENT PROGRESSIVE
sto affiggendo

IMPERFECT PROGRESSIVE
stavo affiggendo

IMPERFECT
affiggevo

PAST DEFINITE
affissi
affiggesti
affisse
affiggemmo
affiggeste
affissero

Note: The main irregular features of the verb are

- the past definite tense
- the past participle

IMPERATIVE
affiggi (tu) affigga (Lei) affiggiamo (noi) affiggete (voi) affiggano (Loro)

PLUPERFECT
avevo affisso

PAST ANTERIOR
ebbi affisso

FUTURE
affiggerò

FUTURE PERFECT
avrò affisso

PRESENT CONDITIONAL
affiggerei

CONDITIONAL PERFECT
avrei affisso

PRESENT SUBJUNCTIVE
affigga

PERFECT SUBJUNCTIVE
abbia affisso

IMPERFECT SUBJUNCTIVE
affiggessi

PLUPERFECT SUBJUNCTIVE
avessi affisso

Affisse **lo sguardo sul cane.**	*He fixed* his gaze on the dog.
Cosa ha ***affisso?***	What did *he put up?*
—***Affiggo*** **il poster qui?**	—*Should I put up* the poster here?
—Lo ***affiggerei*** **laggiù.**	—*I would put it up* down there.

PRESENT GERUND	*PAST PARTICIPLE*
affliggendo	**afflitto**

PRESENT INDICATIVE	*PRESENT PERFECT*
affliggo	ho afflitto
PRESENT PROGRESSIVE	***IMPERFECT PROGRESSIVE***
sto affliggendo	stavo affliggendo
IMPERFECT	***PAST DEFINITE***
affliggevo	**afflissi** affliggesti **afflisse** affliggemmo affliggeste **afflissero**

Similar verbs

friggere	fry	**soffriggere**	fry lightly
infliggere	inflict	**trafiggere**	run through, pierce
sconfiggere	defeat		

Note: The main irregular features of the verb are

- the past definite tense
- the past participle

IMPERATIVE
affliggi (tu) affliggiamo (noi) affliggete (voi) affligga (Lei) affliggano (Loro)

PLUPERFECT
avevo afflitto

PAST ANTERIOR
ebbi afflitto

FUTURE
affliggerò

FUTURE PERFECT
avrò afflitto

PRESENT CONDITIONAL
affliggerei

CONDITIONAL PERFECT
avrei afflitto

PRESENT SUBJUNCTIVE
affligga

PERFECT SUBJUNCTIVE
abbia afflitto

IMPERFECT SUBJUNCTIVE
affliggessi

PLUPERFECT SUBJUNCTIVE
avessi afflitto

Dubito che *sia afflitto* dai reumatismi.	I doubt that *he suffers from* rheumatism.
***Sono afflitta* dalla sinusite.**	*I suffer from* sinusitis.
***Inflisse* una pena al colpevole.**	*He inflicted* a penalty on the guilty man.
Gli *ha inflitto* un colpo.	*He inflicted* a blow on him.
***Ho soffritto* l'olio nella padella.**	*I fried* the oil lightly in the pan.
L'olio *frigge* nella padella.	The oil *is frying* in the pan.
Il nemico lo *trafisse* con la spada.	The enemy *pierced* him with a sword.
Le parole le *trafissero* il cuore.	The words *pierced* her heart.

PRESENT GERUND	*PAST PARTICIPLE*
alludendo	**alluso**

PRESENT INDICATIVE	***PRESENT PERFECT***
alludo	ho alluso
PRESENT PROGRESSIVE	***IMPERFECT PROGRESSIVE***
sto alludendo	stavo alludendo
IMPERFECT	***PAST DEFINITE***
alludevo	**allusi** alludesti **alluse** alludemmo alludeste **allusero**

Similar verbs

accludere	enclose, attach	**eludere**	elude, evade
concludere	conclude, achieve	**escludere**	exclude
deludere	disappoint, frustrate	**illudere**	deceive, delude, fool
disilludere	disillusion	**includere**	include

Note: The main irregular features of the verb are

- the past definite tense
- the past participle

IMPERATIVE
alludi (tu) alluda (Lei) alludiamo (noi) alludete (voi) alludano (Loro)

PLUFERFECT
avevo alluso

FUTURE
alluderò

PRESENT CONDITIONAL
alluderei

PRESENT SUBJUNCTIVE
alluda

IMPERFECT SUBJUNCTIVE
alludessi

PAST ANTERIOR
ebbi alluso

FUTURE PERFECT
avrò alluso

CONDITIONAL PERFECT
avrei alluso

PERFECT SUBJUNCTIVE
abbia alluso

PLUPERFECT SUBJUNCTIVE
avessi alluso

***Si alludeva* a questo durante la discussione ieri.**	This *was alluded to* during the discussion yesterday.
***Accludiamo* un listino prezzi.**	*We enclose* a price list.
***Inclusi* Giovanni nel numero degli invitati.**	*I included* Giovanni in the guest list.
***Ho escluso* alcuni nomi.**	*I excluded* some names.
***Fu escluso* dall'elenco.**	*He was excluded* from the list.
Non *abbiamo concluso* niente oggi.	*We haven't achieved* anything today.
La faccenda *fu conclusa*.	The matter *was concluded.*

PRESENT GERUND	*PAST PARTICIPLE*
andando	andato

PRESENT INDICATIVE	*PRESENT PERFECT*
vado	sono andato / a
vai	sei andato / a
va	è andato / a
andiamo	siamo andati / e
andate	siete andati / e
vanno	sono andati / e

PRESENT PROGRESSIVE	*IMPERFECT PROGRESSIVE*
sto andando	stavo andando

IMPERFECT	*PAST DEFINITE*
andavo	andai

Note: **andare** is the only verb of this type. The main irregular features of the verb are

- the present indicative and the present subjunctive tenses
- the future stem

IMPERATIVE
va (tu) **vada** (Lei) andiamo (noi) andate (voi) **vadano** (Loro)

PLUPERFECT
ero andato

FUTURE
andrò

PRESENT CONDITIONAL
andrei

PRESENT SUBJUNCTIVE
vada
vada
vada
andiamo
andiate
vadano

IMPERFECT SUBJUNCTIVE
andassi

PAST ANTERIOR
fui andato / a

FUTURE PERFECT
sarò andato / a

CONDITIONAL PERFECT
sarei andato / a

PERFECT SUBJUNCTIVE
sia andato / a

PLUPERFECT SUBJUNCTIVE
fossi andato / a

— *Vado* in città, vuoi venire anche tu?
— Grazie no, *sono* già *andata* ieri.
— *Va', andiamoci* insieme.

— Certo è un peccato che *tu vada* da sola.

— Penso che Gianna *sia andata* oggi in città.
— Sarà *andata* senz'altro al mercato.

— *I'm going* to town, do you want to come too?
— No thanks, *I* already *went* yesterday.
— *Go on, let's go* together.

— It's certainly a pity that *you are going* alone.

— I think Gianna *went* to town today.
— *She must have gone* to the market for sure.

PRESENT GERUND	*PAST PARTICIPLE*
annettendo	**annesso**

PRESENT INDICATIVE
annetto

PRESENT PROGRESSIVE
sto annettendo

IMPERFECT
annettevo

PRESENT PERFECT
ho annesso

IMPERFECT PROGRESSIVE
stavo annettendo

PAST DEFINITE
annettei / **annessi**
annettesti
annetté / **annesse**
annettemmo
annetteste
annetterono / **annessero**

Similar verb

connettere connect

Note: The main irregular features of the verb are

- the past definite tense
- the past participle

IMPERATIVE
annetti (tu) annetta (Lei) annettiamo (noi) annettete (voi) annettano (Loro)

PLUPERFECT
avevo annesso

PAST ANTERIOR
ebbi annesso

FUTURE
annetterò

FUTURE PERFECT
avrò annesso

PRESENT CONDITIONAL
annetterei

CONDITIONAL PERFECT
avrei annesso

PRESENT SUBJUNCTIVE
annetta

PERFECT SUBJUNCTIVE
abbia annesso

IMPERFECT SUBJUNCTIVE
annettessi

PLUPERFECT SUBJUNCTIVE
avessi annesso

***Annettiamo* un pieghevole.**	*We attach* a brochure.
Dubito che *sia stato annesso.*	I doubt that *it has been annexed.*
Questi fatti *sono* strettamente *connessi.*	These facts *are* closely *linked.*
Giovanni *connesse* i due fili.	Giovanni *connected* the two wires.

PRESENT GERUND
apparendo

PAST PARTICIPLE
apparso

PRESENT INDICATIVE
appaio / apparisco
appari / apparisci
appare / apparisce
appariamo
apparite
appaiono / appariscono

PRESENT PERFECT
sono apparso / a

PRESENT PROGRESSIVE
sto apparendo

IMPERFECT PROGRESSIVE
stavo apparendo

IMPERFECT
apparivo

PAST DEFINITE
apparvi / apparii / apparsi
apparisti
apparve / apparí / apparse
apparimmo
appariste
apparvero / apparirono / apparsero

Similar verbs

***comparire** appear
***scomparire** disappear, die; to cut a poor figure
***trasparire** shine through

Note: The verb **apparire** follows a similar pattern to the verb **finire,** but is irregular in the past participle and past definite tenses as well as having optional spelling changes in the present indicative and present subjunctive tenses.

IMPERATIVE

apparisci / **appari** (tu)	apparisca / **appaia** (Lei)	appariamo (noi)
apparite (voi)	appariscano / **appaiano** (Loro)	

PLUPERFECT
avevo apparso

PAST ANTERIOR
fui apparso / a

FUTURE
apparirò

FUTURE PERFECT
sarò apparso / a

PRESENT CONDITIONAL
apparirei

CONDITIONAL PERFECT
sarei apparso / a

PRESENT SUBJUNCTIVE
appaia / apparisca
appaia / apparisca
appaia / apparisca
appariamo
appariate
appaiano / appariscano

PERFECT SUBJUNCTIVE
sia apparso / a

IMPERFECT SUBJUNCTIVE
apparissi

PLUPERFECT SUBJUNCTIVE
fossi apparso / a

Gli studenti *appaiono* intelligenti.	The students *appear* to be intelligent.
Dubito che i cantanti *appaiano* in televisione questa sera.	I doubt that the singers *will appear* on television tonight.
Non credo che *appaiano* pigri.	I don't think *they appear* lazy.
***Apparvero* alla riunione.**	*They appeared* at the reunion.
Giovanni *è scomparso* due giorni fa.	Giovanni *disappeared / died* two days ago.
La luce *traspariva* dalla finestra.	The light *shone* through the window.

PRESENT GERUND	***PAST PARTICIPLE***
aprendo	**aperto**

PRESENT INDICATIVE
apro

PRESENT PERFECT
ho aperto

PRESENT PROGRESSIVE
sto aprendo

IMPERFECT PROGRESSIVE
stavo aprendo

IMPERFECT
aprivo

PAST DEFINITE
aprii / **apersi**
apristi
aprí / **aperse**
aprimmo
apriste
aprirono / **apersero**

Similar verbs

coprire	cover	**scoprire**	discover, uncover
offrire	offer	**soffrire**	suffer
ricoprire	cover, cover again		

Note: **aprire** and the similar verbs follow the pattern of **dormire** except for the irregular past participle and optional past definite forms.

IMPERATIVE
apri (tu) apra (Lei) apriamo (noi) aprite (voi) aprano (Loro)

PLUPERFECT
avevo aperto

PAST ANTERIOR
ebbi aperto

FUTURE
aprirò

FUTURE PERFECT
avrò aperto

PRESENT CONDITIONAL
aprirei

CONDITIONAL PERFECT
avrei aperto

PRESENT SUBJUNCTIVE
apra

PERFECT SUBJUNCTIVE
abbia aperto

IMPERFECT SUBJUNCTIVE
aprissi

PLUPERFECT SUBJUNCTIVE
avessi aperto

—*Apri* la finestra, per piacere.	—*Open* the window please.
—Perché? *Ho* già *aperto* la porta.	—Why? *I have* already *opened* the door.
—*Copri* il bambino, per piacere.	—*Cover* the baby, please.
—Perché? Chi l'*ha scoperto?*	—Why? Who *uncovered* him?
***Hai scoperto* l'America!**	Aren't you clever! (*Lit. You have discovered* America.)
La neve *ricopriva* la cima delle montagne.	The snow *covered* the mountain tops.
Quell'uomo *ha sofferto* tanto.	That man *has suffered* so much.
—Gianni ti *ha offerto* da mangiare?	—*Did* Gianni *offer* you something to eat?
—Penso che mi *abbia offerto* da mangiare.	—I think *he offered* me something to eat.
—Beh, *io* ti *offrirei* da mangiare e da bere.	—Well, *I would offer* you something to eat and drink.

Verbs with irregular past participles

PRESENT GERUND	*PAST PARTICIPLE*
assistendo	**assistito**

PRESENT INDICATIVE assisto	***PRESENT PERFECT*** ho assistito
PRESENT PROGRESSIVE sto assistendo	***IMPERFECT PROGRESSIVE*** stavo assistendo
IMPERFECT assistevo	***PAST DEFINITE*** assistetti / **assistei** assistesti assistette / **assisté** assistemmo assisteste assistettero / **assisterono**

Similar verbs

25A All verbs ending in **-istere**

***consistere di**	consist	**insistere su**	insist (on)
esistere	exist		

Note: The main irregular features of these verbs are in the past participle and the past definite.

25B In addition to verbs ending in **-istere**, there are a number of other verbs that are irregular only in the past participle. These verbs are marked **25B** in the Verb Index:

devolvere	**(devoluto)**	transfer
esigere	**(esatto)**	demand, require
evolvere	**(evoluto)**	evolve
flettere	**(flesso)**	bend
redigere	**(redatto)**	write, compile
riflettere	**(riflesso)**	reflect
seppellire	**(sepolto)**	bury [▶ 6 **finire**]
spandere	**(spanto)**	spread, spill
transigere	**(transatto)**	compromise

IMPERATIVE
assisti (tu) assista (Lei) assistiamo (noi) assistete (voi) assistano (Loro)

PLUPERFECT
avevo assistito

FUTURE
assisterò

PRESENT CONDITIONAL
assisterei

PRESENT SUBJUNCTIVE
assista

IMPERFECT SUBJUNCTIVE
assistessi

PAST ANTERIOR
ebbi assistito

FUTURE PERFECT
avrò assistito

CONDITIONAL PERFECT
avrei assistito

PERFECT SUBJUNCTIVE
abbia assistito

PLUPERFECT SUBJUNCTIVE
avessi assistito

***Vi assisterò* come posso.**	*I will help* you as best I can.
Giovanni *ha assistito ad* una partita di calcio.	Giovanni *attended* a soccer match.
Di* che cosa *è consistito?	What *did it consist of?*
***Insisti* perché lei venga!**	*Insist* that she come!
***Ho insistito sulla* necessità di leggere il libro prima di vedere il film.**	*I insisted on* the necessity of reading the book before seeing the movie / film.

PRESENT GERUND	***PAST PARTICIPLE***
assumendo	**assunto**

PRESENT INDICATIVE
assumo

PRESENT PERFECT
ho assunto

PRESENT PROGRESSIVE
sto assumendo

IMPERFECT PROGRESSIVE
stavo assumendo

IMPERFECT
assumevo

PAST DEFINITE
assunsi
assumesti
assunse
assumemmo
assumeste
assunsero

Similar verbs

desumere	infer, deduce; gather
presumere	presume; rely

Note: The main irregular features of the verb are

- the past definite tense
- the past participle

IMPERATIVE
assumi (tu) assuma (Lei) assumiamo (noi) assumete (voi) assumino (Loro)

PLUPERFECT	***PAST ANTERIOR***
avevo assunto	ebbi assunto
FUTURE	***FUTURE PERFECT***
assumerò	avrò assunto
PRESENT CONDITIONAL	***CONDITIONAL PERFECT***
assumerei	avrei assunto
PRESENT SUBJUNCTIVE	***PERFECT SUBJUNCTIVE***
assuma	abbia assunto
IMPERFECT SUBJUNCTIVE	***PLUPERFECT SUBJUNCTIVE***
assumessi	avessi assunto

Assunse **un'aria da innocente.**	*He assumed* an air of innocence.
Ho assunto **un impiegato ieri.**	*I hired* a clerk yesterday.
Fu assunto **al Pontificato.**	*He was raised* to the Papacy.
Penso che ***sia assunto*** **in cielo.**	I think that *he was raised* to Heaven.
Da quanto mi dite ***desumo*** **che siete rientrati tardi ieri sera.**	From what you tell me, *I gather* that you came home late last night.
Presumevo **che Stefano fosse ricco.**	*I presumed* that Stefano was rich.
Presume **troppo dalle sue forze.**	*He relies* too much on his strength.

PRESENT GERUND	***PAST PARTICIPLE***
avendo	avuto

PRESENT INDICATIVE	***PRESENT PERFECT***
ho	ho avuto
hai	
ha	
abbiamo	
avete	
hanno	
PRESENT PROGRESSIVE	***IMPERFECT PROGRESSIVE***
sto avendo	stavo avendo
IMPERFECT	***PAST DEFINITE***
avevo	**ebbi**
avevi	avesti
aveva	**ebbe**
avevamo	avemmo
avevate	aveste
avevano	**ebbero**

Note: **avere** is both a full verb unto itself—meaning 'have,' 'own,' 'possess'—and an auxiliary verb. As an auxiliary verb, it is used to form compound tenses of verbs conjugated with **avere** [➤1b and 1c].

***Ho* un fratello e due sorelle.**	*I have* one brother and two sisters.
***Ho* ventidue anni.**	*I am* twenty-two years old. (*Lit. I have* twenty-two years.)
***Ho* due paia di scarpe.**	*I have* two pairs of shoes.

IMPERATIVE
abbi (tu) **abbia** (Lei) abbiamo (noi) **abbiate** (voi) **abbiano** (Loro)

PLUPERFECT
avevo avuto

PAST ANTERIOR
ebbi avuto

FUTURE
avrò

FUTURE PERFECT
avrò avuto

PRESENT CONDITIONAL
avrei

CONDITIONAL PERFECT
avrei avuto

PRESENT SUBJUNCTIVE
abbia
abbia
abbia
abbiamo
abbiate
abbiano

PERFECT SUBJUNCTIVE
abbia avuto

IMPERFECT SUBJUNCTIVE
avessi

PLUPERFECT SUBJUNCTIVE
avessi avuto

—Dubito che Carlo *abbia spedito* quella lettera.	—I doubt whether Carlo *has sent* that letter.
—Penso che *tu abbia ragione.*	—I think *you are right.*
—Comunque *ha detto* che viene domani.	—However, *he said* he is coming tomorrow.
—*Avremo tempo a* convincerlo allora.	—*We'll have time to* convince him, then.
—*Hai intenzione di* spiegargli tutto?	—*Do you intend to* explain everything to him?
—*Ho paura di* dirgli la verità.	—*I am afraid of* telling him the truth.
—Ma non *aveva il diritto di* agire così.	—But *he did* not *have the right to* act like that.

PRESENT GERUND	*PAST PARTICIPLE*
cadendo	caduto

PRESENT INDICATIVE
cado

PRESENT PROGRESSIVE
sto cadendo

IMPERFECT
cadevo

PRESENT PERFECT
sono caduto / a

IMPERFECT PROGRESSIVE
stavo cadendo

PAST DEFINITE
caddi
cadesti
cadde
cademmo
cadeste
caddero

Similar verbs

***accadere** happen
***ricadere** fall again
***scadere** be due, expire

Note: The main irregular features of the verb are

- the past definite tense
- the future stem

IMPERATIVE
cadi (tu) cada (Lei) cadiamo (noi) cadete (voi) cadano (Loro)

PLUPERFECT
ero caduto / a

PAST ANTERIOR
fui caduto / a

FUTURE
cadrò

FUTURE PERFECT
sarò caduto / a

PRESENT CONDITIONAL
cadrei

CONDITIONAL PERFECT
sarei caduto / a

PRESENT SUBJUNCTIVE
cada

PERFECT SUBJUNCTIVE
sia caduto / a

IMPERFECT SUBJUNCTIVE
cadessi

PLUPERFECT SUBJUNCTIVE
fossi caduto / a

I prezzi *cadevano* rapidamente.	The prices *were falling* quickly.
Gli *sono caduti* i capelli.	*He has lost* his hair.
—Cosa *è accaduto?*	—What *has happened?*
—Ho paura che Chiara *sia ricaduta*.	—I am afraid that Chiara *might have fallen again*.
Ho paura che la fattura *scada* domani.	I am afraid that the invoice *is due* tomorrow.

PRESENT GERUND	*PAST PARTICIPLE*
chiedendo	**chiesto**

PRESENT INDICATIVE
chiedo

PRESENT PROGRESSIVE
sto chiedendo

IMPERFECT
chiedevo

PRESENT PERFECT
ho chiesto

IMPERFECT PROGRESSIVE
stavo chiedendo

PAST DEFINITE
chiesi
chiedesti
chiese
chiedemmo
chiedeste
chiesero

Similar verb

richiedere request, ask for

Note: The main irregular features of the verb are

- the past definite tense
- the past participle

IMPERATIVE
chiedi (tu) chieda (Lei) chiediamo (noi) chiedete (voi) chiedano (Loro)

PLUPERFECT
avevo chiesto

PAST ANTERIOR
ebbi chiesto

FUTURE
chiederò

FUTURE PERFECT
avrò chiesto

PRESENT CONDITIONAL
chiederei

CONDITIONAL PERFECT
avrei chiesto

PRESENT SUBJUNCTIVE
chieda

PERFECT SUBJUNCTIVE
abbia chiesto

IMPERFECT SUBJUNCTIVE
chiedessi

PLUPERFECT SUBJUNCTIVE
avessi chiesto

Cosa *ha chiesto* Luigi?	What *did* Luigi *ask?*
Mi *chiese* di uscire con loro.	*He asked* me to go out with them.
***Chiederò* al professore domani.**	*I shall ask* the teacher tomorrow.
Ho paura che Carlo *abbia richiesto* l'impossibile.	I am afraid that Carlo *has asked for* the impossible.

PRESENT GERUND
chiudendo

PAST PARTICIPLE
chiuso

PRESENT INDICATIVE
chiudo

PRESENT PROGRESSIVE
sto chiudendo

IMPERFECT
chiudevo

PRESENT PERFECT
ho chiuso

IMPERFECT PROGRESSIVE
stavo chiudendo

PAST DEFINITE
chiusi
chiudesti
chiuse
chiudemmo
chiudeste
chiusero

Similar verbs

dischiudere	disclose; open
racchiudere	contain; imply
richiudere	close again
rinchiudere	shut in, shut up
schiudere	open, disclose
socchiudere	half-close, leave . . . ajar

Note: The main irregular features of the verb are

- the past definite tense
- the past participle

IMPERATIVE
chiudi (tu) chiuda (Lei) chiudiamo (noi) chiudete (voi) chiudano (Loro)

PLUPERFECT
avevo chiuso

PAST ANTERIOR
ebbi chiuso

FUTURE
chiuderò

FUTURE PERFECT
avrò chiuso

PRESENT CONDITIONAL
chiuderei

CONDITIONAL PERFECT
avrei chiuso

PRESENT SUBJUNCTIVE
chiuda

PERFECT SUBJUNCTIVE
abbia chiuso

IMPERFECT SUBJUNCTIVE
chiudessi

PLUPERFECT SUBJUNCTIVE
avessi chiuso

Ho paura che Antonio *abbia chiuso* a chiave.	I am afraid that Antonio *has locked* up.
Cosa *ha chiuso?*	What *did he close?*
***Socchiuse* la porta**	*He half closed* the door.
***Chiuderei* alle otto.**	*I would close* at eight.
Quella domanda *racchiude* già la risposta.	That question already *implies* the answer.
Elena *fu rinchiusa* nella casa.	Elena *was shut up* in the house.

-iere verbs

PRESENT GERUND	*PAST PARTICIPLE*
cogliendo	**colto**

PRESENT INDICATIVE
colgo
cogli
coglie
cogliamo
cogliete
colgono

PRESENT PERFECT
ho colto

PRESENT PROGRESSIVE
sto cogliendo

IMPERFECT PROGRESSIVE
stavo cogliendo

IMPERFECT
coglievo

PAST DEFINITE
colsi
cogliesti
colse
cogliemmo
coglieste
colsero

Similar verbs

accogliere	welcome
disciogliere	dissolve
distogliere	dissuade, distract
prescegliere	choose from
raccogliere	gather, pick
scegliere	choose
sciogliere	untie; dissolve
togliere	remove

Note: The main irregular features of these verbs are

- the present indicative and subjunctive tenses
- the past definite tense
- the past participle

IMPERATIVE
cogli (tu) **colga** (Lei) **cogliamo** (noi) cogliete (voi)

PLUPERFECT
avevo colto

PAST ANTERIOR
ebbi colto

FUTURE
coglierò

FUTURE PERFECT
avrò colto

PRESENT CONDITIONAL
coglierei

CONDITIONAL PERFECT
avrei colto

PRESENT SUBJUNCTIVE
colga
colga
colga
cogliamo
cogliate
colgano

PERFECT SUBJUNCTIVE
abbia colto

IMPERFECT SUBJUNCTIVE
cogliessi

PLUPERFECT SUBJUNCTIVE
avessi colto

***Colgono* i fiori.**	*They are gathering* flowers.
Lo *colsi* sul fatto.	*I caught* him in the act / red-handed.
Anna *sciolse* la corda.	Anna *untied* the rope.
—Aspetta, ti *sciolgo* subito.	—Wait, *I'll untie* you right away.
—Grazie, è molto meglio *sciolto!*	—Thank you, it is much better *untied.*
—Quale camicia *scegliete?*	—Which shirt are you *choosing*?
—*Scegliamo* quella blu, è carina.	—*We're choosing* the blue one, it's nice.
—Io *avrei scelto* quella rossa!	—I *would have chosen* the red one!
—Adesso non sappiamo quale *scegliere*!	—Now I don't know which *to choose.*

PRESENT GERUND	*PAST PARTICIPLE*
comprimendo	**compresso**

PRESENT INDICATIVE
comprimo

PRESENT PROGRESSIVE
sto comprimendo

IMPERFECT
comprimevo

PRESENT PERFECT
ho compresso

IMPERFECT PROGRESSIVE
stavo comprimendo

PAST DEFINITE
compressi
comprimesti
compresse
comprimemmo
comprimeste
compressero

Similar verbs

deprimere	depress	***imprimersi**	remain impressed
***deprimersi**	become depressed	**opprimere**	oppress
esprimere	express	**reprimere**	repress
imprimere	impress; stamp	**sopprimere**	abolish; eliminate; suppress

Note: The main irregular features of the verb are

- the past definite tense
- the past participle

La macchina l'*ha compresso.*	The machine *compressed* it.
Vorrei *esprimerti* quanto siamo grati.	I would like to *express to you* how grateful we are.

IMPERATIVE

comprimi (tu)	comprima (Lei)	comprimiamo (noi)
comprimete (voi)	comprimano (Loro)	

PLUPERFECT
avevo compresso

PAST ANTERIOR
ebbi compresso

FUTURE
comprimerò

FUTURE PERFECT
avrò compresso

PRESENT CONDITIONAL
comprimerei

CONDITIONAL PERFECT
avrei compresso

PRESENT SUBJUNCTIVE
comprima

PERFECT SUBJUNCTIVE
abbia compresso

IMPERFECT SUBJUNCTIVE
comprimessi

PLUPERFECT SUBJUNCTIVE
avessi compresso

Il governo *soppresse* il giornale.	The government *suppressed* the newspaper.
L'avvocato *ha soppresso* quella clausola.	The lawyer *eliminated* that clause.
Questo tempo lo *deprime.*	This weather is *depressing* him.
Laura *si è* tanto *depressa* oggi.	Laura *has become* so *depressed* today.
Il tiranno *oppresse* il popolo.	The tyrant *oppressed* the people.
Il lavoro mi *opprimeva*.	Work *was getting* me *down.*
***Ha impresso* un timbro sul foglio.**	*He put* a stamp *on* the paper.
Le sue parole *si impressero* nella sua mente.	His words *remained impressed* in her mind.

PRESENT GERUND	***PAST PARTICIPLE***
concedendo	**concesso** / conceduto

PRESENT INDICATIVE concedo	***PRESENT PERFECT*** ho concesso
PRESENT PROGRESSIVE sto concedendo	***IMPERFECT PROGRESSIVE*** stavo concedendo
IMPERFECT concedevo	***PAST DEFINITE*** **concessi** / concedei / concedetti concedesti **concesse** / concedé / concedette concedemmo concedeste **concessero**/ concederono / concedettero

Similar verbs

***accedere** approach; access; comply with
***succedere** happen; succeed

Note: The main irregular features of the verb are

- the past definite tense
- the past participle

IMPERATIVE

concedi (tu)	conceda (Lei)	concediamo (noi)
concedete (voi)	concedano (Loro)	

PLUPERFECT
avevo concesso

PAST ANTERIOR
ebbi concesso

FUTURE
concederò

FUTURE PERFECT
avrò concesso

PRESENT CONDITIONAL
concederei

CONDITIONAL PERFECT
avrei concesso

PRESENT SUBJUNCTIVE
conceda

PERFECT SUBJUNCTIVE
abbia concesso

IMPERFECT SUBJUNCTIVE
concedessi

PLUPERFECT SUBJUNCTIVE
avessi concesso

—Cosa ti è *successo?*	—What *happened* to you?
—Non mi è *successo* niente.	—Nothing *happened* (to me).
—*Concedi* tutto?	—*Do you concede* everything?
—*Concederei* tutto per amore.	—*I would concede* all for love.

PRESENT GERUND	***PAST PARTICIPLE***
conoscendo	conos**ci**uto

PRESENT INDICATIVE
conosco

PRESENT PERFECT
ho conosciuto

PRESENT PROGRESSIVE
sto conoscendo

IMPERFECT PROGRESSIVE
stavo conoscendo

IMPERFECT
conoscevo

PAST DEFINITE
conobbi
conoscesti
conobbe
conoscemmo
conosceste
conobbero

Similar verb

riconoscere recognize

Note: It is important to distinguish between the verbs **conoscere** and **sapere**. **Conoscere** means to know a person or a place, whereas **sapere** means to know a fact or to know how to do something.

The main irregular feature of the verb is

- the past definite tense
- the spelling change in the past participle [➤ 11c(v)]

IMPERATIVE

conosci (tu)	conosca (Lei)	conosciamo (noi)
conoscete (voi)	conoscano (Loro)	

PLUPERFECT
avevo conosciuto

PAST ANTERIOR
ebbi conosciuto

FUTURE
conoscerò

FUTURE PERFECT
avrò conosciuto

PRESENT CONDITIONAL
conoscerei

CONDITIONAL PERFECT
avrei conosciuto

PRESENT SUBJUNCTIVE
conosca

PERFECT SUBJUNCTIVE
abbia conosciuto

IMPERFECT SUBJUNCTIVE
conoscessi

PLUPERFECT SUBJUNCTIVE
avessi conosciuto

— *Conosci* Roma?	— *Do you know* Rome?
— *Conosco* Roma molto bene.	— *I know* Rome very well.
— *Conoscevo* una vecchia signora a Roma.	— *I used to know* an old lady in Rome.
— Non so se la signora abiti ancora a Roma.	— I do not know whether the lady still lives in Rome.

Note: In the last example the verb **sapere** is used because the meaning is 'to know a fact.'

PRESENT GERUND	*PAST PARTICIPLE*
correndo	**corso**

PRESENT INDICATIVE	*PRESENT PERFECT*
corro	ho corso / sono corso/a
PRESENT PROGRESSIVE	***IMPERFECT PROGRESSIVE***
sto correndo	stavo correndo
IMPERFECT	***PAST DEFINITE***
correvo	**corsi** corresti **corse** corremmo correste **corsero**

Similar verbs

†accorrere	run, rush	**†ricorrere**	resort to, turn to
†discorrere	talk, discuss	**†scorrere**	flow
†incorrere	incur	**†soccorrere**	aid, assist
†occorrere	be necessary (*impersonal*)	**†trascorrere**	spend (*time*)
†percorrere	cover, go along, scour		

Note: The main irregular features of the verb are

- the past definite tense
- the past participle

When used transitively, **correre** takes **avere** in its compound tenses; otherwise it takes **essere.**

IMPERATIVE
corri (tu) corra (Lei) corriamo (noi) correte (voi) corrano (Loro)

PLUPERFECT
avevo corso / ero corso/a

FUTURE
correrò

PRESENT CONDITIONAL
correrei

PRESENT SUBJUNCTIVE
corra

IMPERFECT SUBJUNCTIVE
corressi

PAST ANTERIOR
ebbi corso / fui corso/a

FUTURE PERFECT
avrò corso / sarò corso/a

CONDITIONAL PERFECT
avrei corso / sarei corso/a

PERFECT SUBJUNCTIVE
abbia corso / sia corso/a

PLUPERFECT SUBJUNCTIVE
avessi corso / fossi corso/a

Ho paura che Antonia *sia corsa* troppo velocemente.	I am afraid that Antonia *ran* too fast.
***Corri* ad avvisarlo!**	*Run* to warn him!
La strada *corre* lungo il fiume.	The road *runs* alongside the river.
Il fiume *scorre* vicino alia casa.	The river *flows* near the house.
***Corrono* voci poco rassicuranti sul tuo conto.**	*There are* some less-than-reassuring rumors about you.
***Abbiamo corso* il rischio di morire.**	*We ran* the risk of dying.
***Abbiamo percorso* tutti gli Stati Uniti.**	*We have traveled* all over the United States.
La polizia *percorse* la città in cerca dei ladri.	The police *scoured* the town in search of the thieves.
Ne *discorreremo* dopo cena.	*We shall discuss* it after dinner.

PRESENT GERUND	***PAST PARTICIPLE***
crescendo	cresciuto

PRESENT INDICATIVE
cresco

PRESENT PROGRESSIVE
sto crescendo

IMPERFECT
crescevo

PRESENT PERFECT
sono cresciuto / a

IMPERFECT PROGRESSIVE
stavo crescendo

PAST DEFINITE
crebbi
crescesti
crebbe
crescemmo
cresceste
crebbero

Similar verbs

***accrescere**	increase
***decrescere**	decrease, go down
***rincrescere**	regret, be sorry; mind

Note: The main irregular features of the verb are

- the past definite tense
- the spelling change in the past participle [➤11c(v)]

IMPERATIVE
cresci (tu) cresca (Lei) cresciamo (noi) crescete (voi) crescano (Loro)

PLUPERFECT
ero cresciuto / a

PAST ANTERIOR
fui cresciuto / a

FUTURE
crescerò

FUTURE PERFECT
saròcresciuto / a

PRESENT CONDITIONAL
crescerei

CONDITIONAL PERFECT
sarei cresciuto / a

PRESENT SUBJUNCTIVE
cresca

PERFECT SUBJUNCTIVE
sia cresciuto / a

IMPERFECT SUBJUNCTIVE
crescessi

PLUPERFECT SUBJUNCTIVE
fossi cresciuto / a

I miei capelli non *crescono* molto.	My hair *does* not *grow* much.
Antonio è *cresciuto* molto!	Antonio *has grown* a lot.
L'albero è *cresciuto* poco.	The tree *has grown* very little.
Antonella è *cresciuta* in Sardegna.	Antonella *grew up* in Sardinia.
I prezzi non *decrescono* mai!	Prices never *go down*!
***Le rincresce* di non potervi aiutare.**	*She regrets* not being able to help you.
***Ti rincrescerebbe* aprire la porta?**	*Would you mind* opening the door?

PRESENT GERUND	***PAST PARTICIPLE***
cocendo	**cotto**

PRESENT INDICATIVE
cuocio
cuoci
cuoce
cociamo
cocete
cuociono

PRESENT PERFECT
ho cotto

PRESENT PROGRESSIVE
sto cuocendo / cocendo

IMPERFECT PROGRESSIVE
stavo cuocendo / cocendo

IMPERFECT
cocevo

PAST DEFINITE
cossi
cocesti
cosse
cocemmo
coceste
cossero

Note: The main irregular features of the verb are

- the present indicative and subjunctive tenses
- the past definite tense
- the past participle
- the gerund

IMPERATIVE
cuoci (tu) **cuocia** (Lei) **cociamo** (noi) **cocete** (voi) cuociano (Loro)

PLUPERFECT
avevo cotto

PAST ANTERIOR
ebbi cotto

FUTURE
cocerò

FUTURE PERFECT
avrò cotto

PRESENT CONDITIONAL
cocerei

CONDITIONAL PERFECT
avrei cotto

PRESENT SUBJUNCTIVE
cuocia
cuocia
cuocia
cociamo
cociate
cuociano

PERFECT SUBJUNCTIVE
abbia cotto

IMPERFECT SUBJUNCTIVE
cocessi

PLUPERFECT SUBJUNCTIVE
avessi cotto

—Che cosa *hai cotto?*
—Il sugo *è cotto*, ma *sto* ancora *cocendo* la pasta.
—Ma questa pasta *è stracotta!*

—What *have you cooked?*
—The sauce *is cooked*, but *I am* still *cooking* the pasta.
—But this pasta *is overcooked.*

PRESENT GERUND
dando

PAST PARTICIPLE
dato

PRESENT INDICATIVE
do
dài
dà
diamo
date
dànno

PRESENT PERFECT
ho dato

PRESENT PROGRESSIVE
sto dando

IMPERFECT PROGRESSIVE
stavo dando

IMPERFECT
davo

PAST DEFINITE
diedi / detti
desti
diede / dette
demmo
deste
diedero / dettero

Note: The main irregular features of the verb are

- the present indicative and subjunctive tenses
- the past definite tense
- the future stem

IMPERATIVE
dà / dai (tu) **dia** (Lei) diamo (noi) date (voi) **díano** / díeno (Loro)

PLUPERFECT
avevo dato

PAST ANTERIOR
ebbi dato

FUTURE
darò

FUTURE PERFECT
avrò dato

PRESENT CONDITIONAL
darei

CONDITIONAL PERFECT
avrei dato

PRESENT SUBJUNCTIVE
dia
dia
dia
diamo
diate
díano / díeno

PERFECT SUBJUNCTIVE
abbia dato

IMPERFECT SUBJUNCTIVE
dessi

PLUPERFECT SUBJUNCTIVE
avessi dato

— *Dammi* un po' di pane, per favore.	— *Would you give* me some bread please.
— Mah, ti *ho* già *dato* il pane.	— But *I have* already *given* you the bread.
— Io te ne *darei* senza tante storie!	— *I would give* you some without all this fuss.
— Va bene, te lo *do*, basta che stai zitto.	— O.K., *I'll give* it to you, as long as you keep quiet.

PRESENT GERUND	*PAST PARTICIPLE*
decidendo	**deciso**

PRESENT INDICATIVE
decido

PRESENT PROGRESSIVE
sto decidendo

IMPERFECT
decidevo

PRESENT PERFECT
ho deciso

IMPERFECT PROGRESSIVE
stavo decidendo

PAST DEFINITE
decisi
decidesti
decise
decidemmo
decideste
decisero

Similar verbs

coincidere coincide
incidere cut, carve
recidere cut off, amputate

Note: The main irregular features of the verb are

- the past definite tense
- the past participle

IMPERATIVE
decidi (tu) decida (Lei) decidiamo (noi) decidete (voi) decidano (Loro)

PLUPERFECT
avevo deciso

PAST ANTERIOR
ebbi deciso

FUTURE
deciderò

FUTURE PERFECT
avrò deciso

PRESENT CONDITIONAL
deciderei

CONDITIONAL PERFECT
avrei deciso

PRESENT SUBJUNCTIVE
decida

PERFECT SUBJUNCTIVE
abbia deciso

IMPERFECT SUBJUNCTIVE
decidessi

PLUPERFECT SUBJUNCTIVE
avessi deciso

Dubito che Marco *abbia* già *deciso.*	I doubt whether Marco *has decided* yet.
Cosa *ha deciso* Carla?	What *has* Carla *decided?*
***Decise* di partire subito.**	*He decided* to leave immediately.
***Decisi* sul rosso.**	*I decided on* the red.
***Incise* il nome di Maria sull'albero.**	*He carved* Maria's name on the tree.
***Incisi* un disco molti anni fa.**	*I cut* a record many years ago.

PRESENT GERUND	***PAST PARTICIPLE***
dirigendo	**diretto**

PRESENT INDICATIVE
dirigo

PRESENT PROGRESSIVE
sto dirigendo

IMPERFECT
dirigevo

PRESENT PERFECT
ho diretto

IMPERFECT PROGRESSIVE
stavo dirigendo

PAST DEFINITE
diressi
dirigesti
diresse
dirigemmo
dirigeste
diressero

Similar verbs

***dirigersi** make one's way towards, head (for)
erigere erect

Note: The main irregular features of the verb are

- the past definite tense
- the past participle

IMPERATIVE
dirigi (tu) diriga (Lei) dirigiamo (noi) dirigete (voi) dirigano (Loro)

PLUPERFECT
avevo diretto

PAST ANTERIOR
ebbi diretto

FUTURE
dirigerò

FUTURE PERFECT
avrò diretto

PRESENT CONDITIONAL
dirigerei

CONDITIONAL PERFECT
avrei diretto

PRESENT SUBJUNCTIVE
diriga

PERFECT SUBJUNCTIVE
abbia diretto

IMPERFECT SUBJUNCTIVE
dirigessi

PLUPERFECT SUBJUNCTIVE
avessi diretto

***Diresse* la nave verso il porto.**	*He steered* the boat towards the port.
La nave *era diretta* a Livorno.	The ship *was headed* for Livorno.
La lettera *era diretta* a mio padre.	The letter *was addressed* to my father.
***Ho diretto* lo sguardo verso il mare.**	*I turned* my gaze towards the sea.
Lucia *dirige* un'orchestra.	Lucia *conducts* an orchestra.
Mio padre *dirige* una grande società.	My father *manages* a large company.
***Eresse* un gran monumento.**	*He erected* a large monument.
***Si diresse* verso il paese.**	*He headed* towards the village.

PRESENT GERUND	***PAST PARTICIPLE***
discutendo	**discusso**

PRESENT INDICATIVE
discuto

PRESENT PROGRESSIVE
sto discutendo

IMPERFECT
discutevo

PRESENT PERFECT
ho discusso

IMPERFECT PROGRESSIVE
stavo discutendo

PAST DEFINITE
discussi / discutéi
discutesti
discusse / discuté
discutemmo
discuteste
discussero / discuterono

Similar verb

incutere strike, rouse

Note: The main irregular features of the verb are

- the past definite tense
- the past participle

IMPERATIVE
discuti (tu) discuta (Lei) discutiamo (noi) discutete (voi) discutano (Loro)

PLUPERFECT
avevo discusso

PAST ANTERIOR
ebbi discusso

FUTURE
discuterò

FUTURE PERFECT
avrò discusso

PRESENT CONDITIONAL
discuterei

CONDITIONAL PERFECT
avrei discusso

PRESENT SUBJUNCTIVE
discuta

PERFECT SUBJUNCTIVE
abbia discusso

IMPERFECT SUBJUNCTIVE
discutessi

PLUPERFECT SUBJUNCTIVE
avessi discusso

—Ho paura che Carlo *abbia discusso* il problema con Carla.	—I am afraid that Carlo *has discussed* the problem with Carla.
—Cosa *hanno discusso* Carlo e Carla?	—What *did* Carlo and Carla *discuss?*
—*Discussero* l'inquinamento.	—*They discussed* pollution.
***Discuterò* il tema domani.**	*I shall discuss* the essay tomorrow.
***Incusse* terrore nell'anima di Giovanni.**	*He struck* terror into Giovanni.

PRESENT GERUND	*PAST PARTICIPLE*
distinguendo	**distinto**

PRESENT INDICATIVE
distinguo

PRESENT PROGRESSIVE
sto distinguendo

IMPERFECT
distinguevo

PRESENT PERFECT
ho distinto

IMPERFECT PROGRESSIVE
stavo distinguendo

PAST DEFINITE
distinsi
distinguesti
distinse
distinguemmo
distingueste
distinsero

Similar verb

estinguere extinguish

Note: The main irregular features of the verb are

- the past definite tense
- the past participle

IMPERATIVE

distingui (tu)	distingua (Lei)	distinguiamo (noi)
distinguete (voi)	distinguano (Loro)	

PLUPERFECT
avevo distinto

PAST ANTERIOR
ebbi distinto

FUTURE
distinguerò

FUTURE PERFECT
avrò distinto

PRESENT CONDITIONAL
distinguerei

CONDITIONAL PERFECT
avrei distinto

PRESENT SUBJUNCTIVE
distingua

PERFECT SUBJUNCTIVE
abbia distinto

IMPERFECT SUBJUNCTIVE
distinguessi

PLUPERFECT SUBJUNCTIVE
avessi distinto

Al telefono non *distinguo* la tua voce da quella di tua madre.	On the telephone *I can't tell the difference* between your voice and your mother's.
Non riuscivo a *distinguere* chi c'era.	I was not able *to make out* who was there.
I vigili del fuoco *estinsero* le fiamme.	The firemen *put out* the flames.
***Distinse* un uomo all'orizzonte.**	*He made out* a man on the horizon.
Le porgo i miei più *distinti* saluti.	Yours truly.

PRESENT GERUND	***PAST PARTICIPLE***
dividendo	**diviso**

PRESENT INDICATIVE
divido

PRESENT PROGRESSIVE
sto dividendo

IMPERFECT
dividevo

PRESENT PERFECT
ho diviso

IMPERFECT PROGRESSIVE
stavo dividendo

PAST DEFINITE
divisi
dividesti
divise
dividemmo
divideste
divisero

Similar verbs

condividere	share
dividersi	separate

Note: The main irregular features of the verb are

- the past definite tense
- the past participle

IMPERATIVE
dividi (tu) divida (Lei) dividiamo (noi) dividete (voi) dividano (Loro)

PLUPERFECT
avevo diviso

PAST ANTERIOR
ebbi diviso

FUTURE
dividerò

FUTURE PERFECT
avrò diviso

PRESENT CONDITIONAL
dividerei

CONDITIONAL PERFECT
avrei diviso

PRESENT SUBJUNCTIVE
divida

PERFECT SUBJUNCTIVE
abbia diviso

IMPERFECT SUBJUNCTIVE
dividessi

PLUPERFECT SUBJUNCTIVE
avessi diviso

***Dividete* la torta fra di voi!**	*Divide* the cake among you!
Il marmo si *divise* in tre parti.	The marble *broke up* into three parts.
Il Po *si divide* alla foce.	The Po *divides* at its mouth.
Le lotte interne *dividono* il partito.	Internal disputes *are tearing* the party *apart.*
I bambini *condividevano* le caramelle.	The children *shared* the candies.

PRESENT GERUND	***PAST PARTICIPLE***
dolendo	doluto

PRESENT INDICATIVE
dolgo
duoli
duole
doliamo / dogliamo
dolete
dolgono

PRESENT PERFECT
sono doluto / a

PRESENT PROGRESSIVE
sto dolendo

IMPERFECT PROGRESSIVE
stavo dolendo

IMPERFECT
dolevo

PAST DEFINITE
dolsi
dolesti
dolse
dolemmo
doleste
dolsero

Similar verb

***condolersi** sympathize, condole with

Note: The main irregular features of the verb are

- the present indicative and subjunctive tenses
- the past definite tense
- the future stem

IMPERATIVE
duoli (tu) dolga (Lei) dogliamo / doliamo (noi) dolete (voi) dolgano (Loro)

PLUPERFECT
ero doluto / a

PAST ANTERIOR
fui doluto / a

FUTURE
dorrò

FUTURE PERFECT
sarò doluto / a

PRESENT CONDITIONAL
dorrei

CONDITIONAL PERFECT
sarei doluto / a

PRESENT SUBJUNCTIVE
dolga
dolga
dolga
doliamo / dogliamo
doliate / dogliate
dolgano

PERFECT SUBJUNCTIVE
sia doluto / a

IMPERFECT SUBJUNCTIVE
dolessi

PLUPERFECT SUBJUNCTIVE
fossi doluto / a

— Mi *duole* molto la testa.	— My head *is hurting* a lot.
— Mi dispiace che ti *dolga* tanto.	— I am sorry that *it is hurting* you so much.
— Mi *doleva* anche ieri sera.	— *It was* also *aching* yesterday evening.
***Si condolsero* con lui.**	*They sympathized* with him.

PRESENT GERUND	*PAST PARTICIPLE*
dovendo	dovuto

PRESENT INDICATIVE

devo / debbo
devi
deve
dobbiamo
dovete
devono / debbono

PRESENT PERFECT

ho dovuto / sono dovuto / a

PRESENT PROGRESSIVE

sto dovendo

IMPERFECT PROGRESSIVE

stavo dovendo

IMPERFECT

dovevo

PAST DEFINITE

dovei / dovetti

Note: The main irregular features of this modal verb are

- the present indicative and subjunctive tenses
- the future stem

dovere takes **avere** or **essere** according to which one the dependent infinitive takes. However, in practice the auxiliary **avere** is frequently used in speech, when the emphasis is on obligation.

IMPERATIVE
(There is none.)

PLUPERFECT
avevo dovuto / ero dovuto / a

PAST ANTERIOR
ebbi dovuto / fui dovuto / a

FUTURE
dovrò

FUTURE PERFECT
avrò dovuto / sarò dovuto / a

PRESENT CONDITIONAL
dovrei

CONDITIONAL PERFECT
avrei dovuto / sarei dovuto / a

PRESENT SUBJUNCTIVE
deva / debba
deva / debba
deva / debba
dobbiamo
dobbiate
devano / debbano

PERFECT SUBJUNCTIVE
abbia dovuto / sia dovuto / a

IMPERFECT SUBJUNCTIVE
dovessi

PLUPERFECT SUBJUNCTIVE
ebbi dovuto / fossi dovuto / a

***Devono* essere le otto.**	*It must* be eight.
Il treno *deve* arrivare tra poco.	The train *should* arrive soon.
***Avrei dovuto* parlare con la mamma prima di partire.**	*I should have spoken* with my mother before leaving.
***Dovrei* tornare a casa ora.**	*I should* go home now.
Antonio *è dovuto* andare a casa presto.	Antonio *had* to go home early.

PRESENT GERUND	*PAST PARTICIPLE*
espellendo	**espulso**

PRESENT INDICATIVE
espello

PRESENT PROGRESSIVE
sto espellendo

IMPERFECT
espellevo

PRESENT PERFECT
ho espulso

IMPERFECT PROGRESSIVE
stavo espellendo

PAST DEFINITE
espulsi
espellesti
espulse
espellemmo
espelleste
espulsero

Note: The main irregular features of the verb are

- the past definite tense
- the past participle

IMPERATIVE
espelli (tu) espella (Lei) espelliamo (noi) espellete (voi) espellano (Loro)

PLUPERFECT
avevo espulso

PAST ANTERIOR
ebbi espulso

FUTURE
espellerò

FUTURE PERFECT
avrò espulso

PRESENT CONDITIONAL
espellerei

CONDITIONAL PERFECT
avrei espulso

PRESENT SUBJUNCTIVE
espella

PERFECT SUBJUNCTIVE
abbia espulso

IMPERFECT SUBJUNCTIVE
espellessi

PLUPERFECT SUBJUNCTIVE
avessi espulso

— *Hanno espulso* quel ragazzo?
— *Fu espulso* dalla scuola ieri.

— *Have they expelled* that boy?
— *He was expelled* from the school yesterday.

— Io l'*avrei espulso* l'anno scorso!
— Sì, ma non è facile *espellere* alunni.

— *I would have expelled* him last year.
— Yes, but it is not easy *to expel* pupils / students.

PRESENT GERUND	***PAST PARTICIPLE***
esplodendo	**esploso**

PRESENT INDICATIVE
esplodo

PRESENT PROGRESSIVE
sto esplodendo

IMPERFECT
esplodevo

PRESENT PERFECT
sono esploso / a

IMPERFECT PROGRESSIVE
stavo esplodendo

PAST DEFINITE
esplosi
esplodesti
esplose
esplodemmo
esplodeste
esplosero

Similar verbs

ardere burn
corrodere corrode
rodere gnaw

Note: The main irregular features of the verb are

- the past participle
- the past definite tense

IMPERATIVE
esplodi (tu) esploda (Lei) esplodiamo (noi) esplodete (voi) esplodano (Loro)

PLUPERFECT
ero esploso

PAST ANTERIOR
fui esploso / a

FUTURE
esploderò

FUTURE PERFECT
sarò esploso / a

PRESENT CONDITIONAL
esploderei

CONDITIONAL PERFECT
sarei esploso / a

PRESENT SUBJUNCTIVE
esploda

PERFECT SUBJUNCTIVE
sia esploso / a

IMPERFECT SUBJUNCTIVE
esplodessi

PLUPERFECT SUBJUNCTIVE
fossi esploso / a

— La bomba *sarà esplosa* al mercato.	— The bomb *must have exploded* at the market.
— No, è *esplosa* nel negozio.	— No, *it went off* in the shop.
***Esplosi* in una risata.**	*I burst out* laughing.
Poi la sua ira *esplose.*	Then his anger *exploded.*
***Ardevano* i lumi.**	The lights *were shining.*
Il sole *ha arso* la terra.	The sun *has burned* the ground.
I topi *hanno roso* il libro.	The mice *have gnawed* at the book.

PRESENT GERUND	***PAST PARTICIPLE***
essendo	**stato**

PRESENT INDICATIVE	***PRESENT PERFECT***
sono	sono stato / a
sei	sei stato / a
è	è stato / a
siamo	siamo stati / e
siete	siete stati / e
sono	sono stati / e

PRESENT PROGRESSIVE	***IMPERFECT PROGRESSIVE***
sto	stavo

IMPERFECT	***PAST DEFINITE***
ero	**fui**
eri	**fosti**
era	**fu**
eravamo	**fummo**
eravate	**foste**
erano	**furono**

Note: It is important that you learn all tenses of **essere** as it is used in so many compound tenses.

IMPERATIVE
sii (tu) **sia** (Lei) **siamo** (noi) **siate** (voi) **siano** (Loro)

PLUPERFECT
ero stato

PAST ANTERIOR
fui stato / a

FUTURE
sarò

FUTURE PERFECT
sarò stato / a

PRESENT CONDITIONAL
sarei

CONDITIONAL PERFECT
sarei stato / a

PRESENT SUBJUNCTIVE
sia
sia
sia
siamo
siate
siano

PERFECT SUBJUNCTIVE
sia stato / a

IMPERFECT SUBJUNCTIVE
fossi
fossi
fosse
fossimo
foste
fossero

PLUPERFECT SUBJUNCTIVE
fossi stato / a

Oggi *è* difficile trovare lavoro.	Nowadays *it is* difficult to find work.
— Cosa c'*è*?	— What *is* the matter?
— *Sono* disoccupata.	— *I am* unemployed.
— *Sarà* più facile in un'altra città?	— *Might it be* easier in another town?
— Non credo che *sia* così facile.	— I do not think *it is* so easy.
— *Sei* sempre così pessimista?	— *Are you* always such a pessimist?

PRESENT GERUND	*PAST PARTICIPLE*
evadendo	**evaso**

PRESENT INDICATIVE	***PRESENT PERFECT***
evado	sono evaso / a
PRESENT PROGRESSIVE	***IMPERFECT PROGRESSIVE***
sto evadendo	stavo evadendo
IMPERFECT	***PAST DEFINITE***
evadevo	**evasi** evadesti **evase** evademmo evadeste **evasero**

Similar verb

invadere invade

Note: The main irregular features of the verb are

- the past participle
- the past definite tense

IMPERATIVE
evadi (tu) evada (Lei) evadiamo (noi) evadete (voi) evadano (Loro)

PLUPERFECT
ero evaso

PAST ANTERIOR
fui evaso / a

FUTURE
evaderò

FUTURE PERFECT
sarò evaso / a

PRESENT CONDITIONAL
evaderei

CONDITIONAL PERFECT
sarei evaso / a

PRESENT SUBJUNCTIVE
evada

PERFECT SUBJUNCTIVE
sia evaso / a

IMPERFECT SUBJUNCTIVE
evadessi

PLUPERFECT SUBJUNCTIVE
fossi evaso / a

Ho paura che l'uomo *sia* già *evaso* dalla prigione.	I am afraid the man *might have* already *escaped* from the prison / jail.
Purtroppo i ladri *evasero*.	Unfortunately the robbers *escaped*.
Le erbacce *invasero* il mio giardino.	My garden *was overrun* with weeds.
Il fiume *invase* i campi.	The river *flooded* the fields.
Hanno *invaso* il campo.	They *invaded* the field / pitch.
L'imperatore *invase* il paese.	The emperor *invaded* the country.

PRESENT GERUND	***PAST PARTICIPLE***
fondendo	**fuso**

PRESENT INDICATIVE
fondo

PRESENT PROGRESSIVE
sto fondendo

IMPERFECT
fondevo

PRESENT PERFECT
ho fuso

IMPERFECT PROGRESSIVE
stavo fondendo

PAST DEFINITE
fusi
fondesti
fuse
fondemmo
fondeste
fusero

Similar verbs

diffondere	give out, broadcast, diffuse
infondere	instill
profondere	squander
***profondersi in**	be profuse in

Note: The main irregular features of the verb are

- the past definite tense
- the past participle

IMPERATIVE
fondi (tu) fonda (Lei) fondiamo (noi) fondete (voi) fondano (Loro)

PLUPERFECT
avevo fuso

FUTURE
fonderò

PRESENT CONDITIONAL
fonderei

PRESENT SUBJUNCTIVE
fonda

IMPERFECT SUBJUNCTIVE
fondessi

PAST ANTERIOR
ebbi fuso

FUTURE PERFECT
avrò fuso

CONDITIONAL PERFECT
avrei fuso

PERFECT SUBJUNCTIVE
abbia fuso

PLUPERFECT SUBJUNCTIVE
avessi fuso

Il vetraio *ha fuso* il vetro nella fornace.	The glassmaker *melted* the glass in the furnace.
L'artista *fuse* i due colori.	The artist *blended* the two colors / colours.
La notizia *è stata diffusa* per radio.	The news *was broadcast* on the radio.
Claudio *ha infuso* il coraggio a Luigi.	Claudio *instilled* Luigi with courage.
Antonio *profuse il* denaro in divertimenti.	Antonio *squandered* the money on entertainment.
La signora *si profondeva* sempre in lodi.	The lady *was* always *lavish* in her praise.

PRESENT GERUND
giacendo

PAST PARTICIPLE
giaciuto

PRESENT INDICATIVE
giaccio
giaci
giace
giacciamo / giaciamo
giacete
giacciono

PRESENT PERFECT
sono giaciuto / a

PRESENT PROGRESSIVE
sto giacendo

IMPERFECT PROGRESSIVE
stavo giacendo

IMPERFECT
giacevo

PAST DEFINITE
giacqui
giacesti
giacque
giacemmo
giaceste
giacquero

Note: The main irregular features of the verb are

- the present indicative and subjunctive tenses
- the past definite tense
- the insertion of the **-i** in the past participle

IMPERATIVE

giaci (tu)	**giaccia** (Lei)	**giacciamo** / giaciamo (noi)
giacete (voi)	**giacciano** (Loro)	

PLUPERFECT
ero giaciuto / a

PAST ANTERIOR
fui giaciuto / a

FUTURE
giacerò

FUTURE PERFECT
sarò giaciuto / a

PRESENT CONDITIONAL
giacerei

CONDITIONAL PERFECT
sarei giaciuto / a

PRESENT SUBJUNCTIVE
giaccia

PERFECT SUBJUNCTIVE
sia giaciuto / a

IMPERFECT SUBJUNCTIVE
giacessi

PLUPERFECT SUBJUNCTIVE
fossi giaciuto / a

— *Giacque* sulla spiaggia.	— *He lay* on the beach.
— *Giacevano* sull'erba quando siamo arrivati.	— *They were lying* in the grass when we arrived.
— *Giacerei* al sole tutta la giornata!	— *I would lie* in the sun all day long!

PRESENT GERUND	***PAST PARTICIPLE***
giungendo	**giunto**

PRESENT INDICATIVE
giungo

PRESENT PERFECT
sono giunto / a

PRESENT PROGRESSIVE
sto giungendo

IMPERFECT PROGRESSIVE
stavo giungendo

IMPERFECT
giungevo

PAST DEFINITE
giunsi
giungesti
giunse
giungemmo
giungeste
giunsero

Similar verbs

† **aggiungere**	add
† **congiungere**	join, match
† **disgiungere**	separate
† **raggiungere**	catch up with, reach, attain
† **soggiungere**	add

verbs marked † can take **essere** when used intransitively or **avere** when used transitively

Note: The main irregular features of the verb are

- the past definite tense
- the past participle

IMPERATIVE
giungi (tu) giunga (Lei) giungiamo (noi) giungete (voi) giungano (Loro)

PLUPERFECT
ero giunto / a

PAST ANTERIOR
fui giunto / a

FUTURE
giungerò

FUTURE PERFECT
sarò giunto / a

PRESENT CONDITIONAL
giungerei

CONDITIONAL PERFECT
sarei giunto / a

PRESENT SUBJUNCTIVE
giunga

PERFECT SUBJUNCTIVE
sia giunto / a

IMPERFECT SUBJUNCTIVE
giungessi

PLUPERFECT SUBJUNCTIVE
fossi giunto / a

***Giunsi* in Italia all'inizio di giugno.**	I *arrived* in Italy at the beginning of June.
Nessun suono *giungeva* al mio orecchio.	No sound *reached* my ears.
Dopo aver parlato a lungo del problema, *siamo giunti* alla conclusione che non valeva la pena querelare.	After talking about the problem at length, *we reached* the conclusion that it wasn't worth our suing.
Il nonno *è giunto* all'età di novant'anni.	Grandad *has reached* the age of ninety.
Va' avanti, ti *raggiungo* presto.	Go on ahead, *I'll catch up* soon.
Il prezzo *raggiunge* i tre milioni di lire.	The price *comes to* three million lire.
***Congiunsero* le mani per pregare.**	*They joined* their hands to pray.

PRESENT GERUND	***PAST PARTICIPLE***
leggendo	**letto**

PRESENT INDICATIVE
leggo

PRESENT PROGRESSIVE
sto leggendo

IMPERFECT
leggevo

PRESENT PERFECT
ho letto

IMPERFECT PROGRESSIVE
stavo leggendo

PAST DEFINITE
lessi
leggesti
lesse
leggemmo
leggeste
lessero

Similar verb

eleggere elect

Note: The main irregular features of the verb are

- the past definite tense
- the past participle

IMPERATIVE

leggi (tu) legga (Lei) leggiamo (noi) leggete (voi) leggano (Loro)

PLUPERFECT
avevo letto

FUTURE
leggerò

PRESENT CONDITIONAL
leggerei

PRESENT SUBJUNCTIVE
legga

IMPERFECT SUBJUNCTIVE
leggessi

PAST ANTERIOR
ebbi letto

FUTURE PERFECT
avrò letto

CONDITIONAL PERFECT
avrei letto

PERFECT SUBJUNCTIVE
abbia letto

PLUPERFECT SUBJUNCTIVE
avessi letto

Lo *leggo* nei tuoi occhi.	*I can read* it in your eyes.
***Legga* attentamente questa lettera.**	*Read* this letter carefully.
La *lesse* a voce alta.	*He read* it out aloud.
Sa *leggere* la musica *a prima vista.*	He knows how to *sight-read* music.
***Ho letto* fra le righe.**	*I read* between the lines.
Quando non riuscivo a dormire, *leggevo.*	When I could not sleep, *I used to read.*
È stato *eletto* ieri.	He was *elected* yesterday.

PRESENT GERUND	***PAST PARTICIPLE***
mettendo	**messo**

PRESENT INDICATIVE	***PRESENT PERFECT***
metto	ho messo
PRESENT PROGRESSIVE	***IMPERFECT PROGRESSIVE***
sto mettendo	stavo mettendo
IMPERFECT	***PAST DEFINITE***
mettevo	**misi** mettesti **mise** mettemmo metteste **misero**

Similar verbs

ammettere	admit	**permettere**	permit
commettere	commit	**promettere**	promise
compromettere	compromise	**rimettere**	replace
emettere	emit	**scommettere**	bet
frammettere	interpose, insert	**smettere**	stop
immettere	admit, let in	**trasmettere**	transmit
omettere	omit		

Note: The main irregular features of the verb are

- the past definite tense
- the past participle

***Abbiamo messo* il riscaldamento centrale.**	*We put in* central heating.
***Mise* il fazzoletto in tasca.**	*He put* the handkerchief in his pocket.

IMPERATIVE
metti (tu) metta (Lei) mettiamo (noi) mettete (voi) mettano (Loro)

PLUPERFECT
avevo messo

PAST ANTERIOR
ebbi messo

FUTURE
metterò

FUTURE PERFECT
avrò messo

PRESENT CONDITIONAL
metterei

CONDITIONAL PERFECT
avrei messo

PRESENT SUBJUNCTIVE
metta

PERFECT SUBJUNCTIVE
abbia messo

IMPERFECT SUBJUNCTIVE
mettessi

PLUPERFECT SUBJUNCTIVE
avessi messo

Dubito che *abbia messo* da parte quei soldi.	I doubt whether *he has put* that money aside.
***Ho messo* la tavola all'asta.**	*I put* the table up for auction.
***Ha messo* indietro l'orologio.**	*He put* his watch back.
Quanto tempo *ci hai messo* a farlo?	How long *did it take you* to do it?
***Ammettiamo* pure che tu abbia ragione.**	*Let's suppose* (*admit*) that you are right.
Luigi *emise* un grido forte.	Luigi *let out* a loud cry.
Mi *promise* un bel regalo!	*He promised* me a beautiful present.
***Ho smesso* di fumare!**	*I've stopped* smoking!
***Scommetto* che non lo sa!**	*I bet* he does not know it!
***Trasmettevo* alla radio ogni domenica pomeriggio.**	*I used to broadcast* on the radio every Sunday afternoon.

PRESENT GERUND	***PAST PARTICIPLE***
mordendo	**morso**
PRESENT INDICATIVE	***PRESENT PERFECT***
mordo	ho morso
PRESENT PROGRESSIVE	***IMPERFECT PROGRESSIVE***
sto mordendo	stavo mordendo
IMPERFECT	***PAST DEFINITE***
mordevo	**morsi** mordesti **morse** mordemmo mordeste **morsero**

Similar verbs

***mordersi** bite oneself
rimordere bite back; prick

Note: The main irregular features of the verb are

- the past definite tense
- the past participle

IMPERATIVE
mordi (tu) morda (Lei) mordiamo (noi) mordete (voi) mordano (Loro)

PLUPERFECT	***PAST ANTERIOR***
avevo morso	ebbi morso
FUTURE	***FUTURE PERFECT***
morderò	avrò morso
PRESENT CONDITIONAL	***CONDITIONAL PERFECT***
morderei	avrei morso
PRESENT SUBJUNCTIVE	***PERFECT SUBJUNCTIVE***
morda	abbia morso
IMPERFECT SUBJUNCTIVE	***PLUPERFECT SUBJUNCTIVE***
mordessi	avessi morso

Il cane mi *ha morso* il braccio.	The dog *bit* my arm.
Pulci e zanzare *mordono*.	Fleas and mosquitoes *bite*.
Sentiva un vento gelido *mordergli* il viso.	*He felt* an icy wind on his face.
***Mordeva* il freno.**	He was *champing* at the bit.
***Morsero* la polvere.**	*They bit* the dust.
***Mi sono morsa* la lingua.**	*I bit* my tongue.
***Mi sarei morsa* la lingua.**	*I could have* kicked myself.
***Gli rimorse* la coscienza.**	His conscience *pricked* him.

PRESENT GERUND
morendo

PAST PARTICIPLE
morto

PRESENT INDICATIVE
muoio
muori
muore
moriamo
morite
muoiono

PRESENT PERFECT
sono morto / a

PRESENT PROGRESSIVE
sto morendo

IMPERFECT PROGRESSIVE
stavo morendo

IMPERFECT
morivo

PAST DEFINITE
morii

Note: The main irregular features are

- the present indicative and subjunctive tenses
- the past participle

IMPERATIVE
muori (tu) **muoia** (Lei) moriamo (noi) morite (voi) **muoiano** (Loro)

PLUPERFECT
ero morto / a

PAST ANTERIOR
fui morto / a

FUTURE
morrò / morirò

FUTURE PERFECT
sarò morto / a

PRESENT CONDITIONAL
morrei / morirei

CONDITIONAL PERFECT
sarei morto / a

PRESENT SUBJUNCTIVE
muoia
muoia
muoia
moriamo
moriate
muoiano

PERFECT SUBJUNCTIVE
sia morto / a

IMPERFECT SUBJUNCTIVE
morissi

PLUPERFECT SUBJUNCTIVE
fossi morto / a

— *Muoio* dal caldo!	— *I'm dying* from the heat.
— Dubito che *tu muoia* dal caldo!	— I doubt that *you'll die* from the heat.
Dopo una giornata di lavoro, sono stanca *morta!*	After a day's work, I am *dead* tired.

PRESENT GERUND	***PAST PARTICIPLE***
nascendo	**nato**

PRESENT INDICATIVE
nasco

PRESENT PROGRESSIVE
sto nascendo

IMPERFECT
nascevo

PRESENT PERFECT
sono nato / a

IMPERFECT PROGRESSIVE
stavo nascendo

PAST DEFINITE
nacqui
nascesti
nacque
nascemmo
nasceste
nacquero

Similar verb

rinascere be born again

Note: The main irregular features of the verb are

- the past definite tense
- the past participle

IMPERATIVE
nasci (tu) nasca (Lei) nasciamo (noi) nascete (voi) nascano (Loro)

PLUPERFECT
ero nato / a

PAST ANTERIOR
fui nato / a

FUTURE
nascerò

FUTURE PERFECT
sarò nato / a

PRESENT CONDITIONAL
nascerei

CONDITIONAL PERFECT
sarei nato / a

PRESENT SUBJUNCTIVE
nasca

PERFECT SUBJUNCTIVE
sia nato / a

IMPERFECT SUBJUNCTIVE
nascessi

PLUPERFECT SUBJUNCTIVE
fossi nato / a

La bambina *è nata* stamattina.	The baby girl *was born* this morning.
Il morto *era nato* ottantatré anni fa.	The dead man *was born* eighty-three years ago.
Boccaccio *nacque* secoli fa.	Boccaccio *was born* centuries ago.
Deve ancora *nascere* chi saprà risolvere tali problemi.	The man who can solve such problems is yet *to be born*.
Mi sento *rinascere*.	I feel like a new person (*reborn*).
Quando lo rividi, mi *rinacque* l'odio.	When I saw him, my feelings of hatred *began again*.
Gli *nascono* i denti.	*He is cutting* his first teeth.
Il Po *nasce* dal Monviso.	The river Po *has its source* on Monviso.

PRESENT GERUND
parendo

PAST PARTICIPLE
parso

PRESENT INDICATIVE
paio
pari
pare
paiamo
parete
paiono

PRESENT PERFECT
sono parso / a

PRESENT PROGRESSIVE
sto parendo

IMPERFECT PROGRESSIVE
stavo parendo

IMPERFECT
parevo

PAST DEFINITE
parvi
paresti
parve
paremmo
pareste
parvero

Note: The verb **parere** is mostly used impersonally and is consequently rare except for the third persons.

The main irregular features of the verb are

- the present indicative and subjunctive tenses
- the future stem
- the past definite tense
- the past participle

There are also some similarities with the verb **apparire** [► 23].

IMPERATIVE
(There is none.)

PLUPERFECT
ero parso / a

PAST ANTERIOR
fui parso / a

FUTURE
parrò

FUTURE PERFECT
sarò parso / a

PRESENT CONDITIONAL
parrei

CONDITIONAL PERFECT
sarei parso / a

PRESENT SUBJUNCTIVE
paia
paia
paia
paiamo
pariate
paiano

PERFECT SUBJUNCTIVE
sia parso / a

IMPERFECT SUBJUNCTIVE
paressi

PLUPERFECT SUBJUNCTIVE
fossi parso / a

Mi *pare* importante.	It *seems* important to me.
Non mi *pareva* semplice.	It *did* not *seem* easy to me.
Gli *paiono* grandi.	*They seem* big to him.
***Ti parevano* stretti?**	*Did you think* they were narrow?

PRESENT GERUND	***PAST PARTICIPLE***
perdendo	**perso** / perduto

PRESENT INDICATIVE
perdo

PRESENT PROGRESSIVE
sto perdendo

IMPERFECT
perdevo

PRESENT PERFECT
ho perso

IMPERFECT PROGRESSIVE
stavo perdendo

PAST DEFINITE
persi / perdei / perdetti
perdesti
perse / perdé / perdette
perdemmo
perdeste
persero / perderono / perdettero

Similar verb

***perdersi** get lost

Note: The main irregular features of the verb are

- the past definite tense
- the past participle (although it is possible to use the regular past participle)

IMPERATIVE
perdi (tu) perda (Lei) perdiamo (noi) perdete (voi) perdano (Loro)

PLUPERFECT
avevo perso

PAST ANTERIOR
ebbi perso

FUTURE
perderò

FUTURE PERFECT
avrò perso

PRESENT CONDITIONAL
perderei

CONDITIONAL PERFECT
avrei perso

PRESENT SUBJUNCTIVE
perda

PERFECT SUBJUNCTIVE
abbia perso

IMPERFECT SUBJUNCTIVE
perdessi

PLUPERFECT SUBJUNCTIVE
avessi perso

Ho perso **la penna.**	*I lost* the pen.
L'*ho persa* ieri.	*I lost* it (the pen) yesterday.
Gianna *ha perso* un figlio.	Gianna *has lost* a son (through death).
L'anno scorso *ha perso* un anno perché era ammalata.	Last year *she fell* a year behind because she was sick.
Antonio *ha perso* il treno.	Antonio *has missed* the train.
Questo secchio *perde* acqua.	This bucket *is leaking* water.
Mi sono perso **a Firenze.**	*I got lost* in Florence.
È inutile spiegarmi queste cose, *mi* ci *perdo*.	It's no use explaining these things to me, *I can't make head or tail of* them.

PRESENT GERUND	*PAST PARTICIPLE*
persuadendo	**persuaso**

PRESENT INDICATIVE
persuado

PRESENT PERFECT
ho persuaso

PRESENT PROGRESSIVE
sto persuadendo

IMPERFECT PROGRESSIVE
stavo persuadendo

IMPERFECT
persuadevo

PAST DEFINITE
persuasi
persuadesti
persuase
persuademmo
persuadeste
persuasero

Similar verb

dissuadere dissuade

Note: The main irregular features of the verb are

- the past definite tense
- the past participle

IMPERATIVE

persuadi (tu)	persuada (Lei)	persuadiamo (noi)
persuadete (voi)	persuadano (Loro)	

PLUPERFECT
avevo persuaso

PAST ANTERIOR
ebbi persuaso

FUTURE
persuaderò

FUTURE PERFECT
avrò persuaso

PRESENT CONDITIONAL
persuaderei

CONDITIONAL PERFECT
avrei persuaso

PRESENT SUBJUNCTIVE
persuada

PERFECT SUBJUNCTIVE
abbia persuaso

IMPERFECT SUBJUNCTIVE
persuadessi

PLUPERFECT SUBJUNCTIVE
avessi persuaso

Ho avuto difficoltà a *persuader*la.	I had difficulty in *persuading* her.
Finii per *persuader*la a farlo.	*I* finally *persuaded* her to do it.
La *persuasi* che aveva torto.	*I persuaded* her that she was wrong.
L'*ho persuaso* dell'innocenza di Gianni.	*I convinced* him of Gianni's innocence.
***Dissuadi*la dal venire!**	*Dissuade* her from coming!
Nulla la *dissuaderà* dal provare ancora una volta.	Nothing *will dissuade* her from trying one more time.

PRESENT GERUND	*PAST PARTICIPLE*
piacendo	**piaciuto**

PRESENT INDICATIVE	*PRESENT PERFECT*
piaccio	sono piaciuto / a
piaci	
piace	**è piaciuto / a**
piacciamo / piaciamo	
piacete	
piacciono	**sono piaciuti / e**

PRESENT PROGRESSIVE	*IMPERFECT PROGRESSIVE*
sto piacendo	stavo piacendo

IMPERFECT	*PAST DEFINITE*
piacevo	**piacqui**
	piacesti
	piacque
	piacemmo
	piaceste
	piacquero

Similar verbs

***compiacere** please
***dispiacere** displease

Note: The verb **piacere** is mostly used impersonally and is consequently mainly found in the third person singular or plural. The main irregular features of the verb are

- the present indicative and subjunctive tenses
- the past definite tense
- the addition of the **i** in the past participle

IMPERATIVE
piaci (tu) **piaccia** (Lei) piaciamo (noi) piacete (voi) **piacciano** (Loro)

PLUPERFECT
ero piaciuto / a

PAST ANTERIOR
fui piaciuto / a

FUTURE
piacerò

FUTURE PERFECT
sarò piaciuto / a

PRESENT CONDITIONAL
piacerei

CONDITIONAL PERFECT
sarei piaciuto / a

PRESENT SUBJUNCTIVE
piaccia
piaccia
piaccia
piacciamo / piaciamo
piacciate / piaciate
piacciano

PERFECT SUBJUNCTIVE
sia piaciuto / a

IMPERFECT SUBJUNCTIVE
piacessi

PLUPERFECT SUBJUNCTIVE
fossi piaciuto / a

— *Ti piace* la pasta?	— *Do you like* pasta?
— Si, molto, e *mi piacciono* soprattutto gli spaghetti.	— Yes, a lot, and *I* particularly *like* spaghetti.
— *Piacciono* anche a Giovanni?	— *Does* Giovanni *like* it (spaghetti) too?
— Beh, penso che non gli *dispiacciano.*	— Well, I don't think *he dislikes* it (spaghetti).
— So che gli *piacciono di più* i tortellini.	— I know *he prefers* tortellini.
Mi *dispiace,* ma non posso venire stasera.	*I am sorry*, but I cannot come this evening.
L'*ho compiaciuto* nei suoi capricci.	*I humored* his whims.

PRESENT GERUND	***PAST PARTICIPLE***
piangendo	**pianto**

PRESENT INDICATIVE
piango

PRESENT PROGRESSIVE
sto piangendo

IMPERFECT
piangevo

PRESENT PERFECT
ho pianto

IMPERFECT PROGRESSIVE
stavo piangendo

PAST DEFINITE
piansi
piangesti
pianse
piangemmo
piangeste
piansero

Similar verbs

compiangere	pity, sympathize
rimpiangere	regret

Note: The main irregular features of the verb are

- the past definite tense
- the past participle

IMPERATIVE
piangi (tu) pianga (Lei) piangiamo (noi) piangete (voi) piangano (Loro)

PLUPERFECT
avevo pianto

PAST ANTERIOR
ebbi pianto

FUTURE
piangerò

FUTURE PERFECT
avrò pianto

PRESENT CONDITIONAL
piangerei

CONDITIONAL PERFECT
avrei pianto

PRESENT SUBJUNCTIVE
pianga

PERFECT SUBJUNCTIVE
abbia pianto

IMPERFECT SUBJUNCTIVE
piangessi

PLUPERFECT SUBJUNCTIVE
avessi pianto

Luisa *pianse* dal dolore.	Luisa *cried* with pain.
Mi *piangono* gli occhi per il fumo.	My eyes *are watering* because of the smoke.
***Rimpiango* di non esserci andata.**	*I regret* not having gone.
***Compiango* il tuo dolore.**	*I sympathize* with you in your grief.
***Piansi* di rabbia.**	*I cried* with anger.
***Piange* la giovinezza perduta.**	*He weeps* for his lost youth.
Beati quelli che *piangono*.	Blessed are those that *mourn*.
Chi è causa del suo mal, *pianga* se stesso. (*Proverb*)	You have made your bed, now lie in it. *(Proverb)*

PRESENT GERUND	***PAST PARTICIPLE***
piovendo	piovuto

PRESENT INDICATIVE
piove
piovono

PRESENT PERFECT
ha piovuto / è piovuto/a
hanno piovuto / sono piovuti/e

PRESENT PROGRESSIVE
sta piovendo
stanno piovendo

IMPERFECT PROGRESSIVE
stava piovendo
stavano piovendo

IMPERFECT
pioveva
piovevano

PAST DEFINITE
piovvi
piovesti
piovve
piovemmo
pioveste
piovvero

Note: **piovere** and all impersonal verbs associated with weather terms take either **avere** or **essere** almost indifferently. In addition, **piovere** takes **essere** when it is used figuratively to mean 'to pour in' or 'to turn up unexpectedly.' It is irregular only in the past definite tense.

PLUPERFECT	***PAST ANTERIOR***
aveva piovuto / era piovuto/a	ebbe piovuto / fu piovuto/a
avevano piovuto / erano piovuti/e	ebbero piovuto / furono piovuti/e
FUTURE	***FUTURE PERFECT***
pioverà	avrà piovuto / sarà piovuto/a
pioveranno	avranno piovuto / saranno piovuti/e
PRESENT CONDITIONAL	***CONDITIONAL PERFECT***
pioverebbe	avrebbe piovuto / sarebbe piovuto/a
pioverebbero	avrebbero piovuto / sarebbero piovuti/e
PRESENT SUBJUNCTIVE	***PERFECT SUBJUNCTIVE***
piova	abbia piovuto / sia piovuto/a
IMPERFECT SUBJUNCTIVE	***PLUPERFECT SUBJUNCTIVE***
piovesse	ebbe piovuto / fosse piovuto/a

Ha piovuto. / È piovuto.	*It has rained.*
***Piovve* a catinelle.**	*It rained* buckets.
Non ci *piove* sopra.	There's no doubt about it.
Le *piovvero* inviti da ogni parte.	Invitations *showered* upon her from all sides.
La luce *pioveva* nella stanza dalla finestra aperta.	The light *poured into* the room through the open window.
Lettere gli *piovevano* da ogni lato.	Letters *poured in* for him from all sides.

PRESENT GERUND	*PAST PARTICIPLE*
ponendo	**posto**

PRESENT INDICATIVE
pongo
poni
pone
poniamo
ponete
pongono

PRESENT PERFECT
ho posto

PRESENT PROGRESSIVE
sto ponendo

IMPERFECT PROGRESSIVE
stavo ponendo

IMPERFECT
ponevo

PAST DEFINITE
posi
ponesti
pose
ponemmo
poneste
posero

Similar verbs

There are many compounds of **porre,** which follow this pattern.

apporre	affix	**opporre**	oppose
comporre	compose; dial (number)	**posporre**	postpone
decomporre	decompose	**preporre**	place / put before; prefer
disporre	dispose	**presupporre**	presuppose
esporre	expose	**proporre**	propose
frapporre	insert	**riporre**	put again
imporre	impose	**supporre**	suppose
interporre	interpose		

Note: The main irregular features of these verbs are

- the present indicative and subjunctive tenses
- the past definite tense
- the past participle
- the future stem

IMPERATIVE
poni (tu) ponga (Lei) poniamo (noi) ponete (voi) pongano (Loro)

PLUPERFECT
avevo posto

PAST ANTERIOR
ebbi posto

FUTURE
porrò

FUTURE PERFECT
avrò posto

PRESENT CONDITIONAL
porrei

CONDITIONAL PERFECT
avrei posto

PRESENT SUBJUNCTIVE
ponga
ponga
ponga
poniamo
poniate
pongano

PERFECT SUBJUNCTIVE
abbia posto

IMPERFECT SUBJUNCTIVE
ponessi

PLUPERFECT SUBJUNCTIVE
avessi posto

—Allora cosa *proponi* tu?	—So what do you *propose?*
—*Porrei* la sedia qui ed il divano lì.	—*I would put* the chair here and the sofa there.
—No, non mi piace così. Perchè non *poniamo* la sedia accanto al divano?	—No, I don't like it like that. Why don't *we put* the chair next to the sofa?
—*Suppongo* che devo spostare anche la televisione?	—*I suppose* I'll have to move the television as well?
Spensierata, *composi* il numero.	Without thinking, *I dialed* the number.
***Ha esposto* delle camicie in vetrina.**	*He displayed* some shirts in the window.
***Esporrò* le mie idee dopodomani.**	*I will explain* my ideas the day after tomorrow.

PRESENT GERUND	***PAST PARTICIPLE***
potendo	potuto

PRESENT INDICATIVE
posso
puoi
può
possiamo
potete
possono

PRESENT PERFECT
ho potuto / sono potuto/a

PRESENT PROGRESSIVE
sto potendo

IMPERFECT PROGRESSIVE
stavo potendo

IMPERFECT
potevo

PAST DEFINITE
potei

PLUPERFECT
avevo potuto / ero potuto/a

PAST ANTERIOR
ebbi potuto / fui potuto/a

Note: The verb **potere** is a frequently used modal verb. It is important to distinguish between **potere** and **sapere,** both of which can translate the English word 'can.' The verb **potere** denotes physical capability rather than skill.

The main irregular features of the verb are

- the present indicative and subjunctive tenses
- the past definite tense
- the future stem

The imperative is never used.

IMPERATIVE
(There is none.)

FUTURE
potrò

FUTURE PERFECT
avrò potuto / sarò potuto/a

PRESENT CONDITIONAL
potrei

CONDITIONAL PERFECT
avrei potuto / sarei potuto/a

PRESENT SUBJUNCTIVE
possa
possa
possa
possiamo
possiate
possano

PERFECT SUBJUNCTIVE
abbia potuto / sia potuto/a

IMPERFECT SUBJUNCTIVE
potessi

PLUPERFECT SUBJUNCTIVE
avessi potuto / fossi potuto/a

—Mi dispiace, non *posso* andare in città.	—I'm sorry, *I can*'t go into town.
—Ma mi hai detto che *potevi* venire!	—But you said *you could* come!
—Sì, è vero, ma ho tanto da fare. Non ne *posso* più.	—Yes, it's true, but I have so much to do. *I am* completely *exhausted.*
—Nemmeno Carlo *è potuto* venire.	—Not even Carlo *has been able to* come.
—*Avresti potuto* dirmelo prima!	—*You could have* told me before now.

Note: In the last two examples the auxiliary used depends on the auxiliary normally used by the dependent infinitive, not **potere.** Thus, in **è potuto/a venire** the auxiliary is **essere** because **venire** takes **essere;** and in the final sentence **avere** is used because **dire** takes **avere.**

PRESENT GERUND	*PAST PARTICIPLE*
prendendo	**preso**

PRESENT INDICATIVE prendo	*PRESENT PERFECT* ho preso
PRESENT PROGRESSIVE sto prendendo	*IMPERFECT PROGRESSIVE* stavo prendendo
IMPERFECT prendevo	*PAST DEFINITE* **presi** prendesti **prese** prendemmo prendeste **presero**

Similar verbs

apprendere	learn	**intraprendere**	undertake
comprendere	understand, consist of	**sorprendere**	surprise

Note: The main irregular features of the verb are

- the past definite tense
- the past participle.

***Hanno preso* il ladro.**	*They caught* the thief.
***Prendo* lezioni d'italiano.**	*I take* Italian lessons.
Lo *presi* per il collo.	*I took* him by the scruff of his neck.
***Fu preso* dalla paura.**	*He was seized* by fear.
Devi andare a *prendere* la zia.	You've got to go and *get* auntie.
Ho preso* un appartamento *in affitto.	*I rented* an apartment.
Stefano *ha preso* un raffreddore.	Stephen *has caught* a cold.
Tu mi *sorprendi* spesso!	You often *surprise* me!

IMPERATIVE
prendi (tu) prenda (Lei) prendiamo (noi) prendete (voi) prendano (Loro)

PLUPERFECT
avevo preso

FUTURE
prenderò

PRESENT CONDITIONAL
prenderei

PRESENT SUBJUNCTIVE
prenda

IMPERFECT SUBJUNCTIVE
prendessi

PAST ANTERIOR
ebbi preso

FUTURE PERFECT
avrò preso

CONDITIONAL PERFECT
avrei preso

PERFECT SUBJUNCTIVE
abbia preso

PLUPERFECT SUBJUNCTIVE
avessi preso

***Comprese* il suo errore.**	*He understood* what he had done wrong.
La casa *comprende* un salotto, due camere, un bagno e una cucina.	The house *consists of* a lounge, two bedrooms, a bathroom, and a kitchen.
Gianni l'*ha sorpreso* mentre fumava.	Gianni *caught* him smoking.
Il ragazzo *le prese* da suo padre.	The boy *was smacked* by his father.
***Prende* sempre brutti voti.**	*He* always *gets* bad grades.
Non *ha appreso* nulla a scuola.	He *has* not *learned* anything at school.
Quanto *prendi* al mese?	How much *do you earn* a month?
Per chi mi *prendi?*	Whom do *you take* me for?
Che ti *prende?*	What's *the matter* with you?
Non *prendertela!*	*Don't worry about it.*
Se l'*ha presa* a cuore.	*He has taken* it to heart.

PRESENT GERUND	*PAST PARTICIPLE*
proteggendo	**protetto**

PRESENT INDICATIVE	*PRESENT PERFECT*
proteggo	ho protetto
PRESENT PROGRESSIVE	*IMPERFECT PROGRESSIVE*
sto proteggendo	stavo proteggendo
IMPERFECT	*PAST DEFINITE*
proteggevo	**protessi** proteggesti **protesse** proteggemmo proteggeste **protessero**

Note: The main irregular features of the verb are

- the past definite tense
- the past participle

IMPERATIVE

proteggi (tu)	protegga (Lei)	proteggiamo (noi)
proteggete (voi)	proteggano (Loro)	

PLUPERFECT
avevo protetto

PAST ANTERIOR
ebbi protetto

FUTURE
proteggerò

FUTURE PERFECT
avrò protetto

PRESENT CONDITIONAL
proteggerei

CONDITIONAL PERFECT
avrei protetto

PRESENT SUBJUNCTIVE
protegga

PERFECT SUBJUNCTIVE
abbia protetto

IMPERFECT SUBJUNCTIVE
proteggessi

PLUPERFECT SUBJUNCTIVE
avessi protetto

Quest'ombrello ti *proteggerà* dalla pioggia.	This umbrella *will protect* you from the rain.
Il cane *protesse* la casa.	The dog *protected* the house.
Un angelo *protegge* il bambino.	An angel *is protecting* the baby.
Che Dio ti *protegga!*	May God *protect* you!
La fortuna *protegge* gli audaci.	Fortune *favors* the brave.

PRESENT GERUND	***PAST PARTICIPLE***
pungendo	**punto**

PRESENT INDICATIVE
pungo

PRESENT PERFECT
ho punto

PRESENT PROGRESSIVE
sto pungendo

IMPERFECT PROGRESSIVE
stavo pungendo

IMPERFECT
pungevo

PAST DEFINITE
punsi
pungesti
punse
pungemmo
pungeste
punsero

Similar verbs

fungere act as
mungere milk
ungere oil, grease, lubricate, anoint

Note: The main irregular features of the verb are

- the past definite tense
- the past participle

IMPERATIVE
pungi (tu) punga (Lei) pungiamo (noi) pungete (voi) pungano (Loro)

PLUPERFECT avevo punto	***PAST ANTERIOR*** ebbi punto
FUTURE pungerò	***FUTURE PERFECT*** avrò punto
PRESENT CONDITIONAL pungerei	***CONDITIONAL PERFECT*** avrei punto
PRESENT SUBJUNCTIVE punga	***PERFECT SUBJUNCTIVE*** abbia punto
IMPERFECT SUBJUNCTIVE pungessi	***PLUPERFECT SUBJUNCTIVE*** avessi punto

Le rose *pungono.*	Roses *prick.*
Le vespe *pungono.*	Wasps *sting.*
***Mi punsi* la mano.**	*I pricked* my hand.
Gli *punge* il desiderio di vederla.	*He was spurred on* by the wish to see her.
Il freddo mi *pungeva* il viso.	The cold *stung* my face.
***Fu punto* dal rimorso.**	*He was pricked* with remorse.
Mi *punse* la coscienza.	My conscience *pricked* me.
***Munse* la vacca.**	*He milked* the cow.
***Unsero* le ruote.**	*They oiled* the wheels.
***Fu unto* re.**	*He was anointed* king.
L'uomo *funse* da capo.	The man *acted as* leader.

PRESENT GERUND	*PAST PARTICIPLE*
radendo	**raso**

PRESENT INDICATIVE	*PRESENT PERFECT*
rado	ho raso
PRESENT PROGRESSIVE	***IMPERFECT PROGRESSIVE***
sto radendo	stavo radendo
IMPERFECT	***PAST DEFINITE***
radevo	**rasi** radesti **rase** rademmo radeste **rasero**

Similar verb

***radersi** shave oneself

Note: The main irregular features of the verb are

- the past definite tense
- the past participle

IMPERATIVE
radi (tu) rada (Lei) radiamo (noi) radete (voi) radano (Loro)

PLUPERFECT avevo raso	***PAST ANTERIOR*** ebbi raso
FUTURE raderò	***FUTURE PERFECT*** avrò raso
PRESENT CONDITIONAL raderei	***CONDITIONAL PERFECT*** avrei raso
PRESENT SUBJUNCTIVE rada	***PERFECT SUBJUNCTIVE*** abbia raso
IMPERFECT SUBJUNCTIVE radessi	***PLUPERFECT SUBJUNCTIVE*** avessi raso

Mi *ha raso* male.	*He shaved* me badly.
La città *fu rasa* al suolo.	The city *was razed* to the ground.
***Rase* la superficie dell'acqua.**	*It skimmed* the surface of the water.
***Mi rado* ogni mattina.**	*I shave* every morning.

PRESENT GERUND	*PAST PARTICIPLE*
reggendo	**retto**

PRESENT INDICATIVE
reggo

PRESENT PROGRESSIVE
sto reggendo

IMPERFECT
reggevo

PRESENT PERFECT
ho retto

IMPERFECT PROGRESSIVE
stavo reggendo

PAST DEFINITE
ressi
reggesti
resse
reggemmo
reggeste
ressero

Similar verbs

correggere correct
sorreggere support, hold up

Note: The main irregular features of the verb are

- the past definite tense
- the past participle

IMPERATIVE
reggi (tu) regga (Lei) reggiamo (noi) reggete (voi) reggano (Loro)

PLUPERFECT
avevo retto

PAST ANTERIOR
ebbi retto

FUTURE
reggerò

FUTURE PERFECT
avrò retto

PRESENT CONDITIONAL
reggerei

CONDITIONAL PERFECT
avrei retto

PRESENT SUBJUNCTIVE
regga

PERFECT SUBJUNCTIVE
abbia retto

IMPERFECT SUBJUNCTIVE
reggessi

PLUPERFECT SUBJUNCTIVE
avessi retto

***Regge* il governo.**	*He is the head of* the government.
Le gambe non mi *reggono*.	I *can*not *stand* on my feet.
Quella corda non lo *reggerà*.	That rope *will* not *hold* him.
La mensola non *reggerà* quei libri.	The shelf *will* not *support* those books.
Non *reggo* il vino.	I *can*not *take* wine.
Questo materiale *regge il fuoco.*	This material *is fireproof.*
Non *reggo* più.	I *can*not *go on.*
Bisogna *correggere* quel bambino.	That child *should be corrected.*
***Hai corretto* i compiti?**	*Have you corrected* the homework?
***Correggerò* il tuo caffè col cognac.**	*I'll lace* your coffee with brandy.
I genitori *hanno sorretto* il bambino.	The parents *supported/held up* the child.

PRESENT GERUND	*PAST PARTICIPLE*
rendendo	**reso**

PRESENT INDICATIVE
rendo

PRESENT PROGRESSIVE
sto rendendo

IMPERFECT
rendevo

PRESENT PERFECT
ho reso

IMPERFECT PROGRESSIVE
stavo rendendo

PAST DEFINITE
resi
rendesti
rese
rendemmo
rendeste
resero

Similar verbs

***arrendersi**	surrender
***rendersi conto di**	realize

Note: The main irregular features of the verb are

- the past definite tense
- the past participle

IMPERATIVE
rendi (tu) renda (Lei) rendiamo (noi) rendete (voi) rendano (Loro)

PLUPERFECT avevo reso	***PAST ANTERIOR*** ebbi reso
FUTURE renderò	***FUTURE PERFECT*** avrò reso
PRESENT CONDITIONAL renderei	***CONDITIONAL PERFECT*** avrei reso
PRESENT SUBJUNCTIVE renda	***PERFECT SUBJUNCTIVE*** abbia reso
IMPERFECT SUBJUNCTIVE rendessi	***PLUPERFECT SUBJUNCTIVE*** avessi reso

Mi *ha reso* il libro ieri.	He *gave* me the book *back* yesterday.
***Rendi*mi la penna che ti ho prestata.**	*Give* me *back* the pen that I lent you.
Questo lavoro non *rende* molto.	This job *is* not well *paid.*
L'amore *rende* felici.	Love *makes* you happy.
Questa notizia lo *rese* incapace di parlare.	This piece of news *left* him speechless.
È difficile *rendere* il senso dell'originale in una traduzione.	It is difficult to *render* the sense of the original in a translation.
Non *mi sono reso conto di* ciò che è successo.	I *did* not *realize* what happened.
I soldati *si sono arresi.*	The soldiers *surrendered.*

PRESENT GERUND	***PAST PARTICIPLE***
ridendo	**riso**

PRESENT INDICATIVE
rido

PRESENT PROGRESSIVE
sto ridendo

IMPERFECT
ridevo

PRESENT PERFECT
ho riso

IMPERFECT PROGRESSIVE
stavo ridendo

PAST DEFINITE
risi
ridesti
rise
ridemmo
rideste
risero

Similar verbs

deridere deride, ridicule
sorridere smile

Note: The main irregular features of the verb are

- the past definite tense
- the past participle

IMPERATIVE
ridi (tu) rida (Lei) ridiamo (noi) ridete (voi) ridano (Loro)

PLUPERFECT
avevo riso

PAST ANTERIOR
ebbi riso

FUTURE
riderò

FUTURE PERFECT
avrò riso

PRESENT CONDITIONAL
riderei

CONDITIONAL PERFECT
avrei riso

PRESENT SUBJUNCTIVE
rida

PERFECT SUBJUNCTIVE
abbia riso

IMPERFECT SUBJUNCTIVE
ridessi

PLUPERFECT SUBJUNCTIVE
avessi riso

Non c'è da *ridere!*	It's not a laughing matter!
Non ci vedo niente da *ridere.*	I can't see anything *to laugh about.*
Ma non farmi *ridere!*	But don't make me *laugh!*
Quella bambina *sorride* sempre.	That girl *is* always *smiling.*
Gianni mi *sorrise.*	Gianni *smiled* at me.
La fortuna gli *sorride.*	Good fortune *smiles* on him.
L'*hanno* deriso.	*They ridiculed* him.
***Risero* alle sue spalle.**	*They laughed* behind his back.
I suoi occhi *risero* di gioia.	Her eyes *sparkled* with happiness.
***Ride* bene chi *ride* ultimo. (*Proverbio*)**	*He* who *laughs* last *laughs* best. (*Proverb*)
La fortuna gli *ride.*	Good luck *smiles* at him.
Chi *ride* il venerdì, piange la domenica.	*Laugh* today, for tomorrow you may cry.

PRESENT GERUND	***PAST PARTICIPLE***
rimanendo	**rimasto**

PRESENT INDICATIVE
rimango
rimani
rimane
rimaniamo
rimanete
rimangono

PRESENT PERFECT
sono rimasto / a

PRESENT PROGRESSIVE
sto rimanendo

IMPERFECT PROGRESSIVE
stavo rimanendo

IMPERFECT
rimanevo

PAST DEFINITE
rimasi
rimanesti
rimase
rimanemmo
rimaneste
rimasero

Note: The main irregular features of the verb are

- the present indicative and subjunctive tenses
- the past definite tense
- the past participle
- the future stem

IMPERATIVE
rimani (tu) **rimanga** (Lei) rimaniamo (noi) rimanete (voi) rimangano (Loro)

PLUPERFECT
ero rimasto / a

PAST ANTERIOR
fui rimasto / a

FUTURE
rimarrò

FUTURE PERFECT
sarò rimasto / a

PRESENT CONDITIONAL
rimarrei

CONDITIONAL PERFECT
sarei rimasto / a

PRESENT SUBJUNCTIVE
rimanga
rimanga
rimanga
rimaniamo
rimaniate
rimangano

PERFECT SUBJUNCTIVE
sia rimasto / a

IMPERFECT SUBJUNCTIVE
rimanessi

PLUPERFECT SUBJUNCTIVE
fossi rimasto / a

—Quanto tempo *rimani* in Italia?	—How long *are you staying* in Italy?
—*Rimango* due settimane.	—*I am staying* two weeks.
—Che ti *rimane* da fare?	—What *have you left* to do?
—*Mi rimane* soltanto la conclusione del tema.	—*I have* only the essay's conclusion *left* to do.
—Dubito che *tu rimanga* fino alla festa allora.	—I doubt that *you are staying* until the party then.

PRESENT GERUND	***PAST PARTICIPLE***
risolvendo	**risolto**

PRESENT INDICATIVE
risolvo

PRESENT PROGRESSIVE
sto risolvendo

IMPERFECT
risolvevo

PRESENT PERFECT
ho risolto

IMPERFECT PROGRESSIVE
stavo risolvendo

PAST DEFINITE
risolsi / risolvei / risolvetti
risolvesti
risolse
risolvemmo
risolveste
risolsero

Similar verbs

assolvere absolve, acquit
dissolvere dissolve
***risolversi di** decide, make up one's mind

Note: The main irregular features of the verb are

- the past definite tense
- the past participle

IMPERATIVE
risolvi (tu) risolva (Lei) risolviamo (noi) risolvete (voi) risolvano (Loro)

PLUPERFECT
avevo risolto

PAST ANTERIOR
ebbi risolto

FUTURE
risolverò

FUTURE PERFECT
avrò risolto

PRESENT CONDITIONAL
risolverei

CONDITIONAL PERFECT
avrei risolto

PRESENT SUBJUNCTIVE
risolva

PERFECT SUBJUNCTIVE
abbia risolto

IMPERFECT SUBJUNCTIVE
risolvessi

PLUPERFECT SUBJUNCTIVE
avessi risolto

Risolse **di farlo lui stesso.**	*He resolved* to do it himself.
Hai risolto **l'equazione?**	*Have you solved* the equation?
Dubito che quel problema *sia stato risolto.*	I doubt whether that problem *has been resolved.*
Si risolse di **andare via.**	*He made up his mind* to go away.
Il ladro *fu assolto.*	The thief *was acquitted.*

PRESENT GERUND	***PAST PARTICIPLE***
rispondendo	**risposto**

PRESENT INDICATIVE
rispondo

PRESENT PROGRESSIVE
sto rispondendo

IMPERFECT
rispondevo

PRESENT PERFECT
ho risposto

IMPERFECT PROGRESSIVE
stavo rispondendo

PAST DEFINITE
risposi
rispondesti
rispose
rispondemmo
rispondestie
risposero

Similar verbs

corrispondere	correspond
nascondere	hide
***nascondersi**	hide (oneself)

Note: The main irregular features of the verb are

- the past definite tense
- the past participle

IMPERATIVE

rispondi (tu)	risponda (Lei)	rispondiamo (noi)
rispondete (voi)	rispondano (Loro)	

PLUPERFECT
avevo risposto

PAST ANTERIOR
ebbi risposto

FUTURE
risponderò

FUTURE PERFECT
avrò risposto

PRESENT CONDITIONAL
risponderei

CONDITIONAL PERFECT
avre risposto

PRESENT SUBJUNCTIVE
risponda

PERFECT SUBJUNCTIVE
abba risposto

IMPERFECT SUBJUNCTIVE
rispondessi

PLUPERFECT SUBJUNCTIVE
avessi risposto

Ha risposto **subito alla mia proposta.**	*He replied* immediately to my proposal.
Risposi **per iscritto.**	*I replied* in writing.
Gianna ***rispose*** **con un cenno del capo.**	Gianna *replied* with a nod of the head.
Io non ***rispondo*** **delle azioni di mio fratello.**	*I can*not *be held responsible* for the actions of my brother.
Questo motore non ***risponde.***	This engine *is* not *responding.*
Nascose **la sua identitá.**	*He hid* his identity.
Nadia e Giulia ***si sono nascoste*** **nel giardino.**	Nadia and Giulia *hid* in the garden.
La descrizione nel pieghevole non ***corrispondeva*** **alla realtà.**	The description in the brochure *did* not *correspond* to reality / give a true picture.

PRESENT GERUND	***PAST PARTICIPLE***
rompendo	**rotto**

PRESENT INDICATIVE
rompo

PRESENT PROGRESSIVE
sto rompendo

IMPERFECT
rompevo

PRESENT PERFECT
ho rotto

IMPERFECT PROGRESSIVE
stavo rompendo

PAST DEFINITE
ruppi
rompesti
ruppe
rompemmo
rompeste
ruppero

Similar verbs

corrompere	corrupt
interrompere	interrupt
irrompere	break into
prorompere	burst out
***rompersi**	break up

Note: The main irregular features of the verb are

- the past definite tense
- the past participle

IMPERATIVE
rompi (tu) rompa (Lei) rompiamo (noi) rompete (voi) rompano (Loro)

PLUPERFECT
avevo rotto

PAST ANTERIOR
ebbi rotto

FUTURE
romperò

FUTURE PERFECT
avrò rotto

PRESENT CONDITIONAL
romperei

CONDITIONAL PERFECT
avrei rotto

PRESENT SUBJUNCTIVE
rompa

PERFECT SUBJUNCTIVE
abbia rotto

IMPERFECT SUBJUNCTIVE
rompessi

PLUPERFECT SUBJUNCTIVE
avessi rotto

Ho rotto **un vaso ieri.**	*I broke* a vase yesterday.
Hai rotto **la tua promessa!**	*You have broken* your promise!
Vorrei ***romperla*** **con quel ragazzo.**	I would like *to break up* with that boy.
La nave ***si ruppe*** **sulle rocce.**	The ship *broke up* on the rocks.
Hai corrotto **tutto!**	*You have corrupted* everything!
Interruppe **la nostra conversazione.**	*He interrupted* our conversation.
Ho interrotto **il viaggio a Firenze.**	*I called off* my trip to Florence.
La corrente è stata ***interrotta*** **per un'ora.**	The electricity was *cut off* for an hour.
I ladri ***irruppero*** **nella casa.**	The thieves *broke into* the house.
La folla ***irruppe*** **nello stadio.**	The crowd *broke into* the stadium.

PRESENT GERUND	*PAST PARTICIPLE*
salendo	salito

PRESENT INDICATIVE
salgo
sali
sale
saliamo
salite
salgono

PRESENT PERFECT
ho salito / sono salito / a

PRESENT PROGRESSIVE
sto salendo

IMPERFECT PROGRESSIVE
stavo salendo

IMPERFECT
salivo

PAST DEFINITE
salii

Similar verb

† **assalire** attack, seize, overcome

Note: The main irregular features of the verb are

- the present indicative and subjunctive tenses
- it takes **avere** when used transitively and **essere** when used intransitively

IMPERATIVE
sali (tu) **salga** (Lei) saliamo (noi) salite (voi) salgano (Loro)

PLUPERFECT
avevo salito / ero salito/a

PAST ANTERIOR
ebbi salito / fui salito/a

FUTURE
salirò

FUTURE PERFECT
avrò salito / sarò salito/a

PRESENT CONDITIONAL
salirei

CONDITIONAL PERFECT
avrei salito / sarei salito/a

PRESENT SUBJUNCTIVE
salga
salga
salga
saliamo
saliate
salgano

PERFECT SUBJUNCTIVE
abbia salito / sia salito/a

IMPERFECT SUBJUNCTIVE
salissi

PLUPERFECT SUBJUNCTIVE
avessi salito / fossi salito/a

—*Saliamo* fino a quel punto lì?	—*Shall we go up* to that point there?
—Io non *salgo* più!	—I'*m* not *going up* any further.
—Che peccato che tu non *salga* lassù—c'è un panorama bellissimo da quel punto.	—What a shame that *you are* not *going up* there—there is a beautiful view from that point.
***Fu assalita* dai dubbi.**	*She was assailed* by doubts.
***Fummo assaliti* dal temporale.**	*We were caught* in the storm.

PRESENT GERUND	*PAST PARTICIPLE*
sapendo	saputo

PRESENT INDICATIVE	*PRESENT PERFECT*
so	ho saputo
sai	
sa	
sappiamo	
sapete	
sanno	
PRESENT PROGRESSIVE	*IMPERFECT PROGRESSIVE*
sto sapendo	stavo sapendo
IMPERFECT	*PAST DEFINITE*
sapevo	**seppi**
	sapesti
	seppe
	sapemmo
	sapeste
	seppero

Note: The verb **sapere** is frequently used as a modal verb. It is important to distinguish between **potere** [➤65] and **sapere,** both of which can translate the English word 'can.' The verb **sapere** denotes skill rather than physical capability.

It is also important to distinguish between the verbs **conoscere** [➤34] and **sapere**, which can both be translated as 'to know' in English. **Conoscere** means to know a person or a place, whereas **sapere** means to know a fact or to know how to do something.

The main irregular features of the verb **sapere** are

- the present indicative and subjunctive tenses
- the past definite tense
- the future stem

IMPERATIVE
sappi (tu) **sappia** (Lei) **sappiamo** (noi) **sappiate** (voi) **sappiano** (Loro)

PLUPERFECT
avevo saputo

PAST ANTERIOR
ebbi saputo

FUTURE
saprò

FUTURE PERFECT
avrò saputo

PRESENT CONDITIONAL
saprei

CONDITIONAL PERFECT
avrei saputo

PRESENT SUBJUNCTIVE
sappia
sappia
sappia
sappiamo
sappiate
sappiano

PERFECT SUBJUNCTIVE
abbia saputo

IMPERFECT SUBJUNCTIVE
sapessi

PLUPERFECT SUBJUNCTIVE
avessi saputo

—*So* suonare il flauto adesso.	—*I know* how to play the flute now.
—Non *saprei* da dove cominciare!	—*I would*n't *know* where to begin!
—Conosci la mia maestra?	—Do you know my teacher?
—No, non la conosco, ma *so* dove abita.	—No, I don't know her, but *I know* where she lives.
—Pare che *sappia* suonare molto bene.	—It seems that she *knows* how to play very well.

PRESENT GERUND	*PAST PARTICIPLE*
scendendo	**sceso**

PRESENT INDICATIVE scendo	*PRESENT PERFECT* ho sceso / sono sceso / a
PRESENT PROGRESSIVE sto scendendo	*IMPERFECT PROGRESSIVE* stavo scendendo
IMPERFECT scendevo	*PAST DEFINITE* **scesi** scendesti **scese** scendemmo scendeste **scesero**

Similar verbs

† **accondiscendere**	consent
† **ascendere**	ascend
† **discendere**	descend

† Like **scendere,** these verbs can take either **avere** or **essere**, depending on whether they are used transitively or intransitively.

Note: The main irregular features of the verb are

- the past definite tense
- the past participle

Sono sceso / a.	*I went downstairs.*
***Scese* le scale correndo.**	*He came* running downstairs.
***Sono scesi* dal tram.**	*They got off* the tram.
La montagna *scende* verso il mare.	The mountain *slopes down* towards the sea.

IMPERATIVE
scendi (tu) scenda (Lei) scendiamo (noi) scendete (voi) scendano (Loro)

PLUPERFECT
avevo sceso / ero sceso / a

PAST ANTERIOR
ebbi sceso / fui sceso / a

FUTURE
scenderò

FUTURE PERFECT
avrò sceso / sarò sceso / a

PRESENT CONDITIONAL
scenderei

CONDITIONAL PERFECT
avrei sceso / sarei sceso / a

PRESENT SUBJUNCTIVE
scenda

PERFECT SUBJUNCTIVE
abbia sceso / sia sceso / a

IMPERFECT SUBJUNCTIVE
scendessi

PLUPERFECT SUBJUNCTIVE
avessi sceso / fossi sceso / a

La temperatura *è scesa* oggi.	The temperature *has gone down* today.
Perché non *scendiamo* al bar a prendere un caffè?	Why *don't we go* to the bar for a coffee?
I capelli le *scendevano* alle spalle.	Her hair *fell over* her shoulders.
***Accondiscese* a una riduzione di prezzo.**	*He consented* to a reduction in price.
***Ascese* al trono.**	*He ascended* to the throne.
I cristiani credono che dopo la Risurrezione Gesú *sia asceso* al cielo.	Christians believe that after his Resurrection, Jesus *ascended to* heaven.
***Discesi* le scale.**	*I went* downstairs.
Il fiume *discende verso* il mare.	The river *flows down* to the sea.

PRESENT GERUND	*PAST PARTICIPLE*
scorgendo	**scorto**

PRESENT INDICATIVE
scorgo

PRESENT PROGRESSIVE
sto scorgendo

IMPERFECT
scorgevo

PRESENT PERFECT
ho scorto

IMPERFECT PROGRESSIVE
stavo scorgendo

PAST DEFINITE
scorsi
scorgesti
scorse
scorgemmo
scorgeste
scorsero

Similar verbs

***accorgersi**	notice
porgere	hand, give, hold out
***risorgere**	rise again, revive
***sorgere**	rise
***sporgere**	project, stick out, jut out
***sporgersi**	lean out

Note: The main irregular features of the verb are

- the past definite tense
- the past participle

In lontananza *scorgevo* una figura di uomo avvicinarsi.	In the distance *I noticed* the shape of a man approach.
Se ne andò senza farsi *scorgere.*	He went away without *being noticed.*
Non vuole farsi *scorgere* da lui.	She does not want him *to notice* her.

IMPERATIVE
scorgi (tu) scorga (Lei) scorgiamo (noi) scorgete (voi) scorgano (Loro)

PLUPERFECT avevo scorto	***PAST ANTERIOR*** ebbi scorto
FUTURE scorgerò	***FUTURE PERFECT*** avrò scorto
PRESENT CONDITIONAL scorgerei	***CONDITIONAL PERFECT*** avrei scorto
PRESENT SUBJUNCTIVE scorga	***PERFECT SUBJUNCTIVE*** abbia scorto
IMPERFECT SUBJUNCTIVE scorgessi	***PLUPERFECT SUBJUNCTIVE*** avessi scorto

Non me ne sono nemmeno *accorto!*	*I did*n't even *notice!*
Non si era *accorta* che pioveva.	She *did*n't *notice* it was raining.
Poi *sorse* una grande discussione.	Then a great discussion *arose.*
Le montagne *sorgono* davanti a me.	The mountains *are looming* in front of me.
Ho visto *sorgere* il sole.	I saw the sun *rise.*
La nebbia *sorse* dal lago.	The fog *rose* from the lake.
Le sue speranze *risorsero.*	His hopes *revived.*
Vi *porgo* i miei più distinti saluti.	Yours sincerely.
È pericoloso *sporgersi* dal finestrino.	It is dangerous *to lean out* of the window.

PRESENT GERUND	***PAST PARTICIPLE***
scrivendo	**scritto**

PRESENT INDICATIVE scrivo	***PRESENT PERFECT*** ho scritto
PRESENT PROGRESSIVE sto scrivendo	***IMPERFECT PROGRESSIVE*** stavo scrivendo
IMPERFECT scrivevo	***PAST DEFINITE*** **scrissi** scrivesti **scrisse** scrivemmo scriveste **scrissero**

Similar verbs

descrivere	describe
iscrivere	enroll, register
***iscriversi**	enroll (oneself)

Note: The main irregular features of the verb are

- the past definite tense
- the past participle

IMPERATIVE
scrivi (tu) scriva (Lei) scriviamo (noi) scrivete (voi) scrivano (Loro)

PLUPERFECT
avevo scritto

PAST ANTERIOR
ebbi scritto

FUTURE
scriverò

FUTURE PERFECT
avrò scritto

PRESENT CONDITIONAL
scriverei

CONDITIONAL PERFECT
avrei scritto

PRESENT SUBJUNCTIVE
scriva

PERFECT SUBJUNCTIVE
abbia scritto

IMPERFECT SUBJUNCTIVE
scrivessi

PLUPERFECT SUBJUNCTIVE
avessi scritto

Come *si scrive* questa parola?	How *do you spell* this word?
Sa *scrivere* la musica.	He knows how *to write* music.
Gli *ho scritto* due righe.	*I wrote* him a note (two lines).
***Scrissi* a casa non appena fui arrivata a Roma.**	*I wrote* home as soon as I arrived in Rome.
Ti *iscrivo* al club?	*Shall I enroll* you (as a member) in the club?
***Mi sono iscritto* all'università.**	*I enrolled* at the university.
***Descrisse* la scena in montagna.**	*He described* the scene in the mountains.
Vorrei *descrivere* un'ampia curva.	I would like *to describe* a wide curve.

PRESENT GERUND	*PAST PARTICIPLE*
scotendo	**scosso**

PRESENT INDICATIVE
scuoto
scuoti
scuote
scotiamo
scotete
scuotono

PRESENT PERFECT
ho scosso

PRESENT PROGRESSIVE
sto scuotendo

IMPERFECT PROGRESSIVE
stavo scuotendo

IMPERFECT
scotevo

PAST DEFINITE
scossi
scotesti
scosse
scotemmo
scoteste
scossero

Similar verbs

percuotere	beat, strike
ripercuotere	beat again
***ripercuotersi**	reverberate, affect
riscuotere	collect, cash

Note: The main irregular features of the verb are

- the past definite tense
- the past participle

IMPERATIVE
scuoti (tu) scuota (Lei) scotiamo (noi) scotete (voi) scuotano (Loro)

PLUPERFECT	***PAST ANTERIOR***
avevo scosso	ebbi scosso
FUTURE	***FUTURE PERFECT***
scoterò	avrò scosso
PRESENT CONDITIONAL	***CONDITIONAL PERFECT***
scoterei	avrei scosso
PRESENT SUBJUNCTIVE	***PERFECT SUBJUNCTIVE***
scuota	abbia scosso
IMPERFECT SUBJUNCTIVE	***PLUPERFECT SUBJUNCTIVE***
scotessi	avessi scosso

Scosse **l'albero.**	*He shook* the tree.
Scuote **la testa.**	*He shakes* his head.
Fu scossa **dalla notizia.**	*She was shaken* by the news.
Ho riscosso **l'assegno.**	*I cashed* the check.
La sua influenza *si ripercosse* su tutti i colleghi.	His influence *reverberated* on all his colleagues.
Lo *percosse* a morte.	*He struck* him dead.

PRESENT GERUND	***PAST PARTICIPLE***
solendo	**solito**

PRESENT INDICATIVE

soglio
suoli
suole
sogliamo
solete
sogliono

IMPERFECT	***PAST DEFINITE***
solevo	solei
solevi	solesti
soleva	
solevamo	
solevate	
solevano	

Note: The main irregular features of the verb are

- the present indicative
- the past participle
- **solere** is a 'defective verb' (**verbo difettivo**), which means that some forms of it exist but not others. The other forms either never existed or have fallen out of use. In their place, one uses corresponding tenses of verbal expressions **essere solito** and **avere l'abitudine / la consuetudine.**

PRESENT SUBJUNCTIVE
soglia
soglia
soglia
sogliamo
sogliate
sogliano

IMPERFECT SUBJUNCTIVE
solessi
solessi
solesse
solessimo
soleste
solessero

***Soleva* alzarsi tardi ogni giorno.**	*He used to* get up late every day.
Oggi lavora di più di quanto *soleva* fare due anni fa.	Nowadays he works more than *he used to* two years ago.
***Suole* alzarsi di buon'ora.**	He usually gets up early.
Ogni sera al tramonto del sole le ragazze *solevano* andare a fare una passeggiata.	Every evening at sunset the girls *used to* go for a walk.
La domenica *siamo soliti* pranzare all'una.	On Sundays *we are used to* having dinner at one.
Come *si suol* dire, 'Meglio tardi che mai'!	As they say, 'Better late than never'!
***Ci sogliamo* ritrovare a casa dei genitori ogni domenica.**	*We are used to* meeting at the parents' house every Sunday.

PRESENT GERUND	***PAST PARTICIPLE***
spargendo	**sparso**

PRESENT INDICATIVE
spargo

PRESENT PERFECT
ho sparso

PRESENT PROGRESSIVE
sto spargendo

IMPERFECT PROGRESSIVE
stavo spargendo

IMPERFECT
spargevo

PAST DEFINITE
sparsi
spargesti
sparse
spargemmo
spargeste
sparsero

Similar verbs

aspergere	sprinkle
***emergere**	emerge
immergere	immerse
sommergere	submerge

Note: The main irregular features of the verb are

- the past definite tense
- the past participle

IMPERATIVE
spargi (tu) sparga (Lei) spargiamo (noi) spargete (voi) spargano (Loro)

PLUPERFECT
avevo sparso

PAST ANTERIOR
ebbi sparso

FUTURE
spargerò

FUTURE PERFECT
avrò sparso

PRESENT CONDITIONAL
spargerei

CONDITIONAL PERFECT
avrei sparso

PRESENT SUBJUNCTIVE
sparga

PERFECT SUBJUNCTIVE
abbia sparso

IMPERFECT SUBJUNCTIVE
spargessi

PLUPERFECT SUBJUNCTIVE
avessi sparso

***Sparse* fiori sulla tomba.**	*He scattered* flowers on the grave.
***Ho sparso* zucchero sulla torta.**	*I sprinkled* sugar on the cake.
Il lume *spargeva* una luce fioca.	The lamp *shed* a dim light.
***Sparge* una notizia ai quattro venti!**	He always tells everyone!
Il prete *aspergerà* l'acqua sul bambino.	The priest *will sprinkle* water on the baby.
Le onde *avevano sommerso* la barca.	The waves *had submerged* the boat.
L'*ho immerso* in acqua.	*I immersed* it in water.
Una sirena *è emersa* dall'acqua.	A mermaid *emerged* from the water.

PRESENT GERUND	*PAST PARTICIPLE*
spegnendo	**spento**

PRESENT INDICATIVE
spengo
spegni
spegne
spegniamo
spegnete
spengono

PRESENT PERFECT
ho spento

PRESENT PROGRESSIVE
sto spegnendo

IMPERFECT PROGRESSIVE
stavo spegnendo

IMPERFECT
spegnevo

PAST DEFINITE
spensi
spegnesti
spense
spegnemmo
spegneste
spensero

Note: The main irregular features of the verb are

- the present indicative and subjunctive tenses
- the past definite tense
- the past participle

IMPERATIVE
spegni (tu) **spenga** (Lei) spegniamo (noi) spegnete (voi) spengano (Loro)

PLUPERFECT
avevo spento

PAST ANTERIOR
ebbi spento

FUTURE
spegnerò

FUTURE PERFECT
avrò spento

PRESENT CONDITIONAL
spegnerei

CONDITIONAL PERFECT
avrei spento

PRESENT SUBJUNCTIVE
spenga
spenga
spenga
spegniamo
spegniate
spengano

PERFECT SUBJUNCTIVE
abbia spento

IMPERFECT SUBJUNCTIVE
spegnessi

PLUPERFECT SUBJUNCTIVE
avessi spento

Gianna *spense* la luce nella sala.	Gianna *turned off* the light in the room.
***Spenta* la luce, cominciò ad avere paura.**	When the light *went off,* she began to be afraid.
«Ho paura che il fantasma *spenga* ogni luce nella casa», disse.	"I am afraid that the ghost *will turn off* every light in the house," she said.

PRESENT GERUND	***PAST PARTICIPLE***
spingendo	**spinto**

PRESENT INDICATIVE
spingo

PRESENT PERFECT
ho spinto

PRESENT PROGRESSIVE
sto spingendo

IMPERFECT PROGRESSIVE
stavo spingendo

IMPERFECT
spingevo

PAST DEFINITE
spinsi
spingesti
spinse
spingemmo
spingeste
spinsero

Similar verbs

dipingere	paint
fingere	pretend
respingere	push back
sospingere	push, drive

Note: The main irregular features of the verb are

- the past definite tense
- the past participle

IMPERATIVE
spingi (tu) spinga (Lei) spingiamo (noi) spingete (voi) spingano (Loro)

PLUPERFECT
avevo spinto

FUTURE
spingerò

PRESENT CONDITIONAL
spingerei

PRESENT SUBJUNCTIVE
spinga

IMPERFECT SUBJUNCTIVE
spingessi

PAST ANTERIOR
ebbi spinto

FUTURE PERFECT
avrò spinto

CONDITIONAL PERFECT
avrei spinto

PERFECT SUBJUNCTIVE
abbia spinto

PLUPERFECT SUBJUNCTIVE
avessi spinto

Spingete!	*Push!*
Che cosa ti *ha spinto* a partire così presto?	What *has driven* you to leave so early?
Mio padre mi *spinge* a studiare di più.	My father *is urging* me to study harder.
***Spinse* Luigi dentro.**	*He pushed* Luigi inside.
***Spinse* l'amore fino al ridicolo.**	*She carried* her love to ridiculous extremes.
***Hai spinto* quello scherzo oltre i limiti.**	*You have pushed* that joke too far.
***Respinsero* la folla.**	*They pushed back* the crowd.
La fame la *sospinse* a rubare.	Hunger *drove* her to steal.
***Finsi* di essere addormentata.**	*I pretended* I was asleep.
L'anno scorso *dipinsi* sette quadri, mentre quest'anno ne *ho dipinto* appena due.	Last year *I painted* seven pictures, whereas this year I barely painted two.

PRESENT GERUND	***PAST PARTICIPLE***
stando	stato

PRESENT INDICATIVE

sto
stai
sta
stiamo
state
stanno

PRESENT PERFECT

sono stato / a

IMPERFECT

stavo

PAST DEFINITE

stetti
stesti
stette
stemmo
steste
stettero

Note: The verb **stare** often takes over the duties of **essere,** and indeed the verb **essere** *borrows* the past participle of **stare.**

The main irregular features of the verb are

- the present indicative and subjunctive tenses
- the imperfect subjunctive tense
- the past definite tense
- the future stem

IMPERATIVE
sta / sta' / stai (tu) **stia** (Lei) stiamo (noi) state (voi) stiano (Loro)

PLUPERFECT
ero stato

PAST ANTERIOR
fui stato / a

FUTURE
starò

FUTURE PERFECT
sarò stato / a

PRESENT CONDITIONAL
starei

CONDITIONAL PERFECT
sarei stato / a

PRESENT SUBJUNCTIVE
stia
stia
stia
stiamo
stiate
stiano

PERFECT SUBJUNCTIVE
sia stato / a

IMPERFECT SUBJUNCTIVE
stessi
stessi
stesse
stessimo
steste
stessero

PLUPERFECT SUBJUNCTIVE
fossi stato / a

— Come *stai* oggi? **— *Sto* un po meglio, grazie.**	— How *are you* today? — *I am* a little better, thank you.
***Stettero* tre giorni a Roma e due in provincia.**	*They stayed* three days in Rome and two in the country.
***Stavo* per andarmene quando arrivò Maurizio.**	I was about to leave when Maurizio arrived.

PRESENT GERUND	*PAST PARTICIPLE*
stringendo	**stretto**

PRESENT INDICATIVE
stringo

PRESENT PROGRESSIVE
sto stringendo

IMPERFECT
stringevo

PRESENT PERFECT
ho stretto

IMPERFECT PROGRESSIVE
stavo stringendo

PAST DEFINITE
strinsi
stringesti
strinse
stringemmo
stringeste
strinsero

Similar verbs

costringere force
restringere narrow, tighten

Note: The main irregular features of the verb are

- the past definite tense
- the past participle

IMPERATIVE
stringi (tu) stringa (Lei) stringiamo (noi) stringete (voi) stringano (Loro)

PLUPERFECT	***PAST ANTERIOR***
avevo stretto	ebbi stretto
FUTURE	***FUTURE PERFECT***
stringerò	avrò stretto
PRESENT CONDITIONAL	***CONDITIONAL PERFECT***
stringerei	avrei stretto
PRESENT SUBJUNCTIVE	***PERFECT SUBJUNCTIVE***
stringa	abbia stretto
IMPERFECT SUBJUNCTIVE	***PLUPERFECT SUBJUNCTIVE***
stringessi	avessi stretto

Mi *strinse* la mano.	He *shook* my hand.
***Strinsi* mia figlia tra le braccia.**	*I hugged* my daughter.
***Ha stretto* la moneta in mano.**	*He gripped* the coin in his hand.
Devo *stringere* la cinghia.	I must *tighten* my belt.
Mi *hanno costretto* ad andarmene.	*They forced* me out.
Mi *ha costretto* a venire stasera.	*He made* me come this evening.
Ho fatto *restringere* il vestito.	I have had the dress *taken in.*

PRESENT GERUND	***PAST PARTICIPLE***
struggendo	**strutto**

PRESENT INDICATIVE
struggo

PRESENT PROGRESSIVE
sto struggendo

IMPERFECT
struggevo

PRESENT PERFECT
ho strutto

IMPERFECT PROGRESSIVE
stavo struggendo

PAST DEFINITE
strussi
struggesti
strusse
struggemmo
struggeste
strussero

Similar verb

distruggere destroy

Note: The main irregular features of the verb are

- the past definite tense
- the past participle

IMPERATIVE
struggi (tu) strugga (Lei) struggiamo (noi) struggete (voi) struggano (Loro)

PLUPERFECT
avevo strutto

PAST ANTERIOR
ebbi strutto

FUTURE
struggerò

FUTURE PERFECT
avrò strutto

PRESENT CONDITIONAL
struggerei

CONDITIONAL PERFECT
avrei strutto

PRESENT SUBJUNCTIVE
strugga

PERFECT SUBJUNCTIVE
abbia strutto

IMPERFECT SUBJUNCTIVE
struggessi

PLUPERFECT SUBJUNCTIVE
avessi strutto

***Strussi* la cera.**	*I melted* the wax.
La malattia lo *strugge*.	*He is wasting away* because of the illness / sickness.
***Distrussero* la casa.**	*They destroyed* the house.
***Fu distrutto* dal dolore alla gamba.**	*He was overcome* with the pain in his leg.
Il vino l'*ha distrutto*.	Wine *has been his ruin.*
I bombardamenti *distrussero* tutta la zona.	The bombardments *destroyed* the entire region.

PRESENT GERUND	***PAST PARTICIPLE***
tacendo	tac**i**uto

PRESENT INDICATIVE
taccio
taci
tace
taciamo
tacete
tacciono

PRESENT PERFECT
ho taciuto

PRESENT PROGRESSIVE
sto tacendo

IMPERFECT PROGRESSIVE
stavo tacendo

IMPERFECT
tacevo

PAST DEFINITE
tacqui
tacesti
tacque
tacemmo
taceste
tacquero

Note: The main irregular features of the verb are

- the present indicative and subjunctive tenses
- the past definite tense
- the additional **i** in the past participle

IMPERATIVE
taci (tu) **taccia** (Lei) **tacciamo** (noi) tacete (voi) **tacciano** (Loro)

PLUPERFECT
avevo taciuto

PAST ANTERIOR
ebbi taciuto

FUTURE
tacerò

FUTURE PERFECT
avrò taciuto

PRESENT CONDITIONAL
tacerei

CONDITIONAL PERFECT
avrei taciuto

PRESENT SUBJUNCTIVE
taccia
taccia
taccia
taciamo
taciate
tacciano

PERFECT SUBJUNCTIVE
abbia taciuto

IMPERFECT SUBJUNCTIVE
tacessi

PLUPERFECT SUBJUNCTIVE
avessi taciuto

Il padre *tacque.*	The father *fell silent.*
I ragazzi non *tacquero,* però.	The children *were* not *silent,* however.
***«Tacete»,* disse la mamma.**	"*Be quiet,*" said their mother.
I bambini *tacevano* ed ascoltavano la maestra.	The children *were silent,* and they listened to the teacher.

PRESENT GERUND	*PAST PARTICIPLE*
tendendo	**teso**

PRESENT INDICATIVE
tendo

PRESENT PROGRESSIVE
sto tendendo

IMPERFECT
tendevo

PRESENT PERFECT
ho teso

IMPERFECT PROGRESSIVE
stavo tendendo

PAST DEFINITE
tesi
tendesti
tese
tendemmo
tendeste
tesero

Similar verbs

attendere	wait
contendere	contend
distendere	stretch
estendere	extend
intendere	intend, understand
pretendere	claim
sottintendere	hint at
stendere	spread, stretch out

Note: The main irregular features of the verb are

- the past definite tense
- the past participle

Mi *tese* la mano.	*He stretched out* his hand.
Il cane *ha teso* gli orecchi.	The dog *pricked up* its ears.
***Ho teso* la corda.**	*I pulled* the rope tight.
***Ha teso* le corde del violino.**	*He tightened* the strings of the violin.

IMPERATIVE
tendi (tu) tenda (Lei) tendiamo (noi) tendete (voi) tendano (Loro)

PLUPERFECT avevo teso	***PAST ANTERIOR*** ebbi teso
FUTURE tenderò	***FUTURE PERFECT*** avrò teso
PRESENT CONDITIONAL tenderei	***CONDITIONAL PERFECT*** avrei teso
PRESENT SUBJUNCTIVE tenda	***PERFECT SUBJUNCTIVE*** abbia teso
IMPERFECT SUBJUNCTIVE tendessi	***PLUPERFECT SUBJUNCTIVE*** avessi teso

***Tende* ad ingrassare.**	*She tends* to get fat.
Che colore è? *Tende* al rosso.	What color / colour is it? A reddish color / colour.
***Pretende* di essere un grande artista.**	*He pretends* to be a great artist.
***Pretese* di aver ragione.**	*He claimed* to be right.
***Attendiamo* una pronta risposta.**	*We are waiting* for a prompt reply.
Nessuno gli *contese* i suoi diritti.	No one *contested* his rights.
***Distesi* la mano per aiutare la ragazza.**	*I stretched out* my hand to help the girl.
Che cosa *intendi* fare?	What *do you intend* to do?
***Sottintende* la verità.**	*He is hinting* at the truth.
Giuliana *stese* il bucato sull'erba.	Giuliana *laid out* the washing on the grass.
Mi *ha steso* la mano.	*He streched out* his hand to me.

PRESENT GERUND	*PAST PARTICIPLE*
tenendo	tenuto

PRESENT INDICATIVE
tengo
tieni
tiene
teniamo
tenete
tengono

PRESENT PERFECT
ho tenuto

PRESENT PROGRESSIVE
sto tenendo

IMPERFECT PROGRESSIVE
stavo tenendo

IMPERFECT
tenevo

PAST DEFINITE
tenni
tenesti
tenne
tenemmo
teneste
tennero

Similar verbs

appartenere	belong	**ottenere**	obtain
***astenersi**	abstain	**ritenere**	retain
contenere	contain	**sostenere**	support
detenere	detain, stop	**trattenere**	restrain, detain
mantenere	maintain		

Note: The main irregular features of the verb are

- the present indicative and subjunctive tenses
- the past definite tense
- the future stem

Non riesco più a *tenere* la casa. È troppo lavoro.	I can no longer *keep* the house. It's too much work.
La *terrò* per un altro anno, e poi la vendo.	*I will keep* it for one more year, and then I'll sell it.

IMPERATIVE
tieni (tu) **tenga** (Lei) teniamo (noi) tenete (voi) tengano (Loro)

PLUPERFECT
avevo tenuto

PAST ANTERIOR
ebbi tenuto

FUTURE
terrò

FUTURE PERFECT
avrò tenuto

PRESENT CONDITIONAL
terrei

CONDITIONAL PERFECT
avrei tenuto

PRESENT SUBJUNCTIVE
tenga
tenga
tenga
teniamo
teniate
tengano

PERFECT SUBJUNCTIVE
abbia tenuto

IMPERFECT SUBJUNCTIVE
tenessi

PLUPERFECT SUBJUNCTIVE
avessi tenuto

—A chi *appartiene* quel cane? **—L'*ho ottenuto* l'anno scorso.**	—Whom *does* that dog *belong* to? —*I got* it last year.
Questa bevanda *contiene* alcool.	This drink *contains* alcohol.
Dovrei *astenermi* dall'alcool.	I should *abstain* from drinking alcohol.
***Mantengo* sempre buone relazioni con Giovanni.**	*I* always *maintain* a good relationship with Giovanni.
Il muro *è sostenuto* da lunghi pali.	The wall *is supported* by long poles.
***Sostenne* la sua innocenza.**	*He maintained* his innocence.
***Fu trattenuto* a scuola.**	*He was kept in* at school.

PRESENT GERUND	*PAST PARTICIPLE*
tingendo	**tinto**

PRESENT INDICATIVE
tingo

PRESENT PROGRESSIVE
sto tingendo

IMPERFECT
tingevo

PRESENT PERFECT
ho tinto

IMPERFECT PROGRESSIVE
stavo tingendo

PAST DEFINITE
tinsi
tingesti
tinse
tingemmo
tingeste
tinsero

Similar verbs

attingere draw up, draw out
dipingere paint, portray

Note: The main irregular features of the verb are

- the past definite tense
- the past participle

IMPERATIVE
tingi (tu) tinga (Lei) tingiamo (noi) tingete (voi) tingano (Loro)

PLUPERFECT
avevo tinto

PAST ANTERIOR
ebbi tinto

FUTURE
tingerò

FUTURE PERFECT
avrò tinto

PRESENT CONDITIONAL
tingerei

CONDITIONAL PERFECT
avrei tinto

PRESENT SUBJUNCTIVE
tinga

PERFECT SUBJUNCTIVE
abbia tinto

IMPERFECT SUBJUNCTIVE
tingessi

PLUPERFECT SUBJUNCTIVE
avessi tinto

— *Hai tinto* i capelli?	— *Have you dyed* your hair?
— No, ma *ho tinto* questo vestito di nero!	— No, but *I have dyed* this dress black.
Il sole *tingeva* le montagne di rosa.	The sun *tinged* the mountains with a rosy glow.
***Attinse* l'acqua dal pozzo.**	*He drew out* water from the well.
***Ha dipinto* il ritratto ad olio.**	*He painted* the picture in oils.

PRESENT GERUND	*PAST PARTICIPLE*
torcendo	**torto**

PRESENT INDICATIVE
torco

PRESENT PROGRESSIVE
sto torcendo

IMPERFECT
torcevo

PRESENT PERFECT
ho torto

IMPERFECT PROGRESSIVE
stavo torcendo

PAST DEFINITE
torsi
torcesti
torse
torcemmo
torceste
torsero

Similar verbs

contorcere	contort, distort
***contorcersi**	writhe, twist
***torcersi**	twist, writhe
storcere	twist, wrench

Note: The main irregular features of the verb are

- the past definite tense
- the past participle

IMPERATIVE
torci (tu) torca (Lei) torciamo (noi) torcete (voi) torcano (Loro)

PLUPERFECT
avevo torto

PAST ANTERIOR
ebbi torto

FUTURE
torcerò

FUTURE PERFECT
avrò torto

PRESENT CONDITIONAL
torcerei

CONDITIONAL PERFECT
avrei torto

PRESENT SUBJUNCTIVE
torca

PERFECT SUBJUNCTIVE
abbia torto

IMPERFECT SUBJUNCTIVE
torcessi

PLUPERFECT SUBJUNCTIVE
avessi torto

Vorrei *torcere* il collo a quel ragazzo.	I'd like *to wring* that boy's neck!
***Torse* i panni.**	*He wrung out* the washing.
***Torceva* il naso.**	*He was turning up* his nose.
Anna *ha torto* i fili.	Anna *twisted* the threads.
***Si torceva* dal dolore.**	*He was writhing* in pain.
Tieni la fune diritta, non *storcer*la.	Hold the rope straight, *do*n't *twist* it.

PRESENT GERUND	***PAST PARTICIPLE***
traducendo	**tradotto**

PRESENT INDICATIVE
traduco
traduci
traduce
traduciamo
traducete
traducono

PRESENT PERFECT
ho tradotto

PRESENT PROGRESSIVE
sto traducendo

IMPERFECT PROGRESSIVE
stavo traducendo

IMPERFECT
traducevo

PAST DEFINITE
tradussi
traducesti
tradusse
traducemmo
traduceste
tradussero

Similar verbs

addurre	convey	**introdurre**	introduce
condurre	conduct, lead, drive	**produrre**	produce
dedurre	deduce	**ridurre**	reduce
indurre	induce, induct	**riprodurre**	reproduce
		sedurre	seduce

Note: The main irregular features of the verb are

- the irregular present tense stem
- the irregular future stem
- the past definite tense
- the past participle

***Ho tradotto* il suo ultimo libro.** *I translated* his last book.

IMPERATIVE
traduci (tu) traduca (Lei) traduciamo (noi) traducete (voi) traducano (Loro)

PLUPERFECT
avevo tradotto

PAST ANTERIOR
ebbi tradotto

FUTURE
tradurrò

FUTURE PERFECT
avrò tradotto

PRESENT CONDITIONAL
tradurrei

CONDITIONAL PERFECT
avrei tradotto

PRESENT SUBJUNCTIVE
traduca

PERFECT SUBJUNCTIVE
abbia tradotto

IMPERFECT SUBJUNCTIVE
traducessi

PLUPERFECT SUBJUNCTIVE
avessi tradotto

Dubito che l'opera *sia stata tradotta* in inglese.	I doubt that the work *was translated* into English.
Mi *condusse* al teatro.	*He took* me to the theater / theatre.
***Condussero* una vita miserabile.**	*They led* a miserable life.
Tutte le strade *conducono* a Roma.	All roads *lead* to Rome.
Mi *introdusse* allo studio della lingua italiana.	*He introduced* me to the study of the Italian language.
Quest'albero non *ha prodotto* mai frutta.	This tree *has* never *produced* any fruit.
***Ridusse* la velocità all'angolo della strada.**	*He reduced* his speed at the corner of the road.

PRESENT GERUND	*PAST PARTICIPLE*
traendo	**tratto**

PRESENT INDICATIVE	*PRESENT PERFECT*
traggo **trai** **trae** **traiamo** **traete** **traggono**	ho tratto
PRESENT PROGRESSIVE	*IMPERFECT PROGRESSIVE*
sto traendo	stavo traendo
IMPERFECT	*PAST DEFINITE*
traevo	**trassi** traesti **trasse** traemmo traeste **trassero**

Similar verbs

attrarre	attract
contrarre	contract
distrarre	distract
estrarre	extract
sottrarre	subtract
***sottrarsi**	get out of; shirk

Note: The main irregular features of these verbs are

- the present indicative and subjunctive tenses
- the future stem
- the past definite tense
- the past participle

IMPERATIVE

trai (tu) **tragga** (Lei) traiamo (noi) traete (voi) **traggano** (Loro)

PLUPERFECT

avevo tratto

PAST ANTERIOR

ebbi tratto

FUTURE

trarrò

FUTURE PERFECT

avrò tratto

PRESENT CONDITIONAL

trarrei

CONDITIONAL PERFECT

avrel tratto

PRESENT SUBJUNCTIVE

tragga
tragga
tragga
traiamo
traiate
traggano

PERFECT SUBJUNCTIVE

abbia tratto

IMPERFECT SUBJUNCTIVE

traessi

PLUPERFECT SUBJUNCTIVE

avessi tratto

Non ne *traggo* nessun piacere.	*I don*'t *get* any pleasure from it.
***Trae* origine da una nobile famiglia.**	*He traces* his origins back to a noble family.
La minima cosa lo *distraeva.*	The slightest thing *distracted* him.
Mi sento *attratto* verso quella ragazza.	I feel *attracted* to that girl.
***Sottrai* quattro da dieci.**	*Subtract* four from ten.
Lo *sottrassero* alla morte.	*They rescued* him from death.
Luigi *si sottrasse* al proprio dovere.	Luigi *shirked* his duty.
***Contrasse* una malattia dolorosa.**	*He contracted* a painful illness / sickness.

PRESENT GERUND	*PAST PARTICIPLE*
uccidendo	**ucciso**

PRESENT INDICATIVE
uccido

PRESENT PROGRESSIVE
sto uccidendo

IMPERFECT
uccidevo

PRESENT PERFECT
ho ucciso

IMPERFECT PROGRESSIVE
stavo uccidendo

PAST DEFINITE
uccisi
uccidesti
uccise
uccidemmo
uccideste
uccisero

Similar verb

***uccidersi** kill oneself, commit suicide

Note: The main irregular features of this verb are:

- the past definite tense
- the past participle

IMPERATIVE
uccidi (tu) uccida (Lei) uccidiamo (noi) uccidete (voi) uccidano (Loro)

PLUPERFECT avevo ucciso	***PAST ANTERIOR*** ebbi ucciso
FUTURE ucciderò	***FUTURE PERFECT*** avrò ucciso
PRESENT CONDITIONAL ucciderei	***CONDITIONAL PERFECT*** avrei ucciso
PRESENT SUBJUNCTIVE uccida	***PERFECT SUBJUNCTIVE*** abbia ucciso
IMPERFECT SUBJUNCTIVE uccidessi	***PLUPERFECT SUBJUNCTIVE*** avessi ucciso

***Ha ucciso* un lupo.**	*He killed* a wolf.
***Uccise* l'uomo, sparandogli alla testa.**	*He shot* the man through the head.
***Fu ucciso* in un incidente stradale.**	*He was killed* in a road accident.
***Si uccise* per disperazione.**	*He killed himself* out of despair.

PRESENT GERUND	***PAST PARTICIPLE***
udendo	udito

PRESENT INDICATIVE
odo
odi
ode
udiamo
udite
odono

PRESENT PERFECT
ho udito

PRESENT PROGRESSIVE
sto udendo

IMPERFECT PROGRESSIVE
stavo udendo

IMPERFECT
udivo

PAST DEFINITE
udii

Note: The main irregular features of the verb are

- the present indicative and subjunctive tenses

IMPERATIVE
odi (tu) **oda** (Lei) udiamo (noi) udite (voi) **odano** (Loro)

PLUPERFECT
avevo udito

PAST ANTERIOR
ebbi udito

FUTURE
udirò / udrò

FUTURE PERFECT
avrò udito

PRESENT CONDITIONAL
udirei / udrei

CONDITIONAL PERFECT
avrei udito

PRESENT SUBJUNCTIVE
oda
oda
oda
udiamo
udiate
odano

PERFECT SUBJUNCTIVE
abbia udito

IMPERFECT SUBJUNCTIVE
udissi

PLUPERFECT SUBJUNCTIVE
avessi udito

— L'*hai* mai *udito* cantare?	— *Have you* ever *heard* him sing?
— Non ancora, ma l'*udirò* forse domani.	— Not yet, but *I shall* perhaps *hear* him tomorrow.
Spero che Dio *oda* le mie preghiere!	I hope God *will listen to* my prayers.

PRESENT GERUND	***PAST PARTICIPLE***
uscendo	uscito

PRESENT INDICATIVE
esco
esci
esce
usciamo
uscite
escono

PRESENT PERFECT
sono uscito / a

PRESENT PROGRESSIVE
sto uscendo

IMPERFECT PROGRESSIVE
stavo uscendo

IMPERFECT
uscivo

PAST DEFINITE
uscii

Similar verb

***riuscire** succeed

Note: The main irregular features of the verb are

- the present indicative and subjunctive tenses

IMPERATIVE
esci (tu) **esca** (Lei) usciamo (noi) uscite (voi) **escano** (Loro)

PLUPERFECT
ero uscito

PAST ANTERIOR
fui uscito / a

FUTURE
uscirò

FUTURE PERFECT
sarò uscito / a

PRESENT CONDITIONAL
uscirei

CONDITIONAL PERFECT
sarei uscito / a

PRESENT SUBJUNCTIVE
esca
esca
esca
usciamo
usciate
escano

PERFECT SUBJUNCTIVE
sia uscito / a

IMPERFECT SUBJUNCTIVE
uscissi

PLUPERFECT SUBJUNCTIVE
fossi uscito / a

—A che ora *usciamo* stasera?	—What time *are we going out* tonight?
—Beh, io *esco* alle sette, ma Mario non *esce* fino alle sette e mezzo.	—Well, *I'm going out* at 7:00, but Mario *is* not *going out* till 7:30.
—E Carlo?	—And what about Carlo?
—Non credo che *esca* stasera.	—I don't think *he's going out* tonight.
—Non *sei riuscito* a telefonargli?	—*Did you* not *manage* to call him?
—Sì, ci *sono riuscito,* ma *era uscito* con Antonia.	—Yes, *I did manage to;* but *he had gone out* with Antonia.

PRESENT GERUND
valendo

PAST PARTICIPLE
valso

PRESENT INDICATIVE
valgo
vali
vale
valiamo
valete
valgono

PRESENT PERFECT
sono valso / a

PRESENT PROGRESSIVE
sto valendo

IMPERFECT PROGRESSIVE
stavo valendo

IMPERFECT
valevo

PAST DEFINITE
valsi
valesti
valse
valemmo
valeste
valsero

Similar verb

***prevalere** prevail

Note: The main irregular features of the verb are

- the present indicative and subjunctive tenses
- the past definite tense
- the past participle
- the future stem

IMPERATIVE
vali (tu) **valga** (Lei) valiamo (noi) valete (voi) **valgano** (Loro)

PLUPERFECT
ero valso / a

PAST ANTERIOR
fui valso / a

FUTURE
varrò

FUTURE PERFECT
sarò valso / a

PRESENT CONDITIONAL
varrei

CONDITIONAL PERFECT
sarei valso / a

PRESENT SUBJUNCTIVE
valga
valga
valga
valiamo
valiate
valgano

PERFECT SUBJUNCTIVE
sia valso / a

IMPERFECT SUBJUNCTIVE
valessi

PLUPERFECT SUBJUNCTIVE
fossi valso / a

—Quanto *valgono* queste due statue?	—How much *are* these two statues *worth*?
—Non credo che *valgano* molto.	—I do not think *they are worth* a lot.
—Quella più grande *vale* forse mezzo milione.	—The larger one is perhaps *worth* half a million lire.
Questo biglietto *vale* per 24 ore.	This ticket *is valid* for 24 hours.
Litigarsi per una cosa tale, non *ne vale la pena.*	Fighting for something of the sort *is* not *worth it.*
Dicono cose che non *valgono* a nulla.	They are talking nonsense.

PRESENT GERUND	*PAST PARTICIPLE*
vedendo	**visto** / veduto

PRESENT INDICATIVE
vedo

PRESENT PROGRESSIVE
sto vedendo

IMPERFECT
vedevo

PRESENT PERFECT
ho visto

IMPERFECT PROGRESSIVE
stavo vedendo

PAST DEFINITE
vidi
vedesti
vide
vedemmo
vedeste
videro

Similar verbs

***avvedersi**	perceive
prevedere	foresee
provvedere	provide
rivedere	see again
travedere	be wrong

Note: The main irregular features of the verb are

- the past definite tense
- the past participle (although the regular past participle is also accepted)
- the future stem

IMPERATIVE
vedi (tu) veda (Lei) vediamo (noi) vedete (voi) vedano (Loro)

PLUPERFECT avevo visto	***PAST ANTERIOR*** ebbi visto
FUTURE **vedrò**	***FUTURE PERFECT*** avrò visto
PRESENT CONDITIONAL **vedrei**	***CONDITIONAL PERFECT*** avrei visto
PRESENT SUBJUNCTIVE veda	***PERFECT SUBJUNCTIVE*** abbia visto
IMPERFECT SUBJUNCTIVE vedessi	***PLUPERFECT SUBJUNCTIVE*** avessi visto

—*Vedi* quell'uomo laggiù?	—*Do you see* that man down there?
—Sì, l'*ho visto* anche ieri. Chi è?	—Yes, *I saw* him yesterday as well. Who is he?
—Non lo so. Mai *visto* prima!	—I don't know, *I have* never *seen* him before today.
—Credi che lui ci abbia *visti?*	—Do you think *he has seen* us?
Tu *travedi,* se credi che lui sia colpevole.	You *are making a mistake* if you think he is guilty.
Non *l'ho* mai più *rivista*.	*I* never *saw* her *again*.
Avresti dovuto *preveder*lo.	You should have *foreseen* it.
Ti ferì senza *avvedersene*.	He hurt your feelings without *realizing*.
L'*ho* sempre *provveduto* di tutto.	*I have* always *provided* him with everything.

PRESENT GERUND	***PAST PARTICIPLE***
venendo	**venuto**

PRESENT INDICATIVE
vengo
vieni
viene
veniamo
venite
vengono

PRESENT PERFECT
sono venuto / a

PRESENT PROGRESSIVE
sto venendo

IMPERFECT PROGRESSIVE
stavo venendo

IMPERFECT
venivo

PAST DEFINITE
venni
venisti
venne
venimmo
veniste
vennero

Similar verbs

***avvenire**	happen
***convenire**	agree, gather together
***divenire**	become
***intervenire**	intervene
***pervenire**	reach, arrive
***provenire**	proceed from, come from
†rinvenire	find, discover; recover; come to
***sopravvenire**	arrive; happen
***sovvenire**	aid
***svenire**	faint

Note: The main irregular features of the verb are

- the present indicative and subjunctive tenses
- the past definite tense
- the past participle
- the future stem

IMPERATIVE
vieni (tu) **venga** (Lei) veniamo (noi) venite (voi) vengano (Loro)

PLUPERFECT
ero venuto / a

PAST ANTERIOR
fui venuto / a

FUTURE
verrò

FUTURE PERFECT
sarò venuto / a

PRESENT CONDITIONAL
verrei

CONDITIONAL PERFECT
sarei venuto / a

PRESENT SUBJUNCTIVE
venga
venga
venga
veniamo
veniate
vengano

PERFECT SUBJUNCTIVE
sia venuto / a

IMPERFECT SUBJUNCTIVE
venissi

PLUPERFECT SUBJUNCTIVE
fossi venuto / a

Digli che *venga* subito.	Tell him *to come* at once.
Ha detto che *verrà* domani.	He said *he will come* tomorrow.
Avevo paura che non *venisse* oggi.	I was afraid that *he might* not *come* today.
***Ci conviene* partire subito.**	*We had better* leave immediately.
Il prezzo *è convenuto.*	The price *is agreed upon.*
Non credo che *provenga* da una buona famiglia.	I don't think *he comes* from a good family.
***Svenne* per la fame.**	*He fainted* from hunger.
Antonella *ha rinvenuto* un libro raro.	Antonella *found* a rare book.
La maestra *intervenne* quando vide i due ragazzi bisticciarsi.	The teacher *intervened* when she saw the two boys fighting.

PRESENT GERUND	*PAST PARTICIPLE*
vincendo	**vinto**

PRESENT INDICATIVE
vinco

PRESENT PROGRESSIVE
sto vincendo

IMPERFECT
vincevo

PRESENT PERFECT
ho vinto

MPERFECT CONTINUOUS
stavo vincendo

PAST DEFINITE
vinsi
vincesti
vinse
vincemmo
vinceste
vinsero

Similar verbs

avvincere bind, tie up
convincere convince

Note: The main irregular features of the verb are

- the past definite tense
- the past participle

IMPERATIVE
vinci (tu) vinca (Lei) vinciarno (noi) vincete (voi) vincano (Loro)

PLUPERFECT
avevo vinto

PAST ANTERIOR
ebbi vinto

FUTURE
vincerò

FUTURE PERFECT
avrò vinto

PRESENT CONDITIONAL
vincerei

CONDITIONAL PERFECT
avrei vinto

PRESENT SUBJUNCTIVE
vinca

PERFECT SUBJUNCTIVE
abbia vinto

IMPERFECT SUBJUNCTIVE
vincessi

PLUPERFECT SUBJUNCTIVE
avessi vinto

La sua bellezza mi *vinse.*	I *was won over* by her beauty.
***Hai vinto* un premio?**	*Did you win* a prize?
Il partito *ha vinto*.	The (political) party *has won.*
***Vinsi* di stretta misura.**	*I won* by a short margin.
Il ladro *avvinse* l'uomo.	The robber *tied up* the man.
Mi sono lasciato *vincere* dalla tentazione.	*I yielded* to temptation.
***Fu vinto* dall'ira.**	*He was overcome* by rage.
L'*hai convinto?*	*Did you convince* him?

PRESENT GERUND	***PAST PARTICIPLE***
vivendo	**vissuto**

PRESENT INDICATIVE
vivo

PRESENT PROGRESSIVE
sto vivendo

IMPERFECT
vivevo

PRESENT PERFECT
ho vissuto / sono vissuto/a

IMPERFECT PROGRESSIVE
stavo vivendo

PAST DEFINITE
vissi
vivesti
visse
vivemmo
viveste
vissero

Similar verbs

† rivivere	live again, relive
†sopravvivere	survive; outlive; live on

These verbs, like **vivere** take **avere** when used transitively and **essere** when used intransitively.

Note: The main irregular features of the verb are

- the past definite tense
- the past participle

IMPERATIVE
vivi (tu) viva (Lei) viviamo (noi) vivete (voi) vivano (Loro)

PLUPERFECT
avevo vissuto / ero vissuto/a

PAST ANTERIOR
ebbi vissuto / fui vissuto/a

FUTURE
vivrò

FUTURE PERFECT
avrò vissuto / sarò vissuto/a

PRESENT CONDITIONAL
vivrei

CONDITIONAL PERFECT
avrei vissuto / sarei vissuto/a

PRESENT SUBJUNCTIVE
viva

PERFECT SUBJUNCTIVE
abbia vissuto / sia vissuto/a

IMPERFECT SUBJUNCTIVE
vivessi

PLUPERFECT SUBJUNCTIVE
avessi vissuto / fossi vissuto/a

***Vive* in città da tre anni.**	*He has been living* in town for three years.
***Visse* bene del proprio lavoro.**	*He lived* well from his own work.
Hai di che *vivere?*	Do you have enough *to live on?*
Antonio sa *vivere.*	Antonio knows how *to live!*
Come *si vive* così si muore. (*Proverbio*)	As *we live* so shall we die. (*Proverb*)
Vorrei *rivivere* quei momenti.	I would like *to relive* those moments.
Mi sento *rivivere.*	I feel like a new person.
***Ha sopravvisuto* un terribile incidente stradale.**	*He survived* a terrible road accident.

PRESENT GERUND	*PAST PARTICIPLE*
volendo	voluto

PRESENT INDICATIVE	*PRESENT PERFECT*
voglio	ho voluto / sono voluto/a
vuoi	
vuole	
vogliamo	
volete	
vogliono	
PRESENT PROGRESSIVE	*IMPERFECT PROGRESSIVE*
sto volendo	stavo volendo
IMPERFECT	*PAST DEFINITE*
volevo	**volli**
	volesti
	volle
	volemmo
	voleste
	vollero

Note: The verb **volere** is frequently used as a modal verb, before the infinitive of another verb. It takes **avere** or **essere** according to which one the dependent infinitive takes, although, in speech, **avere** is more common when wishing/wanting is stressed.

The main irregular features of the verb are

- the present indicative and subjunctive tenses
- the past definite tense
- the future stem

IMPERATIVE
vogli (tu) **voglia** (Lei) vogliamo (noi) **vogliate** (voi) **vogliano** (Loro)

PLUPERFECT
avevo voluto / ero voluto/a

FUTURE
vorrò

PRESENT CONDITIONAL
vorrei

PRESENT SUBJUNCTIVE
voglia
voglia
voglia
vogliamo
vogliate
vogliano

IMPERFECT SUBJUNCTIVE
volessi

PAST ANTERIOR
ebbi voluto / fui voluto/a

FUTURE PERFECT
avrò voluto / sarò voluto/a

CONDITIONAL PERFECT
avrei voluto / sarei voluto/a

PERFECT SUBJUNCTIVE
abbia voluto / sia voluto/a

PLUPERFECT SUBJUNCTIVE
avessi voluto / fossi voluto/a

Non capisco ciò che *vuoi dire.*	I don't understand what *you mean.*
***Voglio* rimanere qui in Italia.**	*I want to* stay in Italy.
Non *vorrei* malintesi.	*I would* not *want* any misunderstandings.
Ci *vuole* almeno un'ora per andare da Anna.	*It takes* at least an hour to get to Anna's house.
***Vorresti* accompagnarmi?**	*Would you like* to come with me?
***Avevo voluto* mangiare in quel ristorante.**	*I had wanted to* eat in that restaurant.
La mamma non *volle* che partissimo.	My mother *did* not *want* us to leave.

PRESENT GERUND
volgendo

PAST PARTICIPLE
volto

PRESENT INDICATIVE
volgo

PRESENT PERFECT
ho volto

PRESENT PROGRESSIVE
sto volgendo

IMPERFECT PROGRESSIVE
stavo volgendo

IMPERFECT
volgevo

PAST DEFINITE
volsi
volgesti
volse
volgemmo
volgeste
volsero

Similar verbs

avvolgere	wrap up
coinvolgere	involve
involgere	wrap
ravvolgere	wrap up
rivolgere	turn
sconvolgere	upset
svolgere	unfold

Note: The main irregular features of the verb are

- the past definite tense
- the past participle

IMPERATIVE
volgi (tu) volga (Lei) volgiamo (noi) volgete (voi) volgano (Loro)

PLUPERFECT avevo volto	***PAST ANTERIOR*** ebbi volto
FUTURE volgerò	***FUTURE PERFECT*** avrò volto
PRESENT CONDITIONAL volgerei	***CONDITIONAL PERFECT*** avrei volto
PRESENT SUBJUNCTIVE volga	***PERFECT SUBJUNCTIVE*** abbia volto
IMPERFECT SUBJUNCTIVE volgessi	***PLUPERFECT SUBJUNCTIVE*** avessi volto

Quando arrivi al semaforo, *volgi* a destra.	When you get to the red light, *turn* right.
***Volse* i passi verso la casa.**	*He turned* his steps towards home.
***Volsi* la scenetta a mio vantaggio.**	*I turned* the scene to my advantage.
***Volgo* la vicenda nella mente.**	*I am turning over* the event in my mind.
Il tempo *volge* al brutto.	The weather *is making a turn* for the worse.
***Avvolse* il regalo nella carta.**	*He wrapped up* the present in paper.
***Ho ravvolto* il vaso in molta carta.**	*I have wrapped* the vase in a lot of paper.
***Sconvolsero* i suoi piani.**	*They upset* his plans.
Si è trovato *coinvolto* nello scandalo di cui tutti parlano.	He found himself *involved* in the scandal that is the talk of the day.

C
SUBJECT INDEX

SUBJECT INDEX

The references given here relate to the relevant section in *The verb system in Italian.*

D
VERB INDEX

Verb Index

An **[M]** beside a verb indicates that it is one of the Model Verbs.
An * before a verb indicates that this verb takes **essere**.

A † before a verb indicates that this verb can take **essere** or **avere**; usually, **essere** when it is intransitive and **avere** when it is transitive.

If the verb is usually used impersonally, this is indicated by *(Imp.)*

The number beside the verb indicates the model verb pattern(s) it follows.

A	**abbagliare** *(tr)*	dazzle 13
	abbaiare *(intr)*	bark 13
	abbandonare *(tr)*	abandon, desert, give up 3
	abbassare *(tr)*	depress, turn down (light / window) 3
	abbattere *(tr)*	knock over 4
	***abbattersi su**	hit upon 4, 7
	abbondare *(intr)*	abound 3
	abbotdare *(tr)*	accost 3
	abbottonare *(tr)*	button 3
	abbozzare *(tr)*	draft, sketch 3
	abbracciare *(tr)*	cuddle, embrace 12
	***abbronzarsi** *(intr / refl)*	tan, brown in sun 7
	abitare *(tr)*	live, dwell 3
	abituare *(tr)*	accustom 3
	***abituarsi a** *(intr / refl)*	become accustomed to, get used to 7
	abolire *(tr)*	abolish 6
	abortire *(tr / intr)*	miscarry 6
	***abortire** *(intr)*	fail, come to nothing 6
	***accadere** *(intr)*	occur, happen, turn out transpire *(Imp.)* 28
	accalcarsi *(intr / refl)*	huddle 7, 11
	accarezzare *(tr)*	caress, stroke 3
	accecare *(tr)*	blind 11
	***accedere** *(intr)*	access; approach; comply with 33
	accelerare *(tr / intr)*	speed up, accelerate 3
	accendere *(tr)*	turn on, light, ignite, strike (match) 17 **[M]**
	***accendersi** *(intr)*	go on (of lighting), light up 17, 7

accennare a *(intr)*	refer to, mention 3
accennare di si *(intr)*	nod 3
accentuare *(tr)*	emphasize 3
accertare *(tr)*	assess 3
accettare di *(tr)*	accept 3
acchiappare *(tr)*	catch 3
accludere *(tr)*	enclose, attach 20
***accoccolarsi** *(intr/refl)*	squat, crouch 7
accogliere *(tr)*	welcome 31
accomodare *(tr)*	arrange 3
accomodarsi *(intr/refl)*	come in; sit down 7
accompagnare *(tr)*	accompany, take (for a walk) 3
***accondiscendere a** *(intr)*	consent 79
acconsentire a *(intr)*	accept, agree to 5
***accontentarsi di** *(intr/refl)*	make do with 7
accoppiare *(tr)*	couple 13
***accoppiarsi** *(intr/refl)*	mate 13, 7
accorciare *(tr)*	shorten 12
***accorciarsi** *(intr/refl)*	become shorter, draw in 12, 7
accordare *(tr)*	grant, concede, tune, string (instrument) 3
***accordarsi** *(intr/refl)*	agree 7
***accorgersi di** *(intr/refl)*	notice, take note 80, 7
accorrere *(intr)*	run, rush 35
accrescere *(tr)*	increase 36
accumulare *(tr)*	accumulate, hoard 3
accusare di *(tr)*	accuse (of), charge (criminal) 3
accusare ricevuta di	acknowledge receipt of 3
acquistare *(tr)*	acquire, get 3
adattare *(tr)*	adapt 3
adattare a *(intr)*	adapt to 3
addebitare *(tr)*	charge to account, debit 3
addizionare *(tr)*	count up 3
addolcire *(tr)*	sweeten 6
***addormentarsi** *(intr/refl)*	fall asleep 7
addurre *(tr)*	convey 95
adempire *(tr)*	implement, perform (a function) 6
aderire a *(intr)*	adhere to 6
adorare *(tr)*	adore, worship 3
adottare *(tr)*	adopt 3
aerare *(tr)*	air a room 3
affascinare *(tr)*	charm, fascinate 3
aftermare *(tr)*	affirm, assert 3
afferrare *(tr)*	grasp, snatch, tackle 3
afterrare strettamente *(tr)*	grip 3
affettare *(tr)*	affect, feign, simulate 3
***affezionarsi a** *(intr/refl)*	become fond of, take a liking to 7
affidare *(tr)*	entrust 3
***affidarsi a** *(intr/refl)*	rely on, trust in 7

affiggere *(tr)*	post/put (up), attach; fix 18 **[M]**
affilare *(tr)*	sharpen 3
affittare *(tr)*	hire, rent house, lease out 3
affliggere *(tr)*	suffer from, afflict 19 **[M]**
†affogare *(tr/intr)*	drown 2, 11
affollare *(intr)*	crowd 3
affrettare *(tr)*	hurry 3
***affrettarsi a** *(intr/refl)*	hurry (to) 7
affrontare *(tr)*	confront, stand up to, face 3
agganciare (tr)	hook 12
aggiogare (tr)	yoke 11
aggiornare *(tr)*	adjourn, postpone, write up (diary) 3
***aggiornarsi** *(intr/refl)*	get up to date 7
aggiungere *(tr)*	add, say further, append, add 52
aggiustare *(tr)*	adjust, patch 3
agire *(intr)*	act, do 6
agire per *(intr)*	act for 6
agire seguendo i consigli	act on advice 6
agire su	act on, work on 6
agitare *(tr)*	ruffle, stir, shake, stir, move 3
***agitarsi** *(intr/refl)*	bustle 7
aiutare *(tr)*	aid, assist, help 3
albeggiare *(intr)*	dawn 12
alienare *(tr)*	alienate 3
alimentare *(tr)*	feed 3
allacciare *(tr)*	fasten (seatbelt) 12
allargare *(tr)*	broaden, enlarge, widen 11
allarmare *(tr)*	alarm 3
allattare *(tr)*	nurse (baby), suckle 3
alleggerire *(tr)*	lighten 6
***allenarsi** *(intr/refl)*	exercise 7
allentare *(tr)*	slacken 3
allevare *(tr)*	raise, rear 3
alleviare *(tr)*	alleviate, relieve (pain, anxiety) 13
allineare *(tr)*	align 3
***allinearsi** *(intr/refl)*	line up 7
alloggiare *(tr)*	house 12
alloggiare in *(intr)*	stay (as guest) 12
allontanare *(tr)*	push away 3
***allontanarsi da** *(intr/refl)*	get away from 7
alludere a *(intr)*	allude at, hint at 20 **[M]**
allungare *(tr)*	draw out, become longer, stretch out 11
alterare *(tr)*	alter 3
alternare *(tr)*	alternate 3
alzare *(tr)*	elevate, put up (price), raise, lift 3
alzare *(tr)* **la voce**	speak up 3
alzare gli occhi *(tr)*	look up 3

***alzarsi** *(intr/refl)*	get up, stand, rise to feet 7
amalgamare *(tr)*	amalgamate 3
amare *(tr)*	love 3
ammaccare *(tr)*	bruise 11
***ammalarsi** *(intr/refl)*	become ill, fall ill 7
ammettere di *(tr)*	admit, grant to be true, allow 54
ammiccare a qlcu. *(intr)*	wink 11
amministrare *(tr)*	administer, run, manage 3
ammirare *(tr)*	admire 3
ammobiliare *(tr)*	furnish, equip 13
†ammontare a *(intr/tr)*	number, amount to 3
ammorbidire *(tr)*	soften 6
ammucchiare *(tr)*	heap, pile up 13
***ammucchiarsi** *(intr/refl)*	pile up 13, 7
ammuffire *(intr)*	go moldy 6
amplificare *(tr)*	amplify 11
amputare *(tr)*	amputate 3
analizzare *(tr)*	analyze 3
ancorare *(tr)*	anchor, moor 3
***andare** *(intr)*	go, ride (in car) 21 **[M]**
***andare a fare le spese** *(intr)*	shop 21
***andare a prendere** *(intr)*	go for (e.g., doctor), fetch 21
***andare a trovare** *(tr)*	call on, visit 21
***andare a vapore** *(intr)*	steam, move by steam 21
***andare avanti** *(intr)*	get on, be fast (clock) 21
***andare bene** *(intr)*	fit, be right size, match in color 21
***andare bene a** *(intr)*	suit 21
***andare d'accordo con** *(intr)*	get along with 21
***andare da** *(intr)*	see (doctor) 21
***andare in autobus** *(intr)*	bus 21
***andare in bicicletta** *(intr)*	bike 21
***andare in fretta** *(intr)*	speed 21
***andare in pensione** *(intr)*	retire 21
***andare meglio** *(intr)*	get better 21
***andare pazzo per** *(intr)*	rave about 21
***andarsene** *(refl/intr)*	go away, clear off 21
anestetizzare *(tr)*	anesthetize 3
animare *(tr)*	animate, brighten up 3
annegare *(tr)*	drown 11
†annerire *(tr)*	blacken 6
annettere *(tr)*	attach, add, annex 22 **[M]**
annichilire *(tr)*	annihilate 6
annodare *(tr)*	knot (rope) 3
annoiare *(tr)*	bore 13
***annoiarsi** *(intr/refl)*	be bored 13, 7
annullare *(tr)*	annul, write off, accept loss of 3
***annullarsi** *(intr/refl)*	cancel out 7
annunziare *(tr)*	announce 13

***annuvolarsi** *(intr/refl)*	cloud over 7
ansimare *(intr)*	pant 3
anticipare *(tr)*	advance payment, anticipate 3
appannarsi *(intr/refl)*	become misty 7
apparecchiare *(tr)*	lay (table) 13
***apparire** *(intr)*	appear, seem; make an appearance 23 **[M]**
appartenere *(intr)*	belong 92
***appassire** *(intr)*	wilt, dry up 6
***appellarsi a** *(intr/refl)*	appeal to the law 7
appendere *(tr)*	hang, suspend 17
appianare *(tr)*	even out 3
appiattire *(tr)*	flatten 6
applaudire *(intr)*	applaud, clap 6
applicare *(tr)*	apply, use 11
applicare *(tr)* **le manette a**	handcuff 11
***appoggiarsi** *(intr/refl)*	lean up against (back) 12, 7
apporre *(tr)*	affix 64
apprendere a *(tr)*	learn (to) 66
***apprestarsi a** *(intr/refl)*	get ready to 7
apprezzare *(tr)*	appreciate the value, prize 3
***approfittare di** *(intr)*	take advantage of 3
approfondire *(tr)*	deepen 6
appropriare *(tr)*	appropriate 13
***appropriarsi indebitamente di** *(intr/refl)*	embezzle 13, 7
approssimare *(tr)*	approximate 3
approvare *(tr)*	approve, endorse, pass (a law) 3
aprire *(tr)*	open 24 **[M]**
aprire con chiave *(tr)*	unlock 24
arare *(tr)*	plough 3
arbitrare *(tr)*	arbitrate, umpire, referee, file (IT) 3
ardere *(tr)*	burn 47
armare *(tr)*	arm 3
armonizzare *(intr)*	harmonize, match 3
aromatizzare *(tr)*	flavor/flavour 3
***arrabbiarsi con** *(intr/refl)*	be/get angry, lose one's temper with 13, 7
arrampicare *(tr)*	climb 11
***arrendersi** *(intr/refl)*	capitulate 71, 7
arrestare *(tr)*	arrest, stem, check, stop 3
†arricchire *(intr/tr)*	enrich, grow rich 6
arricciare *(tr)*	curl 12
arrischiare *(tr)*	chance, gamble 13
***arrivare a** *(intr)*	arrive at, get to 2
***arrossire** *(intr)*	blush 6
arrostire *(tr)*	roast 6
arrotondare *(tr)*	approximate, round up (figures) 3
***arrugginirsi** *(intr/refl)*	rust 6, 7
arruolare *(tr)*	enroll in 3

***arruolarsi** *(intr / refl)*	join up army 7
***ascendere** *(intr)*	ascend 79
asciugare *(tr)*	dry, wipe, wipe up 11
ascoltare *(tr)*	listen, listen to 3
aspergere *(tr)*	sprinkle 84
aspettare *(tr)*	expect, hold (telephone), wait 3
***aspettarsi di** *(intr / refl)*	anticipate, expect 7
aspirare a *(intr)*	aspire to 3
assalire *(tr)*	attack, seize, overcome 77
assassinare *(tr)*	assassinate, murder 3
assegnare *(tr)*	allocate, assign, award 3
***assentarsi da** *(intr / refl)*	absent oneself, be absent 7
assicurare *(tr)*	assure, ensure, insure, secure 3
assimilare *(tr)*	assimilate 3
assistere *(tr)*	assist; attend 25 **[M]**
assistere a *(intr)*	be present, stand by, observe, attend 25
associare *(tr)*	associate 12
assolvere *(tr)*	absolve, acquit 74
assomigliare a *(intr)*	resemble 13
***assopirsi** *(intr / refl)*	nod off, doze off 6, 7
assorbire *(tr)*	absorb, soak up 6
assordare *(tr)*	deafen 3
assottigliare *(tr)*	taper, thin down 13
assumere *(tr)*	assume; hire; raise 26 **[M]**
***assumersi** *(intr / refl)*	undertake, assume (responsibility) 26, 7
***astenersi da** *(intr / refl)*	abstain, refrain from 92, 7
astrarre *(tr)*	abstract 96
atomizzare *(tr)*	atomize 3
attaccare *(tr)*	attach, harness, hang up (telephone) 11
attendere *(tr / intr)*	wait 91
atterrire *(tr)*	terrorize 6
attestare *(tr)*	vouch 3
attingere *(tr)*	draw up, draw out
attirare / attrarre *(tr)*	attract, lure 3, 86, 96
attorcigliare *(tr)*	twist 13
attrarre *(tr)*	attract 96
attraversare *(tr)*	come across / over, go across / through 3
attraversare velocemente *(tr)*	shoot (rapids) 3
attribuire *(tr)*	credit with 6
attutire *(tr)*	deaden 6
†aumentare *(intr / tr)*	rise, add to, increase, raise (prices) 3
autorizzare a *(tr)*	authorize, license s.one (to) 3
†avanzare *(intr / tr)*	progress, advance, move / put forward 3
avanzare a fatica *(intr)*	slog away 3

***avanzarsi** *(intr/refl)* advance, go forward 7
avere *(tr)* have 27 **[M]**
avercela con *(tr)* have it in for 27
avere bisogno di *(tr)* need, require 27
avere caldo *(tr)* feel hot 27
avere cura di *(tr)* take care of 27
avere da *(tr)* have to 27
avere disponibile *(tr)* have available 27
avere fiducia in *(tr)* trust 27
avere freddo *(tr)* be/feel cold 27
avere il prurito *(tr)* itch, have an itch 27
avere in mente di *(tr)* have in mind 27
avere l'aria di *(tr)* look (like) 27
avere l'intenzione di *(tr)* think, intend to, be going to 27
avere la diarrea *(tr)* have diarrhea 27
avere luogo *(tr)* take place, happen 27
avere mal di mare *(tr)* be seasick 27
avere paura di *(tr)* be afraid, regret 27
avere qlc. in contrario a *(tr)* object to 27
avere ragione *(tr)* be right 27
avere tendenza ad *(tr)* tend, be inclined to 27
avere torto *(tr)* be wrong 27
avere un rapporto sessuale con *(tr)* have intercourse with 27
avere un ruolo importante *(tr)* star 27
avere uno strappo muscolare *(tr)* have a pulled muscle 27
avere vergogna di *(tr)* be ashamed of 27
avere voglia di *(tr)* want 27
avvedersi *(refl)* perceive 101
avvelenare *(tr)* poison 3
***avvenire** *(intr)* happen *(Imp.)* 102
***avventurarsi** *(intr/refl)* venture 7
avvertire *(tr)* warn, alert 5
***avviarsi verso** *(intr/refl)* make for, move towards 13, 7
avvicinare *(tr)* approach 3
***avvicinarsi a** *(intr)* approach, close in 7
avvincere *(tr)* bind, tie up 103
avvisare *(tr)* advise, inform, notify 3
avvistare *(tr)* sight 3
avvitare *(tr)* screw 3
avvolgere *(tr)* scroll, wrap 106
avvolgersi *(intr)* coil up 106, 7
***azzardarsi** *(intr/refl)* dare (to) 7
***azzuffarsi** *(intr/refl)* brawl 7

B

baciare *(tr)* kiss 13
badare *(intr)* attend, pay attention 3
badare a *(intr)* look after, mind 3
badare di *(intr)* take care to 3
bagnare *(tr)* bathe, dampen, soak, wet 3

	***bagnarsi** *(intr/refl)*	bathe 7
	balbettare *(tr)*	stammer 3
	ballare *(tr)*	dance 3
	barattare *(tr)*	barter 3
	barcollare *(intr)*	stagger, totter 3
	barricare *(tr)*	barricade 11
	basare *(tr)*	base (an argument on) 3
	***bastare** *(intr)*	be enough, be sufficient *(Imp.)* 3
	battere *(tr)*	beat, strike, hit, tap, whip 4
	battere le palpebre *(tr)*	blink 4
	battere violentemente *(tr)*	bang 4
	battezzare *(tr)*	baptize 3
	beccare *(tr)*	peck (chicken) 11
	belare *(intr)*	bleat (animals) 3
	bendare *(tr)*	bandage 3
	benedire *(tr)*	bless 9
	bere *(tr)*	drink 8 **[M]**
	***biforcarsi** *(intr/refl)*	fork (road), branch off 11, 7
	bighellonare *(intr)*	saunter 3
	bilanciare *(tr)*	balance, break even, even up 12
	biodegradare *(tr)*	biodegrade 6
	bisbigliare *(tr)*	whisper 13
	***bisognare** *(intr)*	need *(Imp.)* 3
	bloccare *(tr)*	block, stop 11
	bocciare *(tr)*	fail someone in a test/an exam 12
	boicottare *(tr)*	boycott 3
	bollare *(tr)*	stamp 3
	bollire *(tr)*	boil 5
	bollire lentamente *(tr)*	simmer 5
	bombardare *(tr)*	bomb, shell, bombard 3
	brevettare *(tr)*	patent 3
	brillare *(intr)*	shine, excel 3
	brontolare *(intr)*	growl, grumble, nag 3
	bruciare *(tr)*	burn 12
	brulicare di *(intr)*	crawl with (insects) 11
	bussare *(tr)*	knock 3
	buttare via *(tr)*	throw away 3
C	**cacciare** *(tr)*	hunt, chase, drive away, cause to go 12
	cacciare di frodo *(tr)*	poach 12
	***cadere** *(intr)*	fall (motion) 28 **[M]**
	calare *(tr)*	lower 3
	calare *(tr)*	set, go down 3
	calciare *(tr)*	kick 12
	calcolare *(tr)*	calculate, work out, plan 3
	calmare *(tr)*	calm, allay, quieten 3
	***calmarsi** *(intr/refl)*	calm down 7
	calunniare *(tr)*	slander 13

cinguettare *(intr)*	twitter 3
cintare *(tr)*	fence 3
circolare *(tr)*	circulate, pass round 3
circondare con *(tr)*	encircle, enclose, surround 3
circondare con una siepe *(tr)*	hedge (round) 3
citare *(tr)*	quote 3
civettare *(intr)*	flirt 3
classificare *(tr)*	grade, rank, sort, label, classify 11
coabitare *(intr)*	cohabit 3
coesistere *(intr)*	coexist 25
cogliere *(tr)*	gather 31 **[M]**
coincidere *(intr)*	coincide 39
coinvolgere *(tr)*	involve in 106
colare *(intr/tr)*	leak, strain 3
collaborare *(tr)*	collaborate 3
collocare *(tr)*	place 11
colorare *(tr)*	color in 3
colpire *(tr)*	impress, knock against, shock, smack, strike, hit 6
colpire a morte *(tr)*	shoot dead 6
colpire violentemente *(tr)*	bash 6
coltivare *(tr)*	farm, garden, rear (crops), till (soil) 3
comandare *(intr/tr)*	command, boss about, order 3
combattere *(tr)*	fight, wrestle 4
†cominciare a *(tr)*	begin, get started, initiate, begin, start, commence, take up (pastime) 12
commemorare *(tr)*	commemorate 3
commentare *(tr)*	comment 3
commerciare in *(intr)*	deal in, trade in 12
commettere *(tr)*	commit 54
commuovere *(tr)*	move, affect emotionally 15
commutare *(tr)*	commute 3
comp(e)rare *(tr)*	purchase, buy 1
***comparire** *(intr)*	appear 6
compatire *(tr)*	pity 6
***compiacere** *(intr)*	please 61
compiangere *(tr)*	pity, sympathize 62
compiere / compire *(tr)*	finish, achieve 6
compilare *(tr)*	compile 3
completare *(tr)*	complete 3
complicare *(tr)*	complicate 11
complimentare *(tr)*	compliment 3
comporre *(tr)*	compose music; dial 64
comporre un indice *(tr)*	index 64
comporre il numero *(tr)*	dial telephone number 64
***comportarsi** *(intr/refl)*	behave (animals / humans) 7
comprare *(tr)*	buy, purchase 1 **[M]**

comprare il silenzio di qlcu. *(tr)*	bribe s.one 1
comprendere *(tr)*	include, understand 66
comprimere *(tr)*	compress 32 **[M]**
compromettere *(tr)*	compromise 54
computare *(tr)*	compute 3
comunicare *(intr/tr)*	communicate 11
comunicare per radio *(intr/tr)*	radio 11
concedere a *(tr)*	grant; concede 33 **[M]**
concentrare *(tr)*	concentrate 3
***concentrarsi in** *(intr/refl)*	center on 7
concepire *(tr)*	conceive 6
concludere *(tr)*	conclude 30, 20
concretare *(tr)*	concrete 3
concupire *(tr)*	lust for 6
condannare *(tr)*	condemn 3
condannare qlcu. a *(tr)*	sentence s.one to 3
condensare *(tr)*	condense 3
condire *(tr)*	season (food) 6
condire con pepe *(tr)*	pepper 6
condividere *(tr)*	share 43
condividere *(tr)* **i sentimenti altrui**	sympathize 43
***condolersi** *(intr/refl)*	condole with 44, 7
condurre *(tr)*	conduct, drive, lead, be ahead 95
conferire *(tr)*	confer 6
confermare *(tr)*	confirm 3
confessare *(tr)*	confess 3
confezionare *(tr)*	tailor 3
conficcare *(tr)*	drive in (nail) 11
confidare in *(intr)*	confide in 3
confinare con *(intr)*	border on 3
confondere *(tr)*	bewilder, confuse, muddle up, puzzle 50
***conformarsi a** *(intr/refl)*	comply with, conform to 7
confortare *(tr)*	comfort 3
confrontare *(tr)*	compare 3
confutare *(tr)*	refute 3
congedare *(tr)*	dismiss 38
***congedarsi** *(intr/refl)*	take one's leave 38, 7
congiungere *(tr)*	join, match, graft onto 52
***congratularsi con** *(intr/refl)*	congratulate 7
connettere *(tr)*	connect 54, 22
conoscere *(tr)*	know a person/place 34 **[M]**
conquistare *(tr)*	conquer, win 3
consegnare *(tr)*	deliver, hand in/over 3
consentire *(tr/intr)*	consent 5
conservare *(tr)*	conserve 3
considerare *(tr)*	regard, consider 3
consigliare a qlcu. di *(intr/tr)*	advise s.one to 13
consistere di *(intr)*	consist (of) 25

consolare *(tr)*	console 3
consolidare *(tr)*	consolidate 3
consultare *(tr)*	consult 3
consumare *(tr)*	consume, erode, spend, use up 3
contaminare *(tr)*	contaminate 3
contare *(tr)*	count, number 3
contare su *(intr)*	bank upon, reckon on 3
contemplare *(tr)*	survey, contemplate 3
contendere *(tr/intr)*	contend 91
contenere *(tr)*	contain, store 92
continuare a *(intr)*	carry on, keep going, go on 3
contorcere *(tr)*	twist, contort 94
contrabbandare *(tr)*	smuggle 38
contraddire *(tr)*	contradict 9
contraffare *(tr)*	counterfeit 10
contrarre *(tr)*	contract 96
contrastare *(tr)*	contrast 3
contravvenire *(tr)*	contravene 102
contribuire a *(tr)*	contribute to 6
controllare *(tr)*	check verify, inspect, monitor, service 3
†convenire *(tr/intr)*	agree, gather together *(Imp.)* 102
conversare *(intr)*	converse with 3
convertire *(tr)*	convert 5
convincere a *(tr)*	convict, convince s.one (to) 103
convocare *(tr)*	summon 11
cooperare (intr)	cooperate 3
coordinare *(tr)*	coordinate 3
copiare *(tr)*	copy, write out 13
coprire *(tr)*	cap, cover 24
***coricarsi** *(intr/refl)*	go to bed, lie down 7
coronare *(tr)*	crown 3
correggere *(tr)*	correct 70
†correre a *(tr/intr)*	run, race (to) 35 **[M]**
corrispondere *(intr)*	correspond with 75
corrodere *(tr)*	corrode 47
corrompere *(tr)*	corrupt 76
corrugare *(tr)*	wrinkle 11
corteggiare *(tr)*	court, woo 12
cospirare *(intr)*	conspire against 3
***costare** *(intr)*	cost *(Imp.)* 3
costeggiare *(tr)*	skirt 12
costernare *(tr)*	dismay 3
costituire *(tr)*	constitute 6
costringere a *(tr)*	force, compel (to), constrain, pin down 88
costruire *(tr)*	build, construct, erect 6
costruire un ponte su *(intr)*	bridge (a river) 6
covare *(tr)*	brood over, hatch 3

decifrare *(tr)*	decode 3
declinare *(tr)*	disclaim (responsibility) 3
decollare *(tr)*	take off (plane) 3
decomporre *(tr)*	decompose 64
decorare *(tr)*	decorate 3
***descrescere** *(intr)*	decrease, go down 36
decretare *(tr)*	decree 3
dedicare *(tr)*	dedicate, devote to 11
***dedicarsi a** *(intr/refl)*	devote oneself to 11, 7
dedurre *(tr)*	deduce, deduct, infer 95
definire *(tr)*	define 6
defraudare *(tr)*	defraud 3
degradare *(tr)*	degrade 3
delegare *(tr)*	delegate 11
deliberare *(tr/intr)*	deliberate 3
delineare *(tr)*	outline, sketch out (plans) 3
deludere *(tr)*	disappoint, take in, delude, let down 30, 20
demolire *(tr)*	demolish 6
denudare *(tr)*	bare 3
denunciare *(tr)*	denounce 12
***deperire** *(intr)*	decay, waste away 6
depositare *(tr)*	deposit 3
depositare in una banca *(tr)*	bank (money) 3
deprimere *(tr)*	depress, make sad 32
deridere *(tr)*	deride, ridicule 72
***derivare da** *(intr)*	be derived from, spring, result from 3
derubare *(tr)*	rob 3
descrivere *(tr)*	describe 81
desiderare *(tr)*	desire, long for, want, wish 3
designare *(tr)*	style, design 3
desumere *(tr)*	deduce, assume, infer; gather 26
detenere *(tr)*	detain, stop 92
deteriorare *(tr)*	deteroriate 3
determinare *(tr)*	determine 3
detestare *(tr)*	detest 3
dettare *(tr)*	dictate 3
devastare *(tr)*	devastate 3
deviare *(tr)*	deviate, divert, turn aside 13
devolvere *(intr)*	transfer 4, 25B
diagnosticare *(tr)*	diagnose 11
dibattere *(tr)*	debate 4
dichiarare di *(tr)*	declare, state 3
difendere da *(tr)*	defend from 17
differenziare *(tr)*	differentiate 13
differire *(intr)*	differ 6
diffidare di *(intr)*	distrust 3
diffondere *(tr)*	broadcast 50

digerire *(tr)*	digest 6
digiunare *(intr)*	fast, not eat 3
diluire *(tr)*	dilute, water down 6
***dimagrire** *(intr)*	get thin, slim, eat less 6
dimenticare di *(tr)*	forget (to), leave behind 11 **[M]**
***dimenticarsi di** *(intr/refl)*	forget 11, 7
***dimettersi** *(intr/refl)*	resign 54, 7
†diminuire *(intr/tr)*	decrease, dwindle, diminish, lessen 6
dimostrare *(tr)*	demonstrate, show/prove (innocence) 3
***dipendere da** *(intr)*	depend on 17
dipingere *(tr)*	depict, paint 86, 93
dire di *(tr)*	say, utter remark, tell (to), order 9 **[M]**
dirigere *(tr)*	direct, conduct (music), control, guide 40 **[M]**
***dirigersi verso** *(intr/refl)*	make one's way towards 40, 7
disapprovare *(tr)*	disapprove 3
disarmare *(tr)*	disarm 3
discendere *(tr/intr)*	descend 79
dischiudere *(tr)*	disclose; open 30
disciogliere *(tr)*	dissolve 31
discorrere di *(intr)*	discuss, talk about 35
discutere *(tr)*	discuss, argue, debate, dispute 41 **[M]**
discutere di *(intr)*	talk about 41
disdegnare *(tr)*	scorn 3
disegnare *(tr)*	draw (a picture) 3
diseredare *(tr)*	disinherit 3
disfare *(tr)*	undo, untie, unpack 10
***disfarsi di** *(intr/refl)*	dispose of 10, 7
disgiungere *(tr)*	separate 52
disilludere *(tr)*	disillusion 20
disinfettare *(tr)*	disinfect 3
disintegrare *(tr)*	disintegrate 3
disorganizzare *(tr)*	disorganize 3
dispensare *(tr)*	exempt from 3
disperare *(intr)*	despair 3
disperdere *(intr)*	disperse 59
***dispiacere** *(intr)*	be sorry (for), displease 61
disporre *(tr)*	dispose 64
disprezzare *(tr)*	scorn 3
***dissetarsi** *(intr/refl)*	quench (one's thirst) 7
dissodare *(tr)*	dig up 3
dissolvere *(tr)*	dissolve 74
dissuadere *(tr)*	dissuade 60
distendere *(tr)*	stretch 91
distinguere *(tr)*	distinguish, discern, make out 42 **[M]**

distogliere *(tr)*	distract 31
distorcere *(tr)*	distort 94
distrarre *(tr)*	distract 96
distribuire *(tr)*	deal (cards), distribute, give out, hand out / round, share out 6
districare *(tr)*	disentangle 11
distruggere *(tr)*	destroy 89
disturbare *(tr)*	disturb, trouble, upset 3
disubbidire a *(intr)*	disobey 6
divagare *(intr)*	ramble on 11
***divenire** *(intr)*	become 102
***diventare** *(intr)*	become, turn into 3
***diventare grigio** *(intr)*	go grey (hair) 3
***diventare peggio** *(intr)*	get worse 3
divergere *(intr)*	diverge 84
divertire *(tr)*	amuse 5
***divertirsi a** *(intr / refl)*	amuse / enjoy oneself, have fun (doing) 5, 7
dividere *(tr)*	divide, part, separate, split (cost) 43 **[M]**
dividere a metà *(tr)*	halve 43
divorare *(tr)*	devour 3
divorziare (tr / intr)	divorce, get divorced 13
***divorziarsi** *(intr / refl)*	get divorced 13, 7
***dolere** *(intr)*	ache, hurt 44 **[M]**
domandare *(tr)* **qlco. a qlcu.**	ask someone for something 3
domandare di *(intr)*	ask to 3
***domandarsi** *(intr / refl)*	wonder, ask oneself 7
domare *(tr)*	tame 3
dominare *(tr)*	master 3
dominare dall'alto *(tr)*	overlook 3
donare *(tr)*	donate 3
dondolare *(tr)*	rock, swing 3
dormire *(intr)*	sleep 5 **[M]**
dormire troppo a lungo *(intr)*	oversleep 5
dosare *(tr)*	dose 3
†dovere *(intr)*	have to, must, be obliged to, ought to, should; owe 45 **[M]**
†dovere fare qlco. *(intr)*	be obliged to do sth. 45
drogare *(tr)*	dope, drug 11
drogarsi *(intr / refl)*	become addicted, take drugs 11, 7
dubitare *(tr)*	doubt 3
duplicare *(tr)*	duplicate 11
durare *(intr)*	go on, last 3

E

eccitare *(tr)*	excite, stir, work up (interest) 3
echeggiare *(intr)*	echo 12
editare *(tr)*	edit (IT) 3
educare *(tr)*	educate, train, bring up (children) 11

elaborare *(tr)*	process (data) 3
eleggere *(tr)*	elect 53
elencare *(tr)*	list 11
elettrificare *(tr)*	electrify 11
***elevarsi** *(intr/refl)*	soar (prices) 7
eliminare *(tr)*	delete, eliminate 3
eludere *(tr)*	elude, evade 20
emendare *(tr)*	amend 3
***emergere** *(intr)*	emerge from 84
emettere *(tr)*	send out, emit, utter, pass (sentence) 54
emettere *(tr)* **vapore**	steam, give out vapor/vapour 54
***emigrare** *(intr)*	emigrate, migrate 3
emulsionare *(tr)*	emulsify 3
***entrare in** *(intr)*	enter, come in; get in; come on (stage) 2 **[M]**
***entrare di nascosto in** *(intr)*	steal in 2
***entrare per caso in** *(intr)*	drop in 2
***entusiasmarsi per** *(intr/refl)*	be enthusiastic about 7
equipaggiare *(tr)*	equip 12
***equivalere** *(intr)*	amount to 100
ereditare *(tr)*	succeed, inherit 3
erigere *(tr)*	erect 40
errare *(intr)*	wander, walk aimlessly 3
eruttare *(intr)*	erupt 3
esagerare *(tr)*	exaggerate 3
esalare *(intr)*	exhale 3
esaminare *(tr)*	study, examine carefully 3
esaurire *(tr)*	drain, exhaust, run out of 6
***esaurirsi** *(intr)*	break down (person) 6, 7
esclamare *(tr)*	exclaim 3
escludere *(tr)*	disqualify, except, exclude 30, 20
eseguire *(tr)*	carry out perform, execute 6
esercitare *(tr)*	drill (exercise) 3
esibire *(tr)*	exhibit 6
esigere *(tr)*	require 4, 25B
esiliare *(tr)*	banish 13
***esistere** *(intr)*	exist 25
esitare a *(intr)*	hesitate (to), pause 3
esonerare *(tr)*	exonerate 3
espellere *(tr)*	expel 46 **[M]**
***esplodere** *(intr)*	explode 47 **[M]**
esplorare *(tr)*	explore 3
esporre *(tr)*	expose 64
esportare *(tr)*	export 3
esprimere *(tr)*	say, express (opinion) 32
***essere** *(intr)*	be 48 **[M]**
***essere afoso** *(intr)*	be heavy/sultry 48
***essere a dieta** *(tr)*	diet 48

	***essere avanti** *(intr)*	be fast (clock) 48
	***essere contento** *(intr)*	be pleased 48
	***essere contro** *(intr)*	be against 48
	***essere d'accordo con** *(intr)*	be in agreement, agree (with) 48
	***essere di fronte a** *(intr)*	face, be opposite 48
	***essere disoccupato** *(intr)*	be unemployed 48
	***essere diverso** *(intr)*	be different 48
	***essere dovuto a** *(intr)*	be due to 48
	***essere frequentato da spettri** *(intr)*	be haunted 48
	***essere fuori** *(intr)*	be out 48
	***essere (im)paziente** *(intr)*	be (im)patient 48
	***essere imparentato** *(intr)*	be related (family) 48
	***essere in concorrenza con** *(intr)*	compete with 48
	***essere in disaccordo** *(intr)*	disagree 48
	***essere in periodo di prosperità** *(intr)*	be in a boom 48
	***essere in ritardo** *(intr)*	be delayed, be late 48
	***essere indietro** *(intr)*	be slow (clock) 48
	***essere inguaiato** *(intr)*	be stuck 48
	***essere mite** *(intr)*	be mild 48
	***essere ne di** *(intr)*	become of 48
	***essere necessario** *(intr)*	need, be necessary 48
	***essere nuvoloso** *(intr)*	be cloudy 48
	***essere occupato** *(intr)*	be busy 48
	***essere per** *(intr)*	be for, support 48
	***essere pieno di**	abound with, be full of 48
	***essere promosso** *(intr)*	go up (in school) 48
	***essere responsabile per** *(intr)*	be liable / responsible for 48
	***essere ricco di** *(intr)*	be abundant, abound in 48
	***essere seduto** *(intr)*	sit, be seated 48
	***essere sonnambulo** *(intr)*	walk in one's sleep 48
	***essere stitico** *(intr)*	be constipated 48
	***essere sul punto di** *(intr)*	be about to 48
	***essere umido** *(intr)*	be humid / damp 48
	***essere valido** *(intr)*	be valid 48
	***estendersi** *(intr / refl)*	expand, branch out 91, 7
	estinguere *(tr)*	extinguish 42
	estrarre *(tr)*	extract 96
	evacuare *(tr)*	evacuate 3
	***evadere** *(intr)*	evade, escape 49 **[M]**
	†evaporare *(tr / intr)*	evaporate, vaporize 3
	evidenziare *(tr)*	highlight 13
	evitare *(tr)*	avoid, bypass 3
	evitare di fare qlco.	avoid doing something 3
	evocare *(tr)*	evoke 11
	***evolversi** *(intr / refl)*	evolve, develop 4,25B
F	**fabbricare** *(tr)*	manufacture 11
	facilitare *(tr)*	facilitate 3

fare la cubatura *(intr)*	cube 10
fare la doccia *(tr)*	shower 10
fare la media di *(intr)*	average 10
fare la permanente *(tr)*	perm 10
fare la pubblicità a *(intr)*	publicize 10
fare le fusa *(tr)*	purr 10
fare le prove di *(intr)*	rehearse 10
fare male *(intr)*	ache 10
fare male a *(intr)*	harm 10
fare marcia indietro *(intr)*	back (car) 10
fare notte *(intr)*	get dark 10
fare pagare *(tr)*	charge (prices) 10
fare pareggio *(intr)*	draw in a match 10
fare parte di una giuria *(intr)*	sit on a jury 10
fare pervenire *(tr)*	send in, submit 10
fare piacere a *(intr)*	please 10
fare prigioniero	take prisoner 10
fare pubblicità *(intr)*	advertise 10
fare ricerche *(tr)*	research 10
fare risatine sciocche *(intr)*	giggle 10
fare saltare *(tr)*	blow up, explode 10
fare saltare *(tr)*	pop 10
fare scattare *(tr)*	clock in 10
fare sedere *(tr)*	seat, sit, cause to sit 10
fare segno a qlcu. *(intr)*	wave to s.one 10
fare soffrire a *(intr)*	pain 10
fare solletico a *(intr)*	tickle 10
fare tacere *(tr)*	silence 10
fare torto a *(intr)*	wrong 10
fare traslochi *(tr)*	remove (furniture) 10
fare tutto il possibile per *(intr)*	do everything possible to 10
fare un bilancio *(tr)*	budget 10
fare un brindisi *(tr)*	toast 10
fare un picnic *(tr)*	picnic 10
fare un salto mortale *(tr)*	somersault 10
fare una collezione di *(tr)*	collect (as a hobby) 10
fare una passeggiata *(tr)*	go for a walk 10
fare una trasfusione a *(tr)*	do a blood transfusion 10
fare uno spuntino *(tr)*	have a snack 10
fare vedere a *(intr)*	show 10
faria franca *(intr)*	get away with 10
farne di tutti i colori a *(intr)*	play up 10
***farsi operare** *(intr/refl)*	have an operation 10, 7
***farsi prestare** *(intr/refl)*	borrow 10, 7
***farsi vivo** *(intr/refl)*	show up, turn up 10, 7
fasciare *(tr)*	swaddle (baby) 12
faticare *(intr)*	labour 11
fatturare *(tr)*	bill 3
favorire *(tr)*	favor/favour, treat well, further 6

ferire *(tr)*	injure, wound 6
fermare *(tr)*	stop, prevent 3
***fermarsi** *(intr/refl)*	stop, stall (engine) 7
fermentare *(intr)*	ferment 3
ferrare *(tr)*	shoe (horse) 3
festeggiare *(tr/intr)*	celebrate, feast 12
ficcare *(tr)*	stick, push sth. pointed 11
***fidanzarsi** *(intr/refl)*	get engaged 7
***fidarsi di** *(intr/refl)*	trust 7
***figurarsi** *(intr/refl)*	imagine 7
filare *(tr)*	spin (wool) 3
filtrare *(tr)*	filter, strain (wine) 3
filtrare attraverso *(intr)*	seep through 3
finanziare *(tr)*	finance 13
fingere di *(tr)*	pretend (to) 86
†finire di *(intr/tr)*	finish, end, end up 6 **[M]**
†finire per *(intr)*	end by, finish by 6
***fiorire** *(intr)*	bloom, flower, flourish 6
firmare *(tr)*	sign (signature) 3
fischiare *(intr/tr)*	whistle 13 **[M]**
fissare *(tr)*	fix, gaze at, stare, stare at 3
fissare con caviglie *(tr)*	peg 3
fissare *(tr)* **un appuntamento**	make a date 3
fiutare rumorosamente *(tr)*	sniff 3
flettere *(tr)*	bend 4, 25B
fondare *(tr)*	found 3
fondere *(tr)*	melt, fuse, merge 50 **[M]**
formare *(tr)*	fashion, form 3
formattare *(tr)*	format (IT) 3
fornire *(tr)*	fit out, provide, relay, stock, supply 6
fornire di personale *(tr)*	staff 6
forzare a *(tr)*	force, compel (to) 3
fotocopiare *(tr)*	photocopy, run off, duplicate 13
fotografare *(tr)*	photograph 3
frammettere *(tr)*	interpose, insert 54
frantumare *(tr)*	crush, smash, break 3
***frantumarsi** *(intr/refl)*	shiver 7
frapporre *(tr)*	insert 64
fratturare *(tr)*	fracture 3
fregare *(tr)*	rub, scrub 11
frenare *(tr)*	brake 3
***frenarsi** *(intr/refl)*	control oneself 7
frequentare *(tr)*	attend school, frequent 3
frequentare assiduamente *(tr)*	haunt 3
friggere *(tr)*	fry 19
frizzare *(tr)*	fizz 3
frustrare *(tr)*	foil, frustrate 3
†fuggire *(tr/intr)*	escape, run away, flee 5
fumare *(tr)*	smoke 3

	fungere *(intr)*	act as 68
	funzionare *(intr)*	operate (of machine), work, function 3
G	**galleggiare** *(intr)*	float 12
	garantire *(tr)*	guarantee 6
	†gelare *(intr/tr)*	deepfreeze, freeze 3
	gemere *(intr)*	groan, moan 4
	generare *(tr)*	generate 3
	germogliare *(intr)*	sprout 13
	gettare *(tr)*	chuck, fling, pitch, throw, toss 3
	***ghiacciare** *(intr)*	ice, chill, freeze 12
	***giacere** *(intr)*	lie 51 **[M]**
	giocare a *(intr)*	play, stake (gambling) 11
	giocare a bocce *(intr)*	play bowls 11
	girare *(intr)*	spin, move round, turn 3
	girare intorno a *(intr)*	circle 3
	girare un film *(tr)*	film, shoot a film / movie 3
	***girarsi** *(intr/refl)*	turn around 7
	giudicare da *(tr)*	judge by / on 11
	giudicare male *(tr)*	misjudge 11
	***giungere a** *(intr)*	arrive at, reach 52 **[M]**
	giurare di *(intr)*	swear (to) 3
	giustificare *(tr)*	justify 11
	gocciolare *(tr)*	drip 3
	godere di *(intr)*	enjoy 4
	†gonfiare *(intr/tr)*	inflate, swell 3
	***gonfiarsi di** *(intr/refl)*	bulge with 7
	gorgogliare *(intr)*	bubble 13
	governare *(tr/intr)*	rule, govern 3
	gracchiare *(intr)*	croak 13
	graffiare *(tr)*	scratch 13
	†grandinare *(intr)*	hail (weather) 3
	grattare *(tr)*	scrape, scratch 3
	grattugiare *(tr)*	grate (cheese) 12
	gridare *(tr)*	shout, call out, cry out 3
	grugnire *(intr)*	grunt 6
	guadagnare *(tr)*	earn, gain 3
	guardare *(tr)*	look, look at, watch 3
	guardare furtivamente *(tr)*	peep 3
	***guardarsi da** *(intr/refl)*	beware of 7
	†guarire (intr / tr)	cure, heal, recover, get better 6
	guastare *(tr)*	spoil (fruit) 3
	guerreggiare *(tr)*	war 12
	guidare *(tr)*	drive, lead, guide 3
	gustare *(tr)*	savour, taste (food) 3
I	**idealizzare** *(tr)*	idealize 3
	identificare *(tr)*	identify 11
	ignorare *(tr)*	be unaware of, not know 3

illudere *(tr)*	deceive, delude, fool 20
illuminare *(tr)*	illuminate 3
illustrare *(tr)*	illustrate 3
imballare *(tr)*	pack, package 3
imbarazzare *(tr)*	embarrass 3
imbarcare *(tr)*	embark, ship 11
***imbarcarsi** *(intr/refl)*	board 11, 7
†imbiancare *(intr/tr)*	bleach, turn white 11
imbottigliare *(tr)*	bottle 13
imbucare *(tr)*	post 11
imburrare *(tr)*	butter 3
imitare *(tr)*	mime, imitate 3
immaginare di *(tr)*	imagine, think of 3
***immaginarsi** *(intr/refl)*	imagine 7
immergere *(tr)*	immerse, steep (in liquid) 84
immettere *(tr)*	admit, let in 54
immigrare *(tr)*	immigrate 3
immunizzare *(tr)*	immunize 3
***impadronirsi di** *(intr/refl)*	seize 6, 7
***impallidire** *(intr)*	go white, turn pale 6
imparare a *(tr)*	learn (to) 6
***impazzire** *(intr)*	grow mad/crazy 6
impedire di *(tr)*	forbid, stop, hinder, prevent (from) 6
***impegnarsi a** *(intr/refl)*	commit oneself, undertake (to) 7
***impennarsi** *(intr/refl)*	rear up (horse) 7
impiegare *(tr)*	employ 11
imporre *(tr)*	impose 64
***importare** *(intr)*	care about, matter *(Imp.)* 3
importare *(tr)*	import 3
impressionare *(tr)*	strike, impress 3
imprigionare *(tr)*	imprison 3
imprimere *(tr)*	impress, stamp 32
inalare *(tr)*	inhale 3
inargentare *(tr)*	silver, coat with silver 3
inasprire *(tr)*	exasperate 6
incaricare *(tr)*	commission 11
incartare *(tr)*	wrap up (with paper) 3
incassare *(tr)*	cash 3
incatenare *(tr)*	chain (up) 3
incendiare *(tr)*	fire, set fire to 13
inchiodare *(tr)*	nail down 3
***inciampare** *(intr)*	stumble 3
incidere su *(tr)*	cut, carve, engrave, incise 39
incitare a *(intr)*	urge to 3
inclinare *(tr)*	incline 3
***inclinarsi** *(intr/refl)*	lean 7
includere *(tr)*	comprise, count in, include 20
incollare *(tr)*	stick, glue 3

incolpare *(tr)*	blame 3
***incominciare** *(intr)*	begin 12
†incontrare *(intr / tr)*	run / bump into, meet 3
***incontrarsi con** *(intr / refl)*	meet 7
incoraggiare a *(tr)*	encourage (to) 12
incorniciare *(tr)*	frame (picture) 12
incorporare *(tr)*	incorporate 3
***incorrere in** *(intr)*	incur 35
increspare *(tr)*	ruffle, wrinkle 3
***incrociarsi** *(intr / refl)*	cross, intersect 12, 7
incuneare *(tr)*	wedge 3
incutere *(tr)*	strike, rouse 41
indagare su *(intr)*	investigate 11
†indebolire *(intr / tr)*	weaken 6
indicare *(tr)*	show, indicate 11
indicare a dito *(tr)*	point (with finger) 11
indirizzare *(tr)*	address / send a letter 3
***indirizzarsi** *(intr / refl)*	apply 7
indossare *(tr)*	put on, wear (clothes) 3
indovinare *(tr)*	guess 3
***indugiarsi** *(intr / refl)*	loiter 12, 7
indurire *(tr)*	harden, stiffen 6
***indurirsi** *(intr / refl)*	harden 6, 7
infastidire *(tr)*	bother, worry s.one 6
infettare *(tr)*	infect 3
***infettarsi** *(intr / refl)*	become infected 7
infiammare *(tr)*	inflame 3
infilare *(tr)*	thread 3
***infilarsi** *(intr)*	slip on (clothes) 7
***infischiarsi** *(intr / refl)*	care nothing (about sth.) 13, 7
infliggere *(tr)*	inflict 19
influenzare *(tr)*	influence 3
influire su *(intr)*	influence, affect 6
infondere *(tr)*	instill 50
informare *(tr)*	inform 3
***informarsi di / su** *(intr / refl)*	get information about, ask about 7
ingannare *(tr)*	bluff, cheat, circumvent, deceive, mislead, trick 3
ingessare *(tr)*	plaster 3
inghiottire *(tr)*	swallow 6
***inginocchiarsi** *(intr / refl)*	kneel down 13, 7
ingiuriare qlcu. *(tr)*	call s.one names 13
†ingrassare *(intr / tr)*	fatten put on weight 3
iniettare *(tr)*	inject 3
inizializzare *(tr)*	boot (IT) 3
iniziare a *(tr)*	initiate (s.one) 13
innaffiare *(tr)*	water 13
innalzare *(tr)*	heighten 3
***innamorarsi di** *(intr / refl)*	fall in love 7

***innervosirsi** *(intr/refl)* get nervous 6, 7
innestare la retromarcia *(tr)* reverse (car) 3
inoculare *(tr)* innoculate 3
inoltrare *(tr)* send on (letters) 3
inoltrare una domanda apply (for job) 3
inondare *(tr)* flood, overflow 3
inquinare *(tr)* pollute 3
insaponare *(tr)* soap 3
insegnare a *(tr)* teach (to) 3
inseguire *(tr)* hound, pursue, track 5
inserire *(tr)* write in, insert 6
insistere su *(intr)* insist (on) 25
installare *(tr)* install 3
insultare *(tr)* be rude to, insult 3
integrare *(tr)* integrate 3
intendere *(tr)* mean, intend (to say) 91, 17
***intendersi di** *(intr/refl)* know about, be an expert on 17, 7
intensificare *(tr)* intensify 11
interdire *(tr)* forbid 9
interessare *(tr)* interest *(Imp.)* 3
***interessarsi (a/di)** *(intr/refl)* take an interest in, care 7
interferire *(intr)* interfere 6
interporre *(tr)* interpose 64
interpretare *(tr)* interpret, read/play (a part) 3
interpretare male *(tr)* misinterpret 3
interrogare *(tr)* interrogate, question 11
interrompere *(tr)* interrupt, switch off 76
***intervenire** *(intr)* intervene, chip in, cut off 102
intervistare *(tr)* interview 3
intitolare *(tr)* entitle 3
intraprendere *(tr)* take on, undertake (journey) 66
intravedere *(tr)* glimpse 101
introdurre *(tr)* bring in, introduce 95
***intrudersi** *(intr/refl)* intrude 20, 7
intuire *(tr)* sense 6
inumidire *(tr)* moisten 6
invadere *(tr)* invade 49
***invecchiare** *(intr)* age 13
***invecchiarsi** *(intr/refl)* age, grow old 13, 7
inventare *(tr)* make up, invent 3
investigare *(tr)* investigate 11
investire *(tr)* invest, run down/over (with car) 5
inviare *(tr)* send 13
invidiare *(tr)* envy 13
invitare a *(tr)* ask, invite (to) 3
involgere *(tr)* wrap 106
inzuccherare *(tr)* sugar 3
ionizzare *(tr)* ionize 3
ipotecare *(tr)* mortgage 11

	irrigare *(tr)*	irrigate 11
	irritare *(tr)*	irritate 3
	irrompere *(tr)*	break into a building 76
	***iscriversi** *(intr/refl)*	enroll, register 81, 7
	isolare *(tr)*	isolate, shut off (water, gas) 3
	ispessire *(tr)*	thicken 6
	istruire *(tr)*	instruct 6
	istupidire *(tr)*	stupefy 6
L	***lagnarsi di** *(intr/refl)*	complain about 7
	***lamentarsi di** *(intr/refl)*	complain about 7
	lampeggiare *(tr)*	flash, flash (lightning) 12
	lanciare *(tr)*	throw (a bomb) 12
	lanciare un razzo *(tr)*	launch, lift off (rocket) 12
	***lanciarsi** *(intr/refl)*	dart out 12, 7
	languire *(intr)*	pine 6
	lappare *(intr)*	lap 3
	lasciare *(tr)*	leave, allow to remain 12
	lasciare entrare *(tr)*	allow in, let in, allow to enter 12
	lasciare passare *(tr)*	allow through, let through 12
	lasciare per testamento *(tr)*	bequeath, will 12
	lasciare vuoto *(tr)*	vacate 12
	***lasciarsi cadere** *(intr/refl)*	flop down 12, 7
	lavare *(tr)*	wash 3
	lavare a secco *(tr)*	dry-clean 3
	***lavarsi** *(intr/refl)*	wash oneself, get washed, wash up 7 **[M]**
	lavorare *(tr)*	work 3
	lavorare a maglia *(tr)*	knit 3
	lavorare come uno schiavo *(tr)*	slave, work hard 3
	lavoricchiare *(intr)*	potter about 13
	leccare *(tr)*	lick 11
	legalizzare *(tr)*	legalize 3
	legare *(tr)*	bind, fasten, tie, band together 11
	legare con corde *(tr)*	string 11
	leggere *(tr)*	read 53 **[M]**
	leggere ad alta voce *(tr)*	read aloud 53
	levigare con carta vetrata *(tr)*	sand down 11
	liberare *(tr)*	free, release, rescue, set free, rid of 3
	***librarsi a volo** *(intr/refl)*	soar (of bird) 7
	licenziare *(tr)*	fire (s.one), sack, dismiss 13
	limare *(tr)*	file (wood, metal) 3
	limitare *(tr)*	keep to, limit 3
	***limitarsi a** *(intr/refl)*	confine to 7
	liquefare *(tr)*	liquify, melt 10
	liquidare *(tr)*	pay off debts 3
	lisciare *(tr)*	smooth(e) 12
	litigare con *(intr)*	fall out, quarrel 11

	livellare *(tr)*	level 3
	lodare *(tr)*	praise 1, 3 **[M]**
	***logorarsi** *(intr/refl)*	wear out 7
	lottare contro *(intr)*	struggle against 3
	lottare per *(intr)*	struggle for, fight for 3
	luccicare *(tr)*	gleam 11
	lucidare *(tr)*	shine, polish 3
	lusingare *(tr)*	flatter 11
M	**macchiare** *(tr)*	soil, dirty, spot, mark, stain, blur 13
	macchinare *(tr)*	scheme 3
	maceliare *(tr)*	slaughter 3
	macinare *(tr)*	grind, mill 3
	magnetizzare *(tr)*	magnetize 3
	maledire *(tr)*	curse 9
	maltrattare *(tr)*	mistreat, misuse 3
	***mancare** *(intr)*	be missing, miss, lack 11
	***mancare di** *(intr)*	fail to do sth. 11
	mandare *(tr)*	send 3
	mandare *(tr)* **un fax**	fax 3
	mandare a chiamare *(tr)*	send for s.one 3
	mandare a prendere *(tr)*	send for sth. 3
	mandare fuori *(tr)*	send s.one out 3
	mandare per posta *(tr)*	mail 3
	maneggiare *(tr)*	handle 12
	mangiare *(tr)*	eat 12 **[M]**
	mantenere *(tr)*	abide by / keep, maintain, support, provide for 92
	mantenere la parola *(tr)*	stick to your word 92
	mantenere le proprie posizioni *(tr)*	hold one's own, stand, maintain position 92
	marcare *(tr)*	mark 11
	marciare *(intr)*	march 12
	marinare *(tr)* la scuola	play truant 3
	martellare *(tr)*	hammer 3
	massacrare *(tr)*	massacre 3
	masticare *(tr)*	chew 11
	***maturare** *(intr)*	ripen 3
	mentire *(intr)*	lie, tell a lie 6
	***meravigliarsi di** *(intr/refl)*	be amazed, wonder at 13, 7
	meritare di *(tr)*	deserve 3
	mescolare *(tr)*	jumble up, mix, mix up 3
	mettere *(tr)*	put 54 **[M]**
	mettere all'aria *(tr)*	air 54
	mettere alia prova *(tr)*	test 54
	mettere da parte *(tr)*	put aside, put away, store 54
	mettere fuori *(tr)*	catch out 54
	mettere fuori combattimento *(tr)*	knock out 54
	mettere fuori fase *(tr)*	phase out 54

	mettere in comunicazione *(tr)*	put through (telephone) 54
	mettere in disordine *(tr)*	make a mess of 54
	mettere in fase *(tr)*	phase in 54
	mettere in garage *(tr)*	garage (car) 54
	mettere in moto *(tr)*	start car 54
	mettere in ordine *(tr)*	put in order, tidy up 54
	mettere in pensione *(tr)*	pension off 54
	mettere in relazione a *(intr)*	relate to 54
	mettere insieme *(tr)*	bond, put together 54
	mettere per iscritto *(tr)*	set down on paper 54
	***mettersi a** *(intr/refl)*	begin to 54, 7
	***mettersi a sedere** *(intr/refl)*	sit down 54, 7
	***mettersi al** *(intr/refl)*	set in (of weather) 54, 7
	***mettersi in contatto con** *(intr/refl)*	contact 54, 7
	***mettersi in piedi** *(intr/refl)*	stand up 54, 7
	***mettersi in piega** *(intr/refl)*	set hair 54, 7
	miagolare *(intr)*	mew 3
	mietere *(tr)*	harvest, mow (corn), reap 4
	†migliorare *(intr/tr)*	improve 3
	minacciare di *(tr)*	threaten (to) 12
	mirare a *(intr)*	aim at 3
	mischiare *(tr)*	blend 13
	misurare *(tr)*	survey, measure 3
	modellare *(tr)*	model, mold 3
	modernizzare *(tr)*	modernize 3
	modificare *(tr)*	modify 11
	molestare *(tr)*	molest 3
	moltiplicare *(tr)*	multiply 11
	monopolizzare *(tr)*	monopolize 3
	†montare *(intr/tr)*	ride (bike, horse) 3
	mordere *(tr)*	bite 55 **[M]**
	mordicchiare *(tr)*	nibble 13
	***morire** *(intr)*	die 56 **[M]**
	***morire di fame** *(intr)*	starve 56
	mormorare *(tr)*	murmur 3
	mostrare *(tr)*	show, allow to be seen 3
	motivare *(tr)*	motivate 3
	mudare *(intr)*	molt/moult 3
	muggire *(intr)*	below (animals) 6
	multare *(tr)*	fine (law) 3
	mungere *(tr)*	milk 68
	muovere *(tr)*	move, stir 15 **[M]**
	***muoversi** *(intr/refl)*	move oneself 15, 7
N	**narrare** *(tr)*	narrate, relate (a story) 3
	***nascere** *(intr)*	be born 57 **[M]**
	nascondere *(tr)*	conceal, hide, veil 75
	naufragare *(intr/tr)*	be shipwrecked, sink, go down, wreck 11

	negare *(tr)*	deny 11
	negoziare *(tr)*	negotiate, bargain 13
	neutralizzare *(tr)*	neutralize 3
	†nevicare *(intr)*	snow 11
	nitrire *(intr)*	neigh 6
	noleggiare *(tr)*	charter (plane), hire / rent (car) 12
	nominare *(tr)*	appoint, name, nominate 3
	notare *(tr)*	note, notice 3
	notificare *(tr)*	inform, notify 11
	nuocere a *(intr)*	be bad for, harm 16 **[M]**
	nuotare *(intr)*	swim 3
	nutrire *(tr)*	nourish 6
O	**obiettare** *(tr)*	object 3
	obbligare a *(tr)*	oblige s.one to 11
	***occorrere** *(intr)*	be necessary *(Imp)*. 35
	occupare *(tr)*	occupy, take up (space) 3
	occupare abusivamente *(tr)*	squat, settle illegally 3
	***occuparsi di** *(intr / refl)*	deal with, see about / to, organize 7
	odiare *(tr)*	hate, dislike 13
	offendere *(tr)*	disgust, offend 17
	offrire *(tr)* **a qicu.**	bid hold out, offer, treat s.one, give (present) to s.one 24
	offrire alloggio a *(tr)*	put up, accommodate 24
	offrire di *(intr)*	offer (to) 24
	***offrirsi** *(intr / refl)*	volunteer 24, 7
	omettere *(tr)*	leave out, omit 54
	ondeggiare *(intr)*	flicker 12
	operare *(tr)*	operate 3
	opporre *(tr)*	oppose 64
	***opporsi a** *(intr / refl)*	oppose, be opposed to 64, 7
	opprimere *(tr)*	weigh down, oppress 32
	orbitare *(tr)*	orbit 3
	ordinare *(tr)*	file (papers), order (food) 3
	organizzare *(tr)*	organize 3
	orinare *(intr)*	urinate 3
	ornare *(tr)*	embellish 3
	osare *(intr)*	dare 3
	oscillare *(intr)*	oscillate, sway, range (in amount) 3
	oscurare *(tr)*	darken 3
	ospitare *(tr)*	accommodate, put up, entertain 3
	osservare *(tr)*	notice, observe, remark 3
	ossidare *(tr)*	oxidize 3
	ostacolare *(tr)*	hold up (traffic), thwart 3
	ottenere *(intr)*	come by, obtain 92
	otturare *(tr)*	fill (a tooth) 3
	oziare *(intr)*	idle about 13
P	**pagare** *(tr)*	pay, pay in 11
	***pagare il conto** *(tr)*	check out, pay bill / check 11

palleggiare *(tr)*	dribble (football / soccer) 13
paralizzare *(tr)*	paralyze 3
parcheggiare *(tr)*	park (car) 12
pareggiare *(tr)*	equalize (sport) 12
***parere di** *(intr)*	appear, seem (to) *(Imp)*. 58 **[M]**
parlare di *(tr / intr)*	speak, talk (of) 3 **[M]**
parlare francamente *(intr)*	speak out 3
partecipare a *(intr)*	take part in, participate in 3
parteggiare per *(intr)*	side with, support 12
***partire** *(intr)*	depart, set off, leave 5
***partire per** *(intr)*	leave for 5
†passare *(intr / tr)*	spend (time) 3
***passare a** *(intr)*	pass (an exam) 3
passare *(tr)* **l'aspirapolvere**	vacuum 3
passare a prendere *(tr)*	call for 3
passare a una velocità inferiore *(intr)*	change down (gear) 3
passare a una velocità superiore *(intr)*	change up (gear) 3
passare da *(intr)*	call in 3
passare per *(intr)*	pass by, pass through 3
passeggiare *(intr)*	stroll 12
pattinare *(intr)*	skate 3
peccare *(intr)*	sin 11
pedalare *(intr)*	pedal 3
†peggiorare *(intr / tr)*	worsen 3
pendere *(intr)*	slope, overhang 4
penetrare *(tr)*	penetrate, pierce 3
penetrare a forza *(tr)*	force one's way 3
pensare *(intr / tr)*	think 3
pensare a *(intr)*	think about 3
pensare di *(intr)*	plan, think of (opinion) 3
***pentirsi di** *(intr / refl)*	regret, repent (of) 5, 7
percepire *(tr)*	detect, perceive 6
percorrere *(tr)*	cover, go along, scour 35
percuotere *(tr)*	beat, strike 82
perdere *(tr)*	lose 59 **[M]**
perdere *(tr)* **l'equilibrio**	throw off balance 59
perdere tempo *(intr)*	mess about 59
***perdersi** *(intr / refl)*	get lost 59, 7
perdonare *(tr)*	forgive, pardon 3
perfezionare *(tr)*	perfect 3
perforare *(tr)*	punch (holes) 3
***perire** *(intr)*	perish 6
permettere *(intr)*	permit, allow, let, enable 54
***permettersi** *(intr / refl)*	be allowed 54, 7
***permettersi il lusso di** *(intr / refl)*	afford 54, 7
perseguire *(tr)*	follow up, pursue, search for 5
persistere *(intr)*	keep at, persist 25
persuadere a *(tr)*	persuade 60 **[M]**

***pervenire** *(intr)* arrive at 102
pesare *(tr)* weigh 3
pescare *(tr)* fish 11
pestare *(tr)* stamp (with foot) 3
pettinare *(tr)* comb 3
***piacere a** *(intr)* please, like, be fond of, appeal to 61 **[M]**
piagnucolare *(intr)* snivel, cry 3
piangere *(intr)* cry 62 **[M]**
piantare *(tr)* pitch (tent), plant 3
picchiettare *(intr)* patter (rain) 3
piegare *(tr)* fold 11
pieghettare *(tr)* pleat 3
pigliare *(tr)* take, catch 13
pilotare *(tr)* pilot 3
piluccare *(tr)* peck at 11
†piovere *(intr)* rain *(Imp)*. 63 **[M]**
piovigginare *(intr)* drizzle 3
polverizzare *(tr)* powder, pulverize 3
pompare *(tr)* pump 3
porgere *(tr)* hand, give, hold out 80
porre *(tr)* place, put 64 **[M]**
  porre in scatola *(tr)* box in 64
portare *(tr)* bear, carry, bring; have on, wear 3
  portare a *(intr)* lead to 3
  portare il lutto *(tr)* mourn 3
  portare via *(tr)* carry off, take away 3
posare *(tr)* lay, place 3
posporre *(tr)* postpone 64
possedere *(tr)* possess, have, own 14, 4
potare *(tr)* prune 3
†potere *(intr)* can, be able to 65 **[M]**
pranzare *(intr)* have lunch 3
praticare *(tr)* practice, put into practice 11
precipitare *(tr)* precipitate 3
  ***precipitarsi** *(intr/refl)* rush 7
  ***precipitarsi fuori** *(intr/refl)* burst out 7
  ***precipitarsi in** *(intr/refl)* burst in 7
precisare *(tr)* specify 3
predicare *(tr)* preach 11
predire *(tr)* predict 9
preferire *(tr)* prefer 6
pregare di *(tr)* pray, beg, ask 11
premere *(tr)* press (button) 4
prendere *(tr)* take, catch (train, cold), have, eat 66 **[M]**
  prendere a *(intr)* begin to 66
  prendere d'assalto *(tr)* storm (a building) 66

prendere in considerazione *(tr)*	take into account 66
prendere in trappola *(tr)*	trap 66
prendere le difese di *(tr)*	stand up for 66
prendere nota di *(intr)*	minute, take down (in writing) 66
prendere parte a *(intr)*	take part in 66
prendere per *(intr)*	mistake for 66
prendersi la briga di *(intr/refl)*	take the trouble to 66, 7
prendersela con *(intr)*	be upset with 66, 7
prenotare *(tr)*	book, reserve 3
preoccupare *(tr)*	distress 3
***preoccuparsi di / per** *(intr/refl)*	worry, get worried about 7
preparare *(tr)*	get ready, prepare 3
preparare il terreno *(tr)*	pave the way 3
***prepararsi a** *(intr/refl)*	get prepared for, get ready for 7
preporre *(tr)*	place / put before; prefer 64
prescegliere *(tr)*	choose from 31
prescrivere *(tr)*	prescribe 81
presentare *(tr)*	introduce, present, produce (show) 3
***presentarsi** *(intr/refl)*	arise 7
preservare *(tr)*	preserve 3
presiedere *(tr)*	chair meeting 4
prestare *(tr)*	lend 3
presumere *(tr/intr)*	presume, rely 26
presuporre *(tr)*	presuppose 64
pretendere di *(tr)*	claim, profess (to) 91
***prevalere** *(intr)*	prevail 100
prevedere *(tr)*	foresee 101
privare *(tr)*	rob 3
privare di *(tr)*	do out of, stop s.one having 3
privatizzare *(tr)*	privatize 3
processare *(tr)*	try in court 3
procrastinare *(tr)*	procrastinate 3
procreare *(tr)*	procreate 3
procurare *(tr)*	get 3
produrre *(tr)*	yield, produce 95
produrre vescichetta *(intr)*	blister 95
profittare *(intr)*	profit 3
profittare da *(intr)*	benefit from 3
profondere *(tr)*	squander 50
profondersi in *(intr/refl)*	be profuse in 50
profumare *(tr)*	scent 3
progettare *(tr)*	devise, project 3
programmare *(tr)*	program 3
proibire di *(tr)*	prohibit (from) 6
proiettare *(tr)*	cast 3
prolungare *(tr)*	prolong 11
promettere *(tr)*	promise 54
promettere a qlcu di fare *(intr)*	promise s.one to do sth. 54

promuovere *(tr)* pass (candidate), promote, upgrade 15
pronunciare *(tr)* pronounce 12
proporre di *(tr)* propose (to); table (a bill) 64
prorompere *(intr)* burst out 76
proseguire *(intr)* proceed 5
proseguire *(tr)* prosecute 5
prosperare *(intr)* prosper, flourish, thrive 3
***prostituirsi** *(intr/refl)* prostitute oneself 6, 7
proteggere *(tr)* protect, guard 67 **[M]**
protestare *(tr)* protest 3
provare *(tr)* prove, taste, try on/out, sample 3
provare a *(intr)* try to 3
provare antipatia per *(intr)* dislike 3
provare piacere nel fare *(tr)* delight in doing sth. 3
provare pietà di *(intr)* take pity on 3
***provenire da** *(intr)* come from, issue from 102
provocare *(tr)* challenge 11
provocare un corto circuito *(tr)* short-circuit 11
provvedere a *(intr)* provide for, see to 101
pubblicare *(tr)* bring out, publish, issue 11
pugnalare *(tr)* stab 3
pulire *(tr)* clean, clear out, clear up rubbish 6
pungere *(tr)* prick, sting 68 **[M]**
pungolare *(tr)* prod 3
punire *(tr)* discipline, punish 6
puntare *(tr)* pin 3
puntare a *(intr)* aim at 3
puntellare *(tr)* shore up 3
purificare *(tr)* purify 11
***putrefarsi** *(intr/refl)* rot 10, 7
puzzare di *(intr)* stink of 3

Q

qualificare *(tr)* qualify 11
quantificare *(tr)* quantify 11
quotare *(tr)* quote (prices) 3

R

racchiudere *(tr)* contain; imply 30
raccogliere *(tr)* pick, pick up, rake up (leaves). summon up (courage) 31
raccomandare *(tr)* recommend 3
raccontare *(tr)* report, tell, narrate 3
raddoppiare *(tr)* double 13
raddrizzare *(tr)* straighten 3
radere *(tr)* shave; skim; raze 69 **[M]**
***radersi** *(intr/refl)* shave oneself 69, 7
radiografare *(tr)* X-ray 3
raffinare *(tr)* refine 3
rafforzare *(tr)* strengthen 3

***raffreddarsi** *(intr / refl)*	get / catch cold 7
raggiungere *(tr)*	reach, attain, catch up with 52
ragionare *(intr)*	reason 3
***rallegrarsi** *(intr / refl)*	rejoice 7
rallentare *(tr)*	slow down 3
***rammaricarsi di** *(intr / refl)*	regret, feel sorry for 11, 7
rapinare *(tr)*	hijack 3
rapire *(tr)*	kidnap 6
rappresentare *(tr)*	represent, stage (a play) 3
***rassegnarsi a** *(intr / refl)*	resign oneself to 7
rassomigliare a *(intr)*	take after, resemble 13
rattristate *(tr)*	sadden 3
ravvolgere *(tr)*	wrap up 106
razionare *(tr)*	ration 3
reagire *(intr)*	react 6
realizzare *(tr)*	accomplish, realize, make real 3
***recarsi** *(intr / refl)*	go to 11, 7
recidere *(tr)*	cut off, amputate 39
recitare *(tr)*	act in theater, perform (a play) 3
redigere *(tr)*	draw up (document), compile 4, 25B
refrigerare *(tr)*	refrigerate 3
regalare *(tr)*	give as a present 3
reggere *(tr)*	bear; hold; rule; stand 70 **[M]**
registrare *(tr)*	check in, register, record, video, store data 3
regolare *(tr)*	time, regulate 3
remare *(tr)*	row, paddle 3
rendere *(tr)*	give back; render 71 **[M]**
rendere agro *(tr)*	sour 71
rendere conto di *(intr)*	account for 71
rendere duro come l'acciaio *(tr)*	steel, harden 71
rendere ridicolo *(tr)*	ridicule 71
rendere sicuro *(tr)*	make safe 71
***rendersi conto di** *(intr)*	realize 71, 7
reprimere *(tr)*	repress 32
resistere a *(intr)*	resist, weather 25
respingere *(tr)*	cast off (a boat), push back, reject, turn down 86
respirare *(tr)*	breathe 3
***restare** *(intr)*	stay 3
***restare alzati** *(intr)*	wait up 3
***restare in casa** *(intr)*	stay in / indoors 3
restaurare *(tr)*	restore 3
restituire *(tr)*	restore, give back 6
restringere *(tr)*	narrow, tighten, shrink 88
rettificare *(tr)*	rectify 11
rianimare *(tr)*	revive 3

riassumere *(tr)*	sum up, summarize 26
***riaversi** *(intr/refl)*	come round / to (consciousness) 27, 7
***ribellarsi a** *(intr/refl)*	revolt against 7
ricamare *(tr)*	embroider 3
ricattare *(tr)*	blackmail 3
ricevere *(tr)*	receive, get (letter) 4
ricevere notizie da *(intr)*	hear from 4
richiamare *(tr)*	call back, call up, mobilize, recall 3
richiedere *(tr)*	request, demand, ask for 29
richiudere *(tr)*	close again 30
riciclare *(tr)*	recycle waste 3
ricompensare *(tr)*	compensate for, reward 3
riconciliare *(tr)*	reconcile 13
riconoscere di *(tr)*	spot, recognize 34
ricoprire *(tr)*	cover with, plaster, cover again, roof 24
ricordare a *(intr)*	remind 3
***ricordarsi di** *(intr/refl)*	remember 7
***ricorrere a** *(intr)*	resort to 35
ricostruire *(tr)*	reconstruct 6
ridere di *(intr)*	laugh (at) 72 **[M]**
ridurre *(tr)*	cut back, reduce 95
riempire di *(tr)*	fill, fill in with 5
***riempirsi di** *(intr/refl)*	cram with 5, 7
rifare *(tr)*	redo 10
***riferirsi a** *(intr/refl)*	refer to 6, 7
rifiutare di *(tr)*	decline, refuse (to) 3
riflettere su *(tr)*	reflect on, think over 22, 25B
rifluire *(intr)*	ebb 6
rigare *(tr)*	rule, draw line 11
riguardare *(tr)*	affect, concern 3
***rilassarsi** *(intr/refl)*	relax 7
rimandare *(tr)*	defer, put off, postpone 3
***rimanere** *(intr)*	remain 73 **[M]**
***rimanere indietro** *(intr)*	drop behind 73
***rimanere senza fiato** *(intr)*	gasp, be breathless 73
***rimanere valido** *(intr)*	stand, remain unchanged 73
rimbalzare *(tr)*	bounce 3
rimborsare *(tr)*	refund, reimburse 3
rimediare a *(intr)*	remedy, put right 13
rimettere *(tr)*	replace 54
rimorchiare *(tr)*	tow 13
rimordere *(tr)*	bite back; prick 55
rimpiangere *(tr)*	regret, feel sorry for 62
rimpinzarsi di *(intr/refl)*	guzzle 7
rimproverare *(tr)*	reproach 3
rimuovere *(tr)*	displace 15
rinascere *(tr)*	be born again 57

rinchiudere *(tr)*	shut in, shut up 30
***rincrescere** *(intr)*	regret; mind (*Imp.*) 36
rinforzare *(tr)*	reinforce, steady, make firm 3
rinfrescare *(tr)*	cool, freshen, refresh 11
***rinfrescarsi** *(intr/refl)*	cool down 11, 7
ringraziare *(tr)*	say thank you for, thank 3
rinnovare *(tr)*	renew, renovate 3
rinunciare a *(intr)*	renounce, give up 12
rinvenire *(tr/intr)*	find, discover; recover; come to 102
rinviare *(tr)*	send back 13
riordinare *(tr)*	groom 3
riorganizzare *(tr)*	reorganize 3
riparare *(tr)*	mend, fix, repair, screen, shade, shelter 3
ripercuotere *(tr)*	beat again 82
ripetere *(tr)*	repeat 4
ripiegare *(tr)*	fold up 11
riporre *(tr)*	put again 64
riportare *(tr)*	bring back, take back 3
riposare *(tr)*	rest 3
***riposarsi** *(intr/refl)*	have a rest 7
riprendere *(tr)*	recover, get back 66
riprodurre *(tr)*	reproduce 95
***risalire a** *(intr)*	date back 77
riscaldare *(tr)*	heat, warm up 3
rischiare di *(tr)*	risk, be in danger (of) 13
risciacquare *(tr)*	rinse 3
riscuotere *(tr)*	collect, cash (check) 82
risentire *(tr)*	play back, hear again 5
riservare *(tr)*	reserve 3
risolvere *(tr)*	resolve, solve 74 **[M]**
***risolversi di** *(intr/refl)*	decide, make up one's mind 74, 7
risonare *(intr)*	resonate, resound 3
risorgere *(intr)*	rise again, revive 80
risparmiare *(tr)*	economize, save, spare 13
rispecchiare *(tr)*	reflect, mirror 13
rispettare *(tr)*	respect 3
risplendere *(intr)*	glow 17
rispondere a *(intr)*	reply, answer, rejoin, equivalent to 75 **[M]**
***risultare con** *(intr)*	result in, turn out 3
risuonare *(intr)*	rattle 3
ritardare *(tr)*	delay 3
ritenere di *(tr)*	retain, consider (doing) 92
ritirare *(tr)*	withdraw 3
ritirarsi *(intr/refl)*	drop out, flinch, pull back, stand back 7
***ritornare** *(intr)*	come back, go back, get back, hand back, return 3

	***ritrarsi** *(intr/refl)*	cower 7
	riunire *(tr)*	assemble, put/bring together, gather 6
	riunire in mazzo *(tr)*	bundle up 6
	***riunirsi** *(intr/refl)*	reunite, meet/flock together 6, 7
	riuscire a *(intr)*	manage to (do), succeed 99
	rivedere *(tr)*	see again; revise 101
	rivelare *(tr)*	disclose 3
	***rivivere** *(intr)*	live again, relive 104
	***rivolgersi a** *(intr/refl)*	refer to, speak to 106, 7
	rivoltare *(tr)*	turn inside out 3
	***rizzarsi** *(intr/refl)*	sit up 3
	rodere *(tr)*	gnaw 47
	rombare *(intr)*	rumble 3
	rompere *(tr)*	break 76 **[M]**
	ronzare *(intr)*	buzz 3
	rotolare *(intr/tr)*	roll 3
	rovesciare *(tr)*	capsize, knock over, spill, upset 12
	†rovinare *(intr/tr)*	ruin, spoil, harm, fall to ruin 3
	rubare *(tr)*	pinch, steal 3
	ruotare *(tr)*	wheel 3
	russare *(intr)*	snore 3
S	**sacrificare** *(tr)*	sacrifice 11
	saggiare *(tr)*	sample 12
	salare *(tr)*	salt 3
	saldare *(tr)*	pay up, settle (bill); weld 3
	†salire *(intr/tr)*	go up, climb, mount, come in (of tide) 77 **[M]**
	†salire su *(intr/tr)*	get on, board (bus/train) 77
	†saltare *(intr/tr)*	hop, jump, leap 3
	***saltare (di valvola)** *(intr)*	blow fuse 3
	salutare *(tr)*	hail, greet, see off, say good-bye 3
	salvare *(tr)*	rescue, salvage, save 3
	sanguinare *(intr)*	bleed 3
	sapere *(intr)*	know (a fact), know how to 78 **[M]**
	sapere di *(intr)*	taste of, smack of 78
	sarchiare *(tr)*	weed, hoe 13
	sbadigliare *(intr)*	yawn, gape 13
	***sbagliarsi** *(intr)*	be mistaken 13, 7
	sbalordire *(tr)*	stupefy 6
	sbarcare *(intr)*	land, disembark 11
	sbarrare *(tr)*	dam 3
	sbattere *(tr)*	slam, whip (eggs) 4
	sbloccare *(tr)*	unblock 11
	sborsare *(tr)*	pay out, disburse 3
	sbottonare *(tr)*	unbutton 3
	sbriciolare *(tr)*	crumble 3
	***sbrigarsi** *(intr/refl)*	hurry up, make haste 11, 7

***scadere** *(intr)*	be due, expire (of credit card) 28
scaldare *(tr)*	warm 3
***scalzarsi** *(intr/refl)*	take off shoes 7
scambiare per *(tr)*	mistake for 13
scandalizzare *(tr)*	shock, scandalize 3
***scappare via** *(intr)*	dash/rush away 3
scarabocchiare *(tr)*	scribble 13
scaricare *(tr)*	discharge, unload, download (IT) 11
scartare *(tr)*	scrap 3
***scatenersi** *(intr/refl)*	storm (anger) 92, 7
scattare *(tr)*	snap (photo), trigger off 3
scaturire *(tr)*	well, well up 6
scavare *(tr)*	channel, dig, hollow out, mine, scoop 3
scavare *(tr)* **(un pozzo)**	sink (a well) 3
scegliere di *(tr)*	choose (to), pick select 31
†scendere *(intr/tr)*	go/get/come down, descend 79 **[M]**
†scendere da *(intr/tr)*	get off, get down from 79
scheggiare *(tr)*	chip 12
scherzare *(intr)*	joke 3
schiaffeggiare *(tr)*	slap 12
schiantare *(tr)*	crack 3
schiudere *(tr)*	open, disclose 30
schizzare *(tr)*	sketch 3
sciare *(intr)*	ski sports 12
scintillare *(intr)*	sparkle 3
sciogliere *(tr)*	undo, untie; dissolve 31
***sciogliersi** *(intr/refl)*	melt away 31, 7
scioperare *(tr)*	strike, go on strike 3
sciupare *(tr)*	waste 3
***scivolare** *(intr)*	skid, slide, slip 3
scoccare *(tr)*	shoot (arrow) 11
scodinzolare *(tr)*	wag (tail) 3
scolare *(tr)*	strain (salad) 3
scommettere *(tr)*	bet 54
scommettere su qico.	back, gamble on sth. 54
***scomparire** *(intr)*	fade, disappear, go out of fashion; cut a poor figure 23
***scomporsi** *(intr/refl)*	decompose 64, 7
sconfiggere *(tr)*	defeat, smash (a record) 19
scongiurare *(tr)*	conjure 3
scontare *(tr)*	discount 3
scontentare *(tr)*	dissatisfy 3
***scontrarsi** *(intr/refl)*	crash 7
sconvolgere *(tr)*	upset (person) 106
scopare *(tr)*	sweep 3
***scoppiare** *(intr)*	burst 13
***scoppiare a ridere**	burst out laughing 13

scoprire *(tr)* discover, find out, strike (oil) 24
scoraggiare *(tr)* discourage 12
scorgere *(tr)* notice, perceive 80 **[M]**
***scorrere** *(intr)* flow, glide, stream, flow freely 35
  scorrere *(tr)* browse (books) 35
  ***scorrere lentamente** *(intr)* trickle 35
scottare *(tr)* scorch 3
screditare *(tr)* disparage 3
scricchiolare *(intr)* crackle 3
scrivere *(tr)* write, spell, word-process 81 **[M]**
  scrivere un programma *(tr)* program (IT) 81
  scrivere a macchina *(tr)* type 81
scrollare *(tr)* shrug 3
scrutare *(tr)* look through, scan 3
scuoiare *(tr)* skin 13
scuotere *(tr)* shake 82 **[M]**
scusare *(tr)* excuse, apologize 3
***scusarsi** *(intr/refl)* apologize, say sorry 7
seccare *(tr)* annoy, pester 11
***seccarsi** *(intr/refl)* get annoyed 11, 7
sedere *(tr)* sit (in Parliament, Congress, etc.) 14
***sedersi** *(intr/refl)* sit down 14 **[M]**
sedurre *(tr)* entice, seduce 95
segnalare *(tr)* signal 3
segnare *(tr)* score (sports), sign, check off, mark 3
***segnarsi** *(intr/refl)* cross oneself 7
seguire *(tr)* follow 5
sellare *(tr)* saddle 3
***sembrare** *(intr)* appear, seem *(Imp.)* 3
  ***sembrare di** *(intr)* look, seem, sound (like) 3
seminare *(tr)* sow (seed) 3
sentire *(intr)* feel, hear, smell 5
***sentirsi di** *(intr/refl)* feel (well/unwell) 5, 7
  sentirsi girare la testa *(intr/refl)* feel dizzy 5, 7
separare (da) *(tr)* separate (from) 3
seppellire *(tr)* bury 6, 25B
servire *(tr)* serve, wait on, bowl (cricket) 5
  ***servire da** *(intr)* serve as 5
  ***servire per** *(intr)* be used for 5
***servirsi di** *(intr/refl)* help oneself, use 5, 7
setacciare *(tr)* sieve 12
***sfasciarsi contro** *(intr/refl)* smash into 12, 7
sfidare a *(intr)* challenge to, defy to 3
sfigurare *(tr)* deform 3
sfiorare *(tr)* brush against, graze, sweep past 3
sfogare *(tr)* vent (anger) 11
sfogliare *(tr)* leaf through 13
***sforzarsi di** *(intr/refl)* try hard (to) 7

sfrecciare via *(intr)*	shoot off quickly 12
sfregiare *(tr)*	deface 12
sganciare *(tr)*	unhook, uncouple 12
sgattaiolare *(intr)*	slip away 3
sgelare *(tr)*	defrost, thaw 3
sgobbare *(tr/intr)*	swot (for exam) 3
sgonfiare *(tr)*	deflate 13
sgranare *(tr)*	shell (peas etc.) 3
sgranocchiare *(tr)*	crunch 13
sgridare *(tr)*	scold 3
sgusciare *(intr)*	slip 12
sgusciare *(tr)*	shell, hull 12
sibilare *(tr)*	hiss 3
sigillare *(tr)*	seal 3
significare *(intr)*	denote, mean, signify, represent 11
singhiozzare *(intr)*	sob 3
sintetizzare *(tr)*	synthesize 3
sintonizzare *(tr)*	tune in 3
slacciare *(tr)*	unfasten 12
slegare *(tr)*	loosen 11
slogare *(tr)*	dislocate 11
smaltire *(tr)* **la sbornia**	sober up 6
smantellare *(tr)*	dismantle 3
***smarrirsi** *(intr/refl)*	get lost, wander, go astray 6, 7
smentire *(tr)*	deny 6
smettere di *(intr)*	stop (doing sth.) 54
smuovere *(tr)*	shift; dissuade 15
socchiudere *(tr)* **gli occhi**	half close; squint 30
soccorrere *(tr)*	aid, assist 35
soddisfare *(tr)*	fulfill, satisfy 11
soffiare *(tr)*	blow, blow up (balloon) 13
soffocare *(tr)*	choke, suffocate 11
soffriggere *(intr/tr)*	fry lightly 19
soffrire *(tr)*	suffer, be in pain 5, 24
soggiungere *(tr)*	add 52
sognare di *(intr)*	dream (of) 3
sognare ad occhi aperti *(intr)*	daydream 3
***solere** *(tr)*	be used/accustomed to 83 **[M]**
solidificare *(tr)*	solidify 11
sollevare *(tr)*	heave, hoist, lift (receiver) 3
sollevare con cricco *(tr)*	jack (car) 3
***sollevarsi** *(intr/refl)*	rise, rebel 7
sommergere *(tr)*	submerge 84
sopportare *(tr)*	bear, tolerate, put up with, endure 3
sopprimere *(tr)*	abolish; eliminate; suppress 32
***sopraggiungere** *(intr)*	arrive 52
sopravvenire *(intr)*	arrive; happen 102

***sopravvivere a** *(intr)*	survive, outlive; live on 104
***sorgere** *(intr)*	rise (of sun) 80
sorpassare *(tr)*	overtake 3
sorprendere *(tr)*	surprise 66
soreggere *(tr)*	support, hold up 70
sorridere *(intr)*	smile 72
sorseggiare *(tr)*	sip 12
sorvegliare *(tr)*	supervise 13
sorvolare *(tr)*	hover 3
sospendere *(tr)*	suspend 17
sospettare *(tr)* **qicu. di**	suspect s.one of 3
sospingere *(tr)*	push, urge 86
sospirare *(intr)*	sigh 3
sostenere *(tr)*	allege, maintain, keep up, prop, stand by, support, uphold, back up 92
sostituire *(tr)*	replace, stand in for 6
sottintendere *(tr)*	hint at 91
sottolineare *(tr)*	stress, underline 3
sottomettere *(tr)*	subject 54
***sottomettersi a** *(intr/refl)*	submit to 54, 7
***sottoporsi a** *(intr/refl)*	undergo 64, 7
sottoscrivere *(tr)*	undersign, underwrite 81
sottoscrivere a *(intr)*	subscribe 81
***sottostare** *(intr)*	submit 87
sottovalutare *(tr)*	undervalue 3
sottrarre *(tr)*	subtract 96
sottrarsi *(refl)*	avoid 96
sovraccaricare *(tr)*	overload 11
sovrintendere a *(intr)*	supervise 91
***sovvenire** *(intr)*	aid 102
sovvenzionare *(tr)*	subsidize 3
spaccare *(tr)*	chop, hew, split (wood) 11
spalancare *(tr)*	open wide (door) 11
spandere *(tr/intr)*	spread, spill 25B
sparare *(tr)*	shoot, shoot a goal 3
sparare a *(intr)*	shoot at 3
sparecchiare *(tr)*	clear away 13
spargere *(tr)*	scatter, spread, sprinkle 84 **[M]**
***sparire** *(intr)*	pass away, die, vanish 6
spaventare *(tr)*	frighten, scare, startle, terrify 3
***spaventarsi di** *(intr/refl)*	be alarmed/startled at 7
spazzare *(tr)*	sweep (chimney) 3
spazzolare *(tr)*	brush 3
***specializzarsi in** *(intr/refl)*	specialize 7
specificare *(tr)*	specify 11
speculare *(tr/intr)*	speculate 3
spedire *(tr)*	send, dispatch 6
spegnere *(tr)*	turn off, extinguish, put out 85 **[M]**

spegnersi *(intr/refl)*	go out (of light) 85, 7
spendere *(tr)*	spend money 17
sperare di *(intr)*	hope (to) 3
sperimentare *(tr)*	experiment 3
***spettare a** *(intr)*	be up to, be the duty of *(Imp.)* 3
spezzare *(tr)*	snap, break 3
spiacere *(intr)*	mind (disinterest) 61
spiare *(tr)*	bug, spy on 13
spiccare *(tr)*	stand out (against background) 11
spiegare *(tr)*	explain, give reasons (for), open out (map), spread out (newspaper) 11
spingere a *(tr)*	push, shove, urge (to), jostle 86 **[M]**
splendere *(intr)*	shine (of sun) 17
splendere *(tr)*	flare 17
spogliare *(tr)*	strip, undress 13
***spogliarsi** *(intr/refl)*	get undressed 13, 7
spolverare *(tr)*	dust 3
sporcare *(tr)*	dirty 11
sporgere *(tr)*	project, jut out 80
***sporgersi** *(intr/refl)*	lean out 80, 7
sposare *(tr)*	marry 3
***sposarsi con** *(intr/refl)*	get married to 7
spostare *(tr)*	shift, move 3
sprangare *(tr)*	bar (door) 11
spremere *(tr)*	squeeze 4
spulciare *(tr)*	rid of fleas, examine, debug (IT) 12
spruzzare *(tr)*	splash, spray 3
spumeggiare *(intr)*	foam 12
spuntare *(tr)*	trim (hair) 3
sputare *(tr)*	spit 3
squadrare *(tr)*	square 3
squillare *(tr)*	blare 3
stabilire *(tr)*	appoint, fix, set up, establish 6
stabilire i prezzi di *(intr)*	price 6
stabilire relazioni *(intr)*	liaise (with) 6
***stabilirsi** *(intr/refl)*	settle, settle down 6, 7
stabilizzare *(tr)*	stabilize 3
staccare *(tr)*	detach, disconnect, unstick 11
stampare *(tr)*	print 3
***stancarsi di** *(intr/refl)*	tire of, get tired of 11, 7
standardizzare *(tr)*	standardize 3
***stare** *(intr)*	stay; stand; be 87 **[M]**
***stare attento** *(intr)*	look out, be careful 87
***stare bene** *(intr)*	keep well 87
***stare buono** *(intr)*	be good 87
***stare fermo** *(intr)*	be/keep still 87
***stare fresco** *(intr)*	be in for it 87
***stare fuori** *(intr)*	be outside, away from home 87

***stare in** *(intr)*	stay, remain 87
***stare in ginocchio** *(intr)*	kneel 87
***stare in pensiero** *(intr)*	be worried 87
***stare in piedi** *(intr)*	stand 87
***stare per** *(intr)*	be about to 87
***stare seduto** *(intr)*	be seated 87
***stare sulle spine** *(intr)*	be on tenterhooks 87
***stare tranquillo** *(intr)*	be quiet, calm 87
***stare zitto** *(intr)*	be / keep quiet 87
starnutire *(intr)*	sneeze 6
stendere *(tr)*	lay out, spread out 91
sterzare *(tr)*	steer 3
stillare *(tr)*	distil 3
stimare *(tr)*	appraise, value, estimate, rate 3
stimolare *(tr)*	urge, encourage s.one (to) 3
stirare *(tr)*	iron 3
storcere *(tr)*	twist, writhe, sprain 94
†stordire *(intr / tr)*	be amazed, dumbfound 6
strangolare *(tr)*	strangle 3
strappare *(tr)*	pull, tear 3
strillare *(intr)*	squeal 3
stringere *(tr)*	squeeze, tighten, clamp, narrow, pinch 88 **[M]**
***stringersi** *(intr / refl)*	cling 88, 7
strisciare *(intr)*	crawl, creep 12
strozzare *(tr)*	throttle 3
struggere *(tr)*	melt, consume 89 **[M]**
***struggersi** *(intr / refl)*	pine away 89, 7
strutturare *(tr)*	structure 3
studiare *(tr)*	study, learn 13
***stufarsi di** *(intr / refl)*	get fed up of 7
stupire *(tr)*	amaze 6
***stupirsi di** *(intr / refl)*	wonder, be amazed at 6, 7
subire *(tr)*	suffer, undergo 6
***succedere** *(intr)*	occur, happen; take over *(Imp.)* 33
***succedere a** *(intr)*	come after 33
succhiare *(tr)*	suck 13
sudare *(intr)*	sweat 3
suggerire *(tr)*	suggest 6
suggerire a qlcu. di fare *(intr)*	suggest to s.one to do sth. 6
†suonare *(intr / tr)*	sound, produce sound, play (an instrument), hoot (car), ring (bell) 3
suonare il tamburo *(tr)*	drum 3
superare *(tr)*	exceed, overcome, top, surpass 3
supporre *(intr)*	suppose 64
susseguire *(intr)*	succeed, come next 5
sussultare *(intr)*	jump up 3
svaligiare *(tr)*	burgle 12

svalutare *(tr)*	depreciate, devalue 3
***svanire** *(intr)*	vanish, die away, wear off (of sensation) 6
svantaggiare *(tr)*	handicap 12
svegliare *(tr)*	arouse, awaken, wake (s.one) 13
***svegliarsi** *(intr/refl)*	wake up 13, 7
svelare *(tr)*	reveal, disclose 3
svendere *(tr)*	sell off 4
***svenire** *(intr)*	pass out, faint 102
sviluppare *(tr)*	develop 3
svitare *(tr)*	unscrew 3
svolgere *(tr)*	unfold 106

T

tacere *(intr)*	be silent 90 **[M]**
tagliare *(tr)*	cut, crop, shear 13
tagliare a fette *(tr)*	slice 13
tamponare *(tr)*	stop (wound) 3
tappare *(tr)*	plug, stop up 3
tappezzare *(tr)*	paper (wall) 3
tardare a *(intr)*	delay (in doing sth.) 3
tassare *(tr)*	tax 3
telefonare a *(intr)*	ring up, telephone 3
temere di *(tr)*	fear, dread 4
tendere *(tr)*	stretch out; tend; strain (to limits), tense (muscles) 91 **[M]**
tendere a *(intr)*	stretch out; tend to 91
tendere un'imboscata a *(intr)*	ambush 91
tenere *(tr)*	hold, keep, grasp 92 **[M]**
tenere a *(intr)*	be eager to 92
tenere il broncio *(tr)*	sulk 92
tenere un discorso a *(tr)*	address, give a talk to 92
tenere a freno *(tr)*	bridle 92
tenere conto di *(tr)*	allow for 92
tenere in debito conto *(tr)*	make allowance for 92
tenere indietro *(tr)*	keep back, withhold 92
tenerci a *(intr)*	care a lot about 92
***tenersi iontano** *(intr/refl)*	keep away, abstain 92, 7
tentare di *(tr)*	attempt (to), try, tempt 3
†terminare *(intr/tr)*	end, terminate 3
tessere *(tr)*	weave (threads) 4
testimoniare *(tr)*	bear witness, witness 13
timbrare *(tr)*	stamp (letters) 3
tingere *(tr)*	dye, tint 93 **[M]**
tirare *(tr)*	draw, pull, haul, stretch, extend 3
tirare di scherma *(intr)*	fence (sport) 3
tirare giù *(tr)*	pull down, take down (tent etc.) 3
tirare in lungo *(tr)*	linger 3
tirare vento *(tr)*	be windy 3
toccare *(tr)*	touch 11

***toccare a** *(intr)*	take (turn), be up to *(Imp.)* 11
togliere *(tr)*	draw out, extract, remove, take off (clothes) 31
togliere il nocciolo a *(tr)*	stone (fruit) 31
togliere di mezzo *(tr)*	do away with 31
togliere la comunicazione *(tr)*	ring off 31
tollerare *(tr)*	tolerate 3
torcere *(tr)*	twist, wring 94 **[M]**
tormentare *(tr)*	harass, torment 3
***tornare (a casa)** *(intr)*	go home, turn back 2
torturare *(tr)*	torture 3
tossire *(intr)*	cough 6
tracciare *(tr)*	plot, trace 12
tradire *(tr)*	betray 6
tradurre in / da *(tr)*	translate (into / from) 95 **[M]**
trafiggere *(tr)*	run through, pierce 19
***tramontare** *(intr)*	set (of sun, moon) 3
trangugiare in fretta *(tr)*	gobble up 12
transigere *(intr)*	compromise 4, 25B
trapanare *(tr)*	drill a hole 3
trarre *(tr)*	draw, pull 96 **[M]**
trarre il massimo vantaggio da *(tr)*	make the best of 96
trasalire *(intr)*	start (startled) 77
trascinare *(tr)*	trail, drag 3
***trascorrere(intr)**	pass (of time) 35
trascrivere *(tr)*	transcribe 81
trascurare *(tr)*	neglect 3
trasferire *(tr)*	transfer 6
trasformare in *(tr)*	transform (into) 3
trasgredire *(tr)*	infringe 6
traslocarsi *(intr / refl)*	move (house) 7
trasmettere *(tr)*	pass on, send on (orders), transmit 54
trasparire *(intr)*	shine through 23
trattare *(tr)*	use, treat (person) 3
trattare con *(intr)*	deal with 3
***trattarsi di** *(intr / refl)*	be a matter of, be about 7
trattenere *(tr)*	detain 92
***trattenersi** *(intr / refl)*	holdback, stay, remain 92, 7
travedere *(intr)*	be wrong 101
travestire *(tr)*	disguise 5
trebbiare *(tr)*	thresh 13
tremare *(intr)*	quiver, tremble 3
trionfare *(tr)*	triumph 3
tritare *(tr)*	mince 3
trovare *(tr)*	find, think out (a solution) 3
trovare per caso *(tr)*	chance upon 3
***trovarsi** *(intr / refl)*	stand, be situated / located 7
***truccarsi** *(intr / refl)*	make up (cosmetics) 11, 7